the Dauphin

the truth about Justin Trudeau

by Paul Tuns

FRE3DOM PRESS
CANADA INC.

The Dauphin: The Truth About Justin Trudeau

Freedom Press Canada Inc.
12-111 Fourth Ave., Suite 185
St. Catharines, ON L2S 3P5

Printed in the United States of America

Cover Design: David B. Strutt
Book Design: David Bolton

ISBN: 978-1-927684-18-4

To Patrick, Michael, Kathryn,
Madelyn, Gabriella, and Christopher.

Contents

Introduction

Dauphin: *n. hist.* the title borne by the eldest son of the King of France from 1349 to 1830.

Oxford Encyclopedic English Dictionary

Justin Trudeau, the eldest son of former Prime Minister Pierre Trudeau, rode a wave of nostalgia to rescue the Liberals. Or so the party hopes. But what does Justin Trudeau really believe? And what hints are there, if any, that he would be a good leader, let alone prime minister? Is pedigree enough? Is it a pedigree that should inspire confidence?

Pierre Trudeau rode his charisma to four electoral victories but while Canadians were charmed by the celebrity-politician, he was busy wrecking the country with a brand of liberalism that touched the economy, social issues, and foreign policy. Canadians of a certain age remember the showy leadership of Pierre Trudeau, but forget he was an arrogant and divisive leader.

Justin Trudeau has the charisma, maybe even more than his famous father. Few people believe he has his father's smarts, although as Justin Trudeau said while peddling his book *Common Ground*, he knows he is as smart, or smarter, than anyone else. On November 10, 2014, he told a Toronto audience just that. "I spent my entire life arguing, debating, learning, having deep conversations about everything around the dinner table and in hikes in the woods, talking about history, philosophy … I learned from that I can go toe-to-toe with anyone on an intellectual level." That was Trudeau's reply about what his dad taught him. So apparently he inherited his father's arrogance.

Justin Trudeau has spent nearly three years trying to look moderate when in fact he betrays his natural liberalism whenever he talks about policy with any specificity. That's probably why he prefers to truck in platitudes, without delving into what policies a 21st-century Trudeau Liberal government would

1

pursue. He has attacked the Conservative government while seldom explaining what he would prefer to see them do. For the first 24 months of Trudeau's leadership of the Liberals he was exceeding clear on just two issues: his desire to liberalize Canada's drug laws and celebrating abortion as Canada's highest value and achievement.

As for issues of central importance to Canada's future and voters' hearts, Trudeau provides little comfort. He seems out of his depth on both economic and foreign policy/national security issues.

For nearly two years, Justin Trudeau talked about the middle class without ever offering a satisfactory definition of who qualified as such. He talked about helping the middle class, without telling Canadians how he would go about doing it. Once he started putting forward actual policy, his moderation was cast aside for classic left-wing class warfare. He is a standard-issue tax-and-spend Liberal.

On foreign policy, Trudeau makes gaffes galore and on national security, Justin Trudeau seems more afraid of Conservative attack ads than of terrorists.

For more than two years, Justin Trudeau has dazzled Canadians with his charm, but hidden his agenda. For nearly two years, the Trudeau Liberals led almost every poll, but once he began making substantive policy pronouncements – on fighting ISIS, on domestic anti-terrorism, on taxes and spending – his support fell.

Perhaps Justin Trudeau is an intellectual or political lightweight, cast into the political arena after a stunning victory in a gimmicky charity boxing match. Perhaps he is a dangerous demagogue smart enough to hide his real agenda. Canadians should take a close look at the Dauphin, and not be fooled by the charming smile, nice hair, and political pedigree. They need to understand who Justin Trudeau is and what he wants to do with Canada.

Part I: The Two Trudeaus

Chapter 1: Pierre Trudeau

Pierre Elliott Trudeau dominated Canadian politics from the late 1960s to the mid-1980s, radically changing Canada in the process.

By many accounts, Pierre Trudeau was a popular and successful political leader. According to surveys of historians, Trudeau ranks quite highly. *Maclean's* asked historians in 1997 and 2011 to rank the prime ministers and both times Trudeau finished fifth.

Trudeau is also popular with the public. In 2004, viewers of the CBC's *The Greatest Canadian*, voted Trudeau as the third greatest Canadian, behind Tommy Douglas, who is considered the father of Medicare in Canada, and Terry Fox, who ran across half the country raising funds and awareness for cancer.

But Trudeau is not universally loved. In 2007, the historical magazine *The Beaver* ran a contest, "The Worst Canadians," which Pierre Trudeau "won" by beating three other more recent and contentious prime ministers (Stephen Harper, Jean Chrétien, and Brian Mulroney) and three convicted criminals (Clifford Olson, Paul Bernardo, and Karla Homolka.) One in six of the 15,000 online respondents voted for Trudeau over a three-month period. The editors said the result provided "further evidence of how polarizing his legacy continues to be among Canadians." Notably, *The Beaver*'s panel of experts did not include Trudeau among their list of 10 worst Canadians.

Trudeau became prime minister on April 20, 1968 after replacing Lester Pearson as Liberal leader, and led the party to three consecutive electoral victories between 1969 and 1974. He lost the June 1979 federal election to the hapless Joe Clark, who won a minority government, and soon afterward Trudeau announced his retirement from politics. But as it became evident that Clark's ministry was to be short-lived, Trudeau changed his mind and won a majority government in March 1980. He served a fourth term as prime minister until June 30, 1984.

Trudeau retired as the third-longest serving prime minister, holding office for 15 years and 164 days, about 80 days longer than Wilfrid Laurier, three-and-half years less than John A. Macdonald, and six years less than William Lyon Mackenzie King.

His electoral success is unquestioned, although he did lose to Clark in 1979, was reduced to a minority in 1972 after beating Robert Stanfield's Progressive Conservatives by a mere two seats, and went into a 1974 election in which the result was far from certain (the Liberals won a comfortable 141 of 264 seats.) After his first mandate, in which he won 154 of 264 seats, Trudeau never again won as large a percentage of seats as Stephen Harper did in 2011 (about 54 percent of the seats in the House of Commons), let alone come close to performing as well as John Diefenbaker did in 1958, or Brian Mulroney in 1984. Trudeau is remembered as a universally popular political figure during his time in office, but he was, in fact, greatly divisive and, as evidenced by *The Beaver* poll, reviled by large segments of the population. John English notes in *Just Watch Me: The Life of Pierre Elliott Trudeau, 1968-2000* that from early 1971 through the beginning of 1973, his personal popularity "decreased almost continuously" although it later rebounded. That said, his 1974 return to majority came entirely through his appeal to central Canada, where the Liberals won 115 of their 141 seats; if you didn't include Quebec, the Tories would have won a sizeable minority. In 1978 in the lead-up to the federal election, the *Montreal Gazette* ran a story about Trudeau's uphill battle to re-election: "Election Soon May Be No Cakewalk For PM." In 14 by-elections held between the '74 and '79 elections, the Liberals lost eight and maintained just six of the seats they were defending.

We now erroneously think Trudeau was universally and constantly popular, but he wasn't. Perhaps this isn't surprising. He was an unlikely political leader, let alone candidate for MP. It almost didn't happen.

Liberal Lester Pearson came to power in 1963, defeating the John Diefenbaker government, but only winning a minority government. He hoped to increase the Liberal seat count in the next federal election, but the party was getting pummelled by the press for a series of scandals.

Several ministerial staffers and Pearson's own parliamentary secretary were implicated in assisting alleged drug dealer Luicien Rivard in obtaining bail and from being extradited to the United States, with one ministerial assistant trying to bribe a lawyer acting on behalf of the U.S. government. Justice Minister Guy Favreau refused to prosecute the case, leading Pearson to eventually call an inquiry headed by Justice Frederic Dorian to look into the matter. Favreau was stripped of his duties as justice minister but remained in cabinet. The case became sensational when Rivard escaped from the Bordeaux prison, but even before that the *Toronto Daily Star, Montreal Star,* and *Le Devoir* called for Favreau's resignation and Gerard Pelletier, editor at *La Presse,* called him "unfit" to continue as Pearson's Quebec lieutenant. Pearson dropped Favreau from the cabinet for a week before naming him President of the Privy Council.

The Rivard Affair was not the only scandal during what Richard Gwyn calls in *The Shape of Scandal: A Study of a Government in Crisis, The Winter Scandals of 1964-65.* Maurice Lamontagne, the secretary of state and a former president of the privy council, and Immigration Minister Rene Tremblay, were caught not paying for furniture for their homes from a Montreal store. Minister of state Yvon Dupuis became the first federal cabinet minister in Canada to re-sign under criminal charges related to allegations of accepting a bribe to help a racetrack obtain a license. (He was later acquitted.) Peter Newman in *The Distemper of Our Times: Canadian Politics in Transition, 1963-1968* lists seven scandals that plagued the Pearson government. Most of the scandals involved francophone politicians from Quebec, including the demotion of Favreau, the resignation of Dupuis, and MP Edmund Asselin being pressured not to run again for the Liberals in Notre-Dame-de-Grâce following several controversial land deals. Pearson and top Liberal operatives were worried about the party's ability to maintain its 47 seats, out of 75 in the province.

Looking to change the party's image in the province, Pearson tasked Lamon-tagne, an economist and MP for Outremont who was himself accused of improprieties, and Louis de Gonzague Giguere, a founder of the Canadian Institute of Public Affairs, with the job of finding new talent for the party in Quebec. They recruited Jean Marchand, president of the Confederation of National Trade Unions (formerly the Catholic Workers Confederation of Can-ada), Gérard Pelletier, a recently fired editor of the Montreal daily *La Presse* and former labour activist, and Pierre Trudeau, a law professor at Université de Montréal and a public intellectual who co-founded *Cité Libre* with Pelletier (among others). Michael Vastel said in *The Outsider: The Life of Pierre Elliott Trudeau* the three were supposed to "give the party a new look" and revitalize the Liberals' chances in Quebec.

Born in 1919, Pierre Elliott Trudeau was the son of a wealthy Montreal family. Charlie Trudeau was a lawyer turned businessman who built the Automobile Owners' Association, a series of gas and service stations that would eventually grow to 30 stations. By the late 1920s the family had a maid and a chauffeur, and Pierre attended the elite Collège Jean-de-Brébeuf. In 1932 Charlie Trudeau sold the family business to the Imperial Oil Company for 1 million dollars, a considerable sum at the time. Charlie invested the money and joined the an-glophone elite in Montreal, but died of a heart attack in 1935 when Pierre was just 15 years old. Biographers note that Pierre blamed the social demands of being a Montreal businessman for his father's premature death and began to eschew private enterprise. Pierre became aloof, a trait that was made easier to sustain with the fortune he had inherited from his father.

He travelled extensively and bought books. He excelled at school where he developed a reputation of being a contrarian, including mocking the patronizing of stores owned by Jews and opposing democracy and capitalism. He would later buy a Harley-Davidson and ride it about Montreal wearing a Prussian helmet during World War II.

During World War II he denounced conscription and urged his fellow francophones to resist registering for military service, although he would later enlist with the Canadian Officers' Training Corps while attending law school at the Université de Montréal. Trudeau studied philosophy and was attracted to radical approaches. Max and Monique Nemni describe in their officially sanctioned 2005 book, *Young Trudeau: Son of Quebec, Father of Canada, 1919-1944*, how Trudeau was a bit of a fascist. At the age of 23 he was a leading organizer of LX, a revolutionary group that sought to lead a coup on Quebec. He spoke at a rally in 1942 in which he said, "traitors" should be "impaled alive" and urged the crowd to "eviscerate all the damned bourgeois of Outremont."

He would study politics and economics at Harvard and his politics became more secular. It was there that he learned about the interventionist economist John Maynard Keynes. The Nemnis in their second volume of their intellectual biography, *Trudeau Transformed: The Shaping of a Statesman 1944-1965*, report that he completed the required work toward a doctorate up to the comprehensive examination, but he did not write his PhD thesis. He went to France where he audited courses at the Institut d'Études Politiques de Paris, and under the tutelage of French intellectuals became interested in Soviet communism. At the London School of Economics, influenced by the Fabian socialist Harold Laski, Trudeau settled on democratic socialism as the ideal socio-political system. He debated between becoming a philosopher and a man of action.

By 1949, Trudeau was leaning toward a "man of action" as he moved to Ottawa to work as an economic policy adviser in the Privy Council Office of Liberal Prime Minister Louis St. Laurent after failing to secure a diplomatic post. His prodigious work in the PCO impressed his superiors, but his socialist and pacifist leanings did not. Trudeau would write anonymous attacks on the government in the journal he soon founded, including criticizing the St. Laurent government's involvement in the Korean War.

Trudeau also supported, and later wrote a book about, the 1949 Asbestos Strike, which he described as a seminal event in the resistance to Quebec's political and religious conservatism. (Marchand and Pelletier were also supporters of the strike.) In 1950, he co-founded and edited the journal *Cité Libre*, with Pelletier, which would become a leading voice against the conservatism of Quebec premier Maurice Duplessis.

In 1951, Trudeau returned to Quebec, but was blacklisted from teaching at the Université de Montréal. He was briefly (for a few weeks) banned from entering the United States because of his radical activities. His well-earned reputation as a radical and a trouble-maker had caught up to him, but it did not shut all doors.

He penned a seminal article in *Cité Libre* on "functional politics" in which he urged Quebecers to: "subject to methodical doubt all the political categories relegated to us by the previous generation; the strategy of resistance is no longer conducive to the fulfillment of our society. The time has come to borrow the 'functional' discipline from architecture, to throw to the winds those many prejudices with which the past has encumbered the present, and to build a new man. Let's batter down the totems, let's break the taboos. Better yet, let's consider them null and void. Let us be coolly intelligent." He would later write in an article published in the *Canadian Journal of Economics and Political Science* that English Canadians were imprisoned by the British imperial tradition while French Canadians were imprisoned by their Catholic heritage. His writings in general and his journal in particular gave Trudeau the cache to travel the country, not to canoe in the wilds as he had in his youth, but to meet other intellectuals and power-brokers at think tanks like the Canadian Institute of International Affairs and the Couchiching Institute on Public Affairs.

He dabbled in anti-Duplessis politics, founding the *Rassemblement* and after it floundered, the *Union des Forces Démocratiques,* whose manifesto was penned by Trudeau and published in *Cité Libre.* He became the Union's leader and the *McGill Daily* denounced Trudeau, calling his action that of a dilettante.

Trudeau was close to intellectuals that supported the Co-operative Commonwealth Federation, precursor to today's New Democratic Party, but it is unclear if he ever joined the party himself. He claimed he was unable to support the *deuxnations* approach of the socialist New Democratic Party that replaced the CCF, and joined the Liberals. But he was a fierce critic of his new party.

He denounced Lester Pearson's reversal of Liberal policy on accepting nuclear missiles on Canadian soil (as opposition leader) and the prime minister's establishment of the Royal Commission on Bilingualism and Biculturalism in 1963, which examined the state of biculturalism and bilingualism in Canada.

He called Liberals idiots and referred to the "anti-democratic reflexes of the spineless Liberal herd." He accused the Liberal leadership, including Pearson, of being willing to abandon any principle if it were politically expedient. He said those things in *Cité Libre* in April 1963, in an article about how Pearson, in abandoning Liberal Party policy on defense commitments in relation to NORAD, had traded honour for power. He said he would vote for the NDP in the next election, a party he had earlier disavowed. Instead, Trudeau joined the Liberals and ran for them in Mont Royal.

Trudeau would defend the dissonance between his professed academic views and his political actions saying that as an academic he was free to tell the "absolute truth," but presumably had to be cagier as a politician.

Joining Marchand and Pelletier to rejuvenate the Liberal brand in Quebec, Trudeau thought of running in St. Michel de Napierville, farm country where his paternal grandparents had lived, but the Liberals were not fond of the idea of dropping an intellectual – what journalist Larry Zolf would later call "an Outremont salon socialist" – into that riding as their candidate. He ran in Mount-Royal, a majority Anglophone riding. A Liberal MP from Shawinigan, Jean Chrétien, predicted of the Liberals recruiting Trudeau, "We won't be able to get him elected anywhere." He was wrong. Trudeau won with a comfortable majority, 55 percent. He would win the seat in each of the next five elections with at least three-quarters of the vote and as much as 90 percent.

Trudeau was going to explain why he was abandoning the life of the mind for public life in the political sphere, preparing an article for *Cité Libre* in 1965 that concluded: "The punishment for intelligent citizens who ignore public affairs is to be governed by imbeciles." Pelletier convinced Trudeau to change the ending to a quote from Plato: "The price people pay for taking no interest in public affairs is to be governed by people who are worse than themselves." Nonetheless, the original line is a window into Trudeau's mind and how he viewed his fellow Canadians.

Upon his election to the House of Commons, Pearson named Trudeau his parliamentary secretary, a role suited to the new MPs penchant for travel. In 1967, Trudeau was appointed minister of justice, a role which would vault him into the media spotlight. The following year Trudeau introduced the federal *Divorce Act* which standardized the law of divorce across Canada for the first time and introduced the concept of permanent marriage breakdown as one of the grounds for divorce. He was just warming up for a massive legal change in moral matters.

Pierre Trudeau would be responsible for widespread changes to the Criminal Code with an omnibus bill, the *Criminal Law Amendment Act*, which would reform 109 aspects of the Criminal Code. Most contentiously, the omnibus bill decriminalized consensual homosexual acts between adults, legalized contraception, permitted abortion, and allowed for the creation of lotteries, among many other changes. He famously declared, "there's no place for the state in the bedrooms of the nation," and "what's done in private between adults doesn't concern the Criminal Code" as an explanation for the government's plans to decriminalize homosexual acts, although the line has become more linked to the loosening of abortion law.

Fr. Alphonse de Valk, a historian, said in his booklet *The Secular State*, that, "As Minister of Justice in 1967, Trudeau personally and on his own initiative introduced the Liberal government's proposal for legalizing abortion, ignoring even the hearings which were being conducted on the subject by a joint House-of-Commons/Senate committee. As he explained to the *Calgary Herald* in December 1967, he deliberately placed the abortion item amid 108 other items in an Omnibus Bill in order to weaken resistance to it." That is, by joining literally more than one hundred other issues to his plan to liberalize abortion law, Trudeau was able to conflate opposition to abortion with opposition to other, more popular items in the bill.

Due in part to wrangling over the contentious bill in committee, the *Criminal Law Amendment Act* did not pass before Lester Pearson announced his resignation as leader of the Liberals on December 14, 1967.

Trudeau Rises

In 1968, *Toronto Telegram* columnist Lubor Zink began writing columns warning of the imminent entry of Pierre Trudeau into the Liberal leadership race to replace Lester Pearson. On January 21, 1968, Zink wrote about "the new messiah of the 'progressive' fraternity" who had "yet to declare his candidacy," but for whom "the Trudeau build-up" had already reached fevered pitch as few in the mass media had "serious misgivings" about the young and untested Liberal leader. Zink was a lonely voice decrying the extreme left-wing views of the former socialist academic turned Pearson cabinet minister. Zink said the Left and its cheerleaders in the media saw in Trudeau their best hope for "a model welfare and 'neutralist' state."

The Liberal leadership race culminated in an April 6, 1968 convention. The party was choosing not only a leader, but the next prime minister who would be expected to face the electorate to obtain his (or her) own mandate. The early front-runners were Paul Martin, Secretary of State for External Affairs, who ran twice previously and finished second to Pearson in 1958, Mitchell Sharp, Minister of Finance, and Paul Hellyer, Minister of Transport and former minister of defense. Marchand was thought to be a candidate who might satisfy the Liberal tradition of alternating between anglophone and francophone leaders, but he didn't throw his hat into the ring. Instead, he backed Trudeau, the justice minister but also a one-term MP. Trudeau lacked much of a base within the party, especially outside Quebec.

After a four-month campaign to woo party members at the riding level, just under 2400 delegates were scheduled to attend the convention at the Ottawa Civic Center from April 3-6. Marc Lalonde, an adviser to Pearson, arranged a tour for Trudeau to meet the Liberal premiers, partly to gain their support for constitutional reforms, partly to generate media coverage and increase his profile. In mid-February, Trudeau announced that he would enter the race for Liberal leader. An academic study later found that Trudeau earned a full quarter of media coverage in the leadership race, more than twice the amount one would expect if it was distributed evenly among the nine candidates. His charisma made him popular with the media and (therefore) the public. Polls showed him more than twice as popular as any other candidate in the race (32 percent to Martin's 14). Sharp dropped out of the race days before the convention and endorsed Trudeau, bringing with him an estimated 100 delegates. It might have proved decisive.

Along with Martin and Hellyer, former Minister of Trade and Commerce Robert Winters and Health Minister Allan MacEachen were also running, along with a collection of minor candidates: John Turner, who held various portfolios, most notably Consumer Affairs; Eric Kierans, a former health minister in Quebec; Agriculture Minister Joe Greene; Rev. Lloyd Henderson, a former mayor of Portage la Prairie, Manitoba and unsuccessful independent candidate for MP; Ernest Zundel, a holocaust denier who dropped out before the ballots were cast.

When the first ballot was counted, Trudeau had a significant but not insurmountable lead. He won 752 of the 2388 ballots case, more than the next two combined. Hellyer and Winters had 330 and 292 respectively while Martin and Turner were tied with 277. Greene, MacEachen, and Kierans each had between 103 and 109 votes. Winters appeared to be the stop-Trudeau candidate instead of Hellyer and the CBC cameras caught Judy LaMarsh, a former minister of national health and welfare, telling Hellyer, whom she had supported, to back Winters to prevent a Trudeau victory: "You've got to go to Winters. Don't let that bastard win it, Paul – he isn't even a Liberal." Three candidates, including Martin, who had finished tied for fourth, dropped off the first ballot, and Trudeau grew his lead in the second ballot before Winters closed the gap on the third ballot. Hellyer endorsed Winters. The long convention was sweltering and the concession stands had run out of food. Delegates were eager to get the convention over with, and with three names still on the fourth ballot, Trudeau won 50.9 percent of the vote compared to 40.3 percent for Winters and 8.2 for Turner.

During his victory speech, Trudeau said, "Canada must be progressive. Canada must be a Just Society." Two weeks later he was sworn in as prime minister.

As prime minister, Trudeau set out to radically change the country, to bring in his "Just Society," as he saw it. He sought his own mandate and called an election for June 25. He ran on a campaign of "Vote for New Leadership for All of Canada" which included the social programs that made up his Just Society. He won 45.4 percent of the vote, electing the first Liberal majority since Louis St. Laurent in 1953, taking 154 of 262 seats. The CBC's Larry Zolf said that the electorate shared Trudeau's lifelong "conviction that change even for the sake of change is better than treading windmills or slowly sucking wind."

While some conservative pundits fancy modern Canada Trudeaupia, the fact is that Canada was remade not only by Trudeau, but Pearson.

Although he was in office for a mere five years and never commanded a majority, it was Pearson who radically expanded social programs, establishing the Canada Student Loan Program, the Canada Pension Plan, the Canada Assistance Plan (which got Ottawa in the business of sharing social assistance costs with the provinces), the Guaranteed Income Supplement, and universal health care through the 1966 *Medical Care Act*. Pearson also established a federal labour code and minimum wage, created new regulatory agencies, funded universities, expanded crop insurance, and increased arts funding. Increasingly, government was called upon to intervene in the economic life of business and individuals.

Pearson convened the Royal Commission on Bilingualism and Biculturalism which led directly to institutionalized bilingualism at the federal level, widespread French instruction at the provincial level, with New Brunswick declaring itself officially bilingual, expanded French government services in Ontario and Manitoba, and the creation of the federal department of multiculturalism.

There was a radical reform of the immigration system so that it no longer favoured European immigrants, which led to an influx of visible minorities. He reoriented Canadian foreign policy to multilateral institutions like the United Nations and criticized U.S. policy in Vietnam, on American soil, during a visit to Philadelphia. In 1967, the government passed a moratorium on capital punishment and limited its applicability. The government also liberalized divorce law and set out to permit homosexual acts, contraception, and abortion, although those measures wouldn't pass until Trudeau was Prime Minister.

Pearson also began vandalizing Canada's institutions and gutting its traditions. Historian and sympathetic biographer John English, who later served as a one-term Liberal MP from Kitchener in the 1990s, observed that Pearson moved Canada toward a European welfare state model at the same time he was moving the country away from its European heritage as he shucked colonial imagery and ties. He substituted the old Red Ensign flag with the Red

Maple Leaf, created a joint House-Senate committee to examine the feasibility of making "O Canada" the national anthem and relegate "God Save the Queen" to mere royal anthem, began removing the words royal and imperial from federal institutions, and created the Order of Canada honours system. He merged the Royal Canadian Navy, the Royal Canadian Air Force, and the Canadian Army under the banner of the Armed Forces.

Andrew Cohen states in his Extraordinary Canadians biography of the 14th Prime Minister, "Pearson's time in office was surprisingly experimental and singularly transformative." Historian Blair Neatby said Pearson "fundamentally altered Canadian identity." Pearson's tenure in office was perhaps the most transformative in Canadian history. He normalized having the state interfere in almost every imaginable sphere of human activity in Canada and set a trajectory in which no limits would be placed on government involvement. He set the stage for further incursions by his predecessors, most notably Trudeau.

One might think there was little remaining for Trudeau to do when he got to power. But the next decade-and-a-half would witness further changes. The Just Society was not a set of programs; in this regard it differed from Lyndon Johnson's Great Society in the United States. Instead, it was a two-word guiding principle for a large set of policies that were implemented over 15 years.

Trudeau rose to power during the centenary of Confederation and he embodied the boundless enthusiasm of Canada's promise and potential. Even if Wilfrid Laurier was wrong about the 20th century belonging to Canada, there was little reason the next 100 years wouldn't be one in which Canada would shine. From a near halving of unemployment during the Pearson years to the euphoria of the 1967 World's Fair (Expo 67), and, of course, the historic pride that accompanied the celebration of 100 years of Confederation, the possibilities for Canada seemed limitless.

Abortion

Lester Pearson began exploring liberalization of abortion, contraception, and divorce in 1966 following several years of agitation of feminists and liberal churches, a campaign by the Canadian Medical Association and Canadian Bar Association, and media support from *Chatelaine* and the *Globe and Mail*. The discussion took place in the Standing Committee on Health and Welfare, indicating it would be dealt with as a medical matter not a legal issue. What began as an examination of permitting abortion under very limited circumstances such as cases of rape or incest, or to protect the health of the mother, eventually ballooned to full decriminalization as feminists and the *Globe* editorial writers began clamouring for the right to abortion.

Trudeau was Pearson's justice minister and on December 20, 1967, one day after it was released by the committee, he accepted an interim report even though it hadn't heard all presenters, most notably the Catholic bishops. Trudeau told parliament the government would accept the Health and Welfare committee's recommendation and liberalize Canada's abortion law in an Omnibus Bill. Before the Christmas recess, it passed first reading. The Omnibus Bill was 72 pages long and featured more than 100 clauses on issues as diverse and controversial as contraception, divorce, homosexuality, and abortion, but also technical items such as passport regulations and jury rules; it also permitted lotteries and relaxed marijuana laws. The inclusion of such a wide range of issues was meant to break down opposition to its most controversial components, especially abortion.

The Omnibus Bill maintained abortion as a criminal offense but permitted it when an application for abortion was accepted by the majority of a three-person therapeutic abortion committee (TAC). The abortion had to be carried out in a hospital. These committees were required to consider not only cases where a mother's life was in danger, but when her health "would" or "would be likely" affected by the continuation of the pregnancy, including the emotional health of the mother. Pro-life groups said these therapeutic abortion committees were rubber-stamp committees that effectively created abortion-on-demand. The final report of the Health and Welfare committee, presented to the House in March 1998, acknowledged problems with defining "health" and settled on the World Health Organization's definition of health to include physical, mental, emotional and psychological health.

Trudeau had made a name for himself handling this file as justice minister and after winning the Liberal leadership and becoming prime minister he asked Paul Martin Sr. to take his old job heading up the Justice Department. Martin refused because as a faithful Catholic he could not accept responsibility for re-introducing the Omnibus Bill which Trudeau had made clear would be brought back to the House of Commons. John Turner, another Catholic and fellow leadership contender, was named the new justice minister and in July announced he would re-introduce the Omnibus Bill, saying, "The Prime Minister is committed to it and so am I."

Turner said the changes were merely clarifying the law (against a backdrop of claims of widespread breaking of the law with back-alley abortions). Turner claimed that despite permitting abortions in certain circumstances – which the law did not actually limit – the Omnibus Bill did "not promote abortion" or "authorize the taking of fetal life" because it "simply removes certain categories of abortion from the present place they have on the list of indictable offenses." On May 9, 1969, the Omnibus Bill passed 149-55 (119 Liberals voting with 18 NDP, and 12 PCs, over the objections of 43 Tories, 11 Creditistes, and one Liberal.)

Feminists bristled at women having to get their abortions approved by hospital committees, but there is little evidence TACs refused many requests. Abortion became the second most common hospital procedure after tonsillectomies. Abortionists such as Henry Morgentaler flouted the law with street-front abortion facilities. He would challenge the constitutionality of the law, and in 1988, the Supreme Court of Canada threw out the limited restrictions of Section 251 of the Criminal Code.

The October Crisis

While some people recall Trudeau as a liberal – which he was – he was not doctrinaire. During the October Crisis in 1970 following the separate kidnappings of British trade commissioner James Cross and Quebec Minister of Immigration and Minister of Labour Pierre Laporte by the *Front de Libération du Québec* (FLQ), Trudeau would invoke the *War Measures Act,* the first and only time it has come into effect during peacetime. The FLQ was a terrorist group founded in 1963 to work toward independence for Quebec and it had carried out hundreds of terrorist attacks, mostly robberies and non-fatal bombings. The Quebec government was negotiating for Cross with one cell of the FLQ when another took Laporte. Trudeau mobilized the Armed Forces to provide security in the nation's capital.

In a famous exchange, CBC reporter Tim Ralfe questioned the prime minister about the armed soldiers on Parliament Hill as he entered a government building. Trudeau complained about the "bleeding hearts around who just don't like to see people with helmets and guns. All I can say is, go on and bleed. But it's more important to keep law and order in this society than to be worried about weak-kneed people who don't like the looks of ..." Ralfe interrupted Trudeau's answer, and asked, "At any cost? How far would you go with that? How far would you extend that?" Trudeau replied with a phrase that would come to define his time in office: "Well, just watch me." It was a typical Trudeau shrug to a serious question, even though he was perfectly capable of providing an articulate justification for the policy.

Trudeau was willing to go far to prevent the October Crisis from getting out of hand. Three days after that interview, on October 16, 1970, Trudeau asked the Governor General to proclaim a state of "apprehended insurrection" under the *War Measures Act,* and under the emergency regulations the FLQ was outlawed. Membership in the terrorist group became a criminal act. The police could arrest and detain individuals without charge and they did so to nearly 500 people. The emergency regulations were replaced in November by similar temporary regulations under the *Public Order Temporary Measures Act* which remained in effect until the following April. Basic measures of due process were denied: Habeas corpus (the right of an individual to have his detention confirmed as lawful by a judge) was suspended, suspects could be detained for seven days without being charged (and it could be extended to 21 days at the request of the attorney general), and prisoners were not allowed to meet with lawyers. The military was also dispatched to provide security to key buildings and individuals in Ottawa and Quebec, thereby freeing the police to investigate suspected terrorists.

Two inquiries, the federal Inquiry into Certain Activities of the RCMP and the Keable Commission in Quebec, found that the Trudeau government permitted the Royal Canadian Mounted Police to conduct electronic surveillance and break-ins without warrants. Civil libertarians were aghast with the government. Yet polls at the time found widespread support for Trudeau in English Canada – a Gallup poll in December found that 89 percent of English Canadians supported invoking the *War Measures Act* – but was divisive in Quebec, raising the ire of Quebec nationalism which contributed to the growing sovereignty movement in the province.

Dominique Clément later wrote in the *Journal of Canadian Studies* that the civil and human rights abuses that occurred under the *War Measures Act* were not limited to Quebec and Ottawa, but occurred across the country.

Richard Gwyn in his book on the Trudeau years, *Northern Magus: Pierre Trudeau and Canadians*, said the prime minister "smeared irredeemably his reputation as a champion of civil liberties. No other prime minister has been so severely criticized for crushing civil liberties."

While polls showed popular support for Trudeau, there was organized opposition to the *War Measures Act* from the Canadian Association of University Teachers and the Lawyers' Union, led by Clayton Ruby. Trudeau shrugged off their concerns much like he shrugged off the questions of the CBC's Tim Ralfe.

Gerald Godin, the lone PQ government dissenter against a Liberal motion put forward in the Quebec National Assembly paying homage to Trudeau after his death in 2000, said he would not acknowledge "a man who ... allowed the establishment of a police state in Quebec." While claims about Trudeau's police-state are exaggerated – there was no martial law, not all civil liberties were tossed aside, the media was still able to report on events without censure even if it felt chilled – the violation of civil liberties was still serious, and the wounds lasting.

Foreign policy

Trudeau, according to one of his biographers, Michel Vastel, was fond of neither the military nor the Americans, and it led to an instinctive pacifist posture as both an academic and prime minister.

Historians J.L. Granatstein and Robert Bothwell note in their book *Pirouette: Pierre Trudeau and Canadian Foreign Policy* that foreign affairs took a backseat to domestic policy for Canada's 15th Prime Minister. They said, "When the whole Trudeau record in foreign policy is examined, the inescapable and overwhelming reaction is wonderment at the on-and-off again nature of his interest, the lack of follow-through, the peripatetic nature of his concerns." Trudeau began his ministry reviewing Canadian foreign and defense policies which resulted in a rethinking of Canada's Cold War arrangements. Granatstein and Bothwell said that Trudeau was not just distrustful of NATO, but even ignorant of its history, eventually cutting Canada's contribution to the western alliance by half, while reorienting Canadian defense priorities from defending the country and her allies to international cooperation and peacekeeping. He would later reallocate funds for defense and provide tanks for NATO, but only after seeing a social democrat like West Germany's Helmut Schmidt's appreciation for the organization's role in maintaining peace between the East and West. Still, Canada's military was significantly smaller after Trudeau's years in office.

Trudeau became focused on "helpful fixations" in Africa, Latin America, and southeast Asia, turning Canada away from its historic alliances with the United States and western Europe. Through diplomatic relations including personal visits, trade, and aid, Trudeau sought "lasting improvements in their economies," as the future prime minister said during a 1968 campaign speech.

He increased foreign aid, although never to the one percent of Gross National Product level he promised. He argued for, more than fought for nuclear disarmament, with two speeches at the United Nations marking the most work he did on his goal of ending the "suffocation" of the arms race. More importantly, as Granatstein and Bothwell note, Pierre Trudeau's anti-Americanism angered Canada's largest trading partner while leading Soviet officials to believe he might move Canada away from its western alliance. Of course, Canada would do no such thing, but the friendly personal relations between Trudeau and Soviet party officials worried the United States, and Canada's response to Soviet aggression was muted, including the response to their invasion of Czechoslovakia in 1968, the invasion of Afghanistan in 1989, shutting down the Solidarity uprising in Poland in 1980, and the shooting down of a Korean airliner in 1983. Trudeau saw these developments occurring in the Soviet sphere of influence and thus felt it best to limit Canada's reaction.

Trudeau befriended third-world dictators and seemed to enjoy traveling the Globe for photo-ops with some of the worst tyrants on the planet. Historian Michael Bliss said that Trudeau was less concerned with tangible foreign policy, such as contributing militarily to strategic alliances, than with engaging in a dialogue of ideas. Trudeau said he wanted Canada to "sway the world with the force of its ideals." Granatstein and Bothwell called him "an adventurer in ideas with great articulation and little commitment." But ironically the growing distance between Canada and its historic allies made Canada a less beneficial partner to many countries in the developing world who had previously viewed good relations with Canada as the way to enter Washington's good graces. Not any longer. In the estimation of historians such as Bliss, Granatstein, and Bothwell, Canada became less relevant on the global stage under Trudeau.

Bliss said Trudeau would, "aid and abet the socialist politicians, some of whom were dreamers, some bloody dictators, who emerged in the 1950s." The most famous of these was Cuban President Fidel Castro. On January 26, 1976, Trudeau became the first western leader to visit communist Cuba. His communist hosts plastered the city with Trudeau posters and a quarter-million Cubans filled the streets to see the Canadian prime minister. The timing was inopportune. Castro had just sent troops to fight in Angola's Civil War and Canada's allies questioned Trudeau's judgement. How could he lend Castro the prestige of the historic meeting at precisely the time they had collectively condemned Cuba's military involvement in an internal African dispute?

While Trudeau claimed that he raised the issue of Angola in private, the video footage of the Canadian leader raising arms with the Cuban dictator and yelling, "Viva Cuba" and "Viva Castro," while expressing his wish "long-live Prime Minister and Commander-in-Chief, Fidel Castro" left a very different impression. And as Bob Plamandon reported in *The Truth about Trudeau*, the prime minister was overheard by reporters saying that Canada would be easier to govern "the Cuban way."

At the end of this fourth and final term, Trudeau launched his peace initiative. Worried that East-West tensions were dangerously high, mostly due to Ronald Reagan's supposed bellicosity, he traveled around the world meeting leaders and pleading for world peace. Bliss said, "Almost no one outside of his office, and perhaps not many people inside it, believed the tour had any effect." The American view, according to Bliss, was that Trudeau was acting like a "leftist high on pot."

Economy

Trudeau was an economist by training but his government was unable to arrest the economic problems the country faced in the 1970s. Globally, the 1970s offered economic suffering and anxiety. Stagflation hammered both Canada and the United States as unemployment and inflation rose. For the first time in Canada, the number of unemployed people exceeded 500,000 (throughout the

1950s and '60s that number fluttered between 197,000 and 466,000). Inflation rose above 5 percent in the early 1970s and reached double digits by the end of the decade. Mix in rapidly rising oil prices and fears of gas shortages, along with lower economic productivity after the boom of the previous two decades, and the economy seemed constantly on the precipice of disaster.

The Trudeau governments spent most of the decade reacting to the economic reality, flitting from one set of policies to another.Whether Trudeau's policies helped or not is debatable. In 1969, Trudeau established the federal Prices and Incomes Commission, pressuring private businesses to voluntarily restrict profits. Inflation rates fell the following two years to 3.3 percent and 2.9 percent, but it was only a temporary relief as inflation later worsened.

Two years later, the Liberal government reduced corporate tax rates, which have led some observers to claim a quid pro quo and, worse, an abandonment by Trudeau of his principles. Colin Campbell said that parliamentary review of the Carter Royal Commission on Tax Reform gutted most the commission's corporate tax proposals, providing "the first instance in which Trudeau's lip-service to social democratic ideals collapsed under pressure from the business community."

Trudeau initially brought a degree of restraint to government spending after the 1969 election, but when the 1973 election approached, he opened the spigots: Ottawa increased equalization payments to the provinces and invested in infrastructure, expanded employment training, youth employment programs, and temporary worker programs, and reduced taxes on low income workers. The Trudeau Liberals were reduced to a minority government in 1972, with a 10-point swing toward the Tories almost costing the Grits re-election. Robert Stanfield led the Tories to win 107 seats, two short of the Liberals. The NDP held the balance of power with 31 seats. (There were also 15 Social Credit MPs and two others elected.)

Trudeau was dependent on NDP support to get legislation passed. Buying NDP support was not cheap as the government increased unemployment insurance benefits while expanding coverage; the result was an increase in the total UIC cost from $891 million in 1971 to $1.87 billion the following year.

The 1973 budget increased family allowance and old age assistance payments. At the same time it reduced income and business taxes and indexed basic personal tax exemption. Deficits accumulated continued to accumulate.

In 1974, the Liberals regained their majority but it was far from certain when the Writ was dropped whether Trudeau would remain as prime minister. Robert Stanfield was widely admired (later called the best prime minister Canada never had). The Tories maintained their 1972 support, but a four-point upswing for the Liberals helped them pick up 32 seats and a majority.

The government undertook a Priorities Exercise in 1974/75 and ignored both economic growth and inflation and contained only vague references to regional development. As it groped around for answers to the economic challenges of high inflation, unemployment, and energy prices, Trudeau's government abandoned its own Priorities Exercise in October 1975 in favour of wage and price controls, a policy supported by the business community and opposed by organized labour.

Throughout the '70s, Trudeau budgets would increase and decrease the benefits and definitions of programs as they reacted ineptly to the slightest movement in economic indicators. The Trudeau government filled its 1978 pre-election budget with gifts to companies. At the same time, the Liberals had antagonized working Canadians with mandatory wage controls and back-to-work legislation. (From 1950 through 1965, the federal government ordered labour back to work five times, but from 1966 through 1980, the Pearson-Trudeau years, the government passed back-to-work legislation 45 times.)

Unable to turn the economy around, the Liberals attempted to redirect the agenda to national unity. (They had help when the Parti Quebecois attained power in 1976.) But in June 1979 Joe Clark interrupted the Trudeau reign when it eked out a narrow minority despite the Tories earning 480,000 fewer votes than the Liberals. The Clark Tories fell when they lost a budget vote in December 1979. Trudeau, who had earlier announced he was retiring, changed his mind.

Trudeau was convinced by interim Liberal leader, Allan MacEachen, to stay. MacEachen offered two reasons. The first was that it was Trudeau's "duty" to help defeat the separatists in Quebec. The Tellier Group, a Quebec consulting company, told Trudeau's inner circle that the "no" side for the impending referendum on sovereignty was a mere five points ahead of the "yes" side in the polls. The second, and perhaps more important reason, was his duty to help bring the Liberals back to government. MacEachen came with a poll in hand showing that the Liberals were more likely to return to power with Trudeau at the helm than if he was not.

Trudeau informed his Liberal caucus that he had changed his mind about retiring to raise his family in Montreal, away from the political intrigue of Ottawa, and that he would, indeed, stay to lead the party. "In response to an urgent appeal from the national caucus and the Liberal Party executive, I have decided to resume the leadership of our party in the election campaign that is now underway," he told his Liberal colleagues. "In light of the serious problems confronting Canada, it was my duty to once again undertake the leadership of my party."

National energy program

Trudeau's finance minister, Allan J. MacEachen, introduced the National Energy Program in his budget following the 1980 election. After oil prices more than doubled in 1979 and early 1980, the federal government unilaterally created the NEP to provide energy self-sufficiency, redistribute wealth from the oil-producing Alberta to the federal government, reduce costs for eastern energy consumers, and increase Canadian ownership of the oil industry. Trudeau had already increased government involvement in the energy market when it created Petro-Canada, a Crown Corporation, in 1975 to explore, develop, market, and refine Canada's oil resources. It was a nationalist response to the view that American companies controlled the oil patch. By 1980, Trudeau thought that Ottawa needed to become more involved in the energy sector.

The NEP was a wide-ranging set of policies that included grants for oil drilling, higher taxes on the oil industry, a larger mandate for Petro-Canada, and increased government control of offshore oil and gas discoveries. MacEachen said that the measures would limit oil price increases. Trudeau thought that global oil prices were going to continue to increase, but they began falling by 1982. The oil sector, heavily regulated by the federal government at a time when most of the West was deregulating their oil industry, was less flexible and couldn't easily cope with volatile global oil prices. Journalist David Frum called the NEP, "the single worst economic decision of Canada's 20th century."

The program proved unnecessary, was poor economics, and was bad policy for the energy sector. But the NEP's real impact was political, deepening national divisions. Alberta Premier Peter Lougheed resented the loss of control over natural resources, which was constitutionally the jurisdiction of provinces. He also resented sending money to Ottawa in the form of higher taxes paid by Alberta companies. Most importantly, he resented the unilateral actions of the federal government as Trudeau acted without consulting the western premiers and the Liberals had no MPs west of Manitoba.

Lougheed threatened to stop sending Alberta oil to eastern Canada and "Let the eastern bastards freeze in the dark" became a popular bumper sticker on cars in the province. Albertans viewed Ottawa with greater suspicion, believing that the Toronto-to-Montreal axis controlled the country, or at least the governing Liberal Party. There was growing western alienation, if not outright support for separation. When oil prices cratered in 1982, the hard-hit west blamed Ottawa. The whole ordeal cemented the Liberal Party's unpopularity in much of western Canada.

Trudeau, the former economist and a strong federalist, fumbled the NEP on both economic and federalist grounds. During the second half of the mandate, Jean Chrétien, now the minister of energy, mines and resources, began to dismantle parts of the program.

The Charter

In the 1980 campaign, Trudeau ran on constitutional reform and repatriation. To be fair, Trudeau had made a career of opposing Quebecois nationalism and had previously attempted to change the constitution with a meeting of premiers and civil servants at the Victoria Conference of June 1971. The so-called Victoria Charter set out social policy and constitutional change that would have modernized the British North America Act. Quebec ended up vetoing it and Trudeau put constitutional reform on the backburner.

After taking up the cause of the victorious "no" side in the sovereignty association referendum in Quebec, Trudeau focused on the constitution once again. He wanted a made-in-Canada constitution.

The repatriated constitution and Charter of Rights obtained several goals for Trudeau. It cut the link to Britain (and, Trudeau argued, strengthened the Canadian nation), guaranteed collective rights for Canada's founding peoples, established civil rights in connection to the liberal administrative state, gave the courts enhanced power to create law rather than merely interrupt it, and eroded the cultural distinctiveness of the provinces.

Quebec's separatist Parti Quebecois government would not agree to the new constitution, but Trudeau went ahead with it anyway. His actions fed Quebec nationalism and led to a decade of constitutional wrangling among Ottawa and the provinces. Mulroney twice attempted to bring Quebec into the constitutional fold, which only further stoked separatist sentiment in the province.

Critics of the Charter say it has diminished the role of parliament by inviting the courts to endlessly adjudicate rights claims. While neither abortion nor same-sex marriage are mentioned in the Charter, the Supreme Court of Canada threw out Canada's limited abortion restrictions claiming that they violated the equal treatment and security of the person clauses. Lower courts threw out the traditional definition of marriage under the Charter's equality clause. Likewise, judges, not elected representatives, have dictated policy on prostitution, euthanasia, voting rights for prisoners, and services that refugees must be provided by the state, among a host of issues.

Trudeau Legacy

Except for the nine-month Clark interruption, Trudeau was in power for 16 years, which is impressive in itself but unusual in the politically turbulent 1970s.

Like Pearson, Trudeau was transformative. "By 1984," Larry Zolf would say, "the speed and volume of Trudeau's legislative reforms were unequaled in Canadian history." That is debatable, but if one looks at the Pearson and Trudeau ministries as one project, it is obvious that the Liberal Party set out to fundamentally change Canada.

Trudeau had liberalized abortion, divorce, and homosexuality laws, opened the floodgates of immigration, introduced the *Official Languages Act*, instituted unprecedented state intervention in the economy through wage and price controls, set up Petro Canada, given Canada a new constitution, and regularly sided with dictators in global affairs at the expense of the country's western allies.

Journalist Larry Zolf said, "Socialism is a state of mind; Trudeau is now and has always been a state-of-mind socialist." That is, he wasn't a member of a socialist party, but "Trudeau's socialism was only slightly to the right of David Lewis," the long-time NDP leader. For Trudeau, Zolf explains, "Socialism was the vindication and defense of Big Bureaucratic economic and social power." Thus, his "perpetual bailouts" of private enterprise from Dome to de Havilland, because for Trudeau's socialism "not only does the state guarantee the rules of the marketplace, the state guarantees the marketplace itself." Zolf said upon Trudeau's retirement in 1984 that the Liberal prime minister "was still the most successful socialist in Canadian history" who "could very well be Canada's Last Best Socialist."

Trudeau is remembered for his charisma and flamboyancy. Trudeaumania was a term coined by journalist Lubor Zink in 1968 who used it to describe the cult-like celebrity, the feverish zeal young Canadians, especially youth and women, had for the cool new leader. Pierre Elliott Trudeau famously jumped into a swimming pool with his clothes on and pirouetted behind the queen. He dated stars like actress Barbara Streisand and guitarist Leona Boyd. (Joni Mitchell told an American audience that Pierre Trudeau made her "wet" but that might have been from afar.) More importantly, he had a way with words that could cut down a political opponent or uplift his own ideas. At a time when politicians were still boring – Pearson, Stanfield, and Lewis did not exactly ooze personable-ness – Trudeau had style.

But Pierre Trudeau also had substance. The problem for five electorates is that there was seldom much substance on the campaign trail. Despite his cry for a Just Society, Trudeau didn't really enunciate what that would entail. There was little debate over the grand visions of the parties at the time, because the media and half the public seemed enamoured by Trudeau's style. One might wonder whether his flashiness was a shield behind which Trudeau could hide his agenda to move the country hard-left as he did.

Chapter 2: The Decline of the Liberal Party

Pierre Trudeau states in his memoirs that by 1984 he was becoming tired of politics and wanted to spend more time with his three sons, who he had custody of following the finalization of his divorce from Margaret. Perhaps also influencing his decision were polls showing that the country was ready for a change and the Liberals were going to be defeated if Trudeau was still leading the party.

Trudeau's resignation in the spring of 1984 left the party with two major contenders for the Liberal leadership: John Turner and Jean Chrétien. Turner and Chrétien both served as finance and justice minister under Trudeau and they represented the right and left of the party respectively. Turner was the golden boy, with Bay Street connections. He was seen as a moderate, a Business Liberal who finished third in the 1968 leadership race that chose Trudeau as leader. It was widely believed that only Turner could continue the Liberal Party's hold on power. Chrétien seemed awkward partly because the left side of his face was partially paralysed due to a childhood attack of Bell's palsy. But perhaps more worrying for Liberals was that Chrétien was seen to be on the Left of the party (despite the fact that he balanced the federal budget as Trudeau's finance minister in the late '70s.)

Both men were central players in several signature achievements of Trudeau's time in office. Turner was justice minister in 1969 when the Trudeau government passed the Omnibus Bill (1969) legalizing contraception and abortion, and was instrumental in mollifying Catholic opposition to the bill. Turner left federal politics in 1975 for Bay Street and over time, as Paul Litt reports in *Elusive Destiny: The Political Vocation of John Napier Turner*, the former cabinet minister came to resent Trudeau's long tenure which blocked his own presumed prime ministership.

Chrétien was justice minister when Trudeau negotiated the repatriated constitution and was instrumental in getting recalcitrant provinces on board, most famously working with Saskatchewan Justice Minister Roy Romanow and Ontario Justice Minister Roy McMurtry in the kitchen of the Government's Conference Center in Ottawa, the so-called Kitchen Accord. During these unofficial negotiations, he convinced the provinces to drop demands for an opt-out clause in the Charter of Rights and Freedom, which would be replaced by the notwithstanding clause authorizing governments to temporarily override certain sections of the Charter for up to five years.

Turner and Chrétien strongly disliked each other and fought a nasty leadership campaign. The bad blood between them went back to 1978 when Turner penned a criticism of Chrétien's budget in a corporate newsletter. Chrétien held a grudge. They would be joined in the race by five other candidates, all white men who held various portfolios under Trudeau, but in June 1984, Turner won 54 percent of the vote on the second ballot.

Turner's tenure as prime minister would last a little longer than two months, the shortest of any Liberal. He would finish the Trudeau mandate from 1980, and called an election for September. Internal polls showed an uptick in Liberal support so Turner called an election about nine months earlier than he had to. He had the Governor General dissolve parliament on July 4 and call an election for September 4. Being out of elected politics for nearly a decade may have contributed to the fact that he was an inept campaigner. He used antiquated terms when talking about policy ("make-work programs" instead of "job creation") and seemed to be a throwback to another era when he was caught patting Liberal Party President Iona Campagnolo on her bottom. But worse, he appointed more than 200 Liberals to patronage positions on Trudeau's recommendation (and another 70 of his own choosing). Inexplicably, Turner challenged Progressive Conservative Brian Mulroney in the leaders' debate on his patronage plans. The Tory leader turned the attack around on the patronage appointments Turner himself made earlier that summer. Turner feebly claimed, "I had no option." Mulroney responded: "You had an option, sir. You could have said, 'I am not going to do it. This is wrong for Canada, and I am not going to ask Canadians to pay the price.' You had an option, sir, to say 'no' and you chose to say, 'yes' to the old attitudes and the old stories of the Liberal Party. That sir, if I may say respectfully, that is not good enough for Canadians."

While it was unlikely the Liberals would have won the general election, especially with declining support in Quebec and no support in the West, the exchange was seen as the nail in the Liberal coffin. The Tories won more than half the votes cast and 211 of 282 seats. The Liberals had their worst electoral showing in 117 years of Confederation, winning just 28 percent of the vote and 40 seats, just ten more than the third place NDP.

Despite the terrible showing, Turner kept the leadership. After the disastrous campaign that saw the Liberals reduced to 40 seats, Chrétien refused to publicly support the Liberal leader when asked by journalists. At the 1986 Liberal convention, Turner would obtain the support of 75 percent of delegates to remain leader despite a backroom campaign against him by not only longtime nemesis, Chrétien, but key Liberal strategist Keith Davey.

Turner led the Liberals again in 1988, the famous free trade election. Turner, with his connections to big business, vacillated in 1987 on whether to back the Tories and the Canada-U.S. Free Trade Agreement. He eventually opposed the agreement, thereby splitting the anti-free trade vote between Liberals and the NDP, and Mulroney was returned to power in November albeit with a smaller majority of 169 of 295 seats. The Liberals more than doubled their 1984 result, winning 83 seats, and the NDP grew their caucus from 30 to 43.

Despite the improvement, leaders seldom get a chance to lose a third election in a row. Turner resigned in May 1989 and a leadership race was called for the following June. Chrétien, who had been working behind the scenes to undermine Turner, was set for his second leadership campaign. Joining him was Paul Martin, a first-term MP and former executive with Power Corporation-owned Canada Steamship Lines, whose father thrice ran and lost the Liberal leadership, including in 1968 against Trudeau. MPs Sheila Copps, Tom Wappel, and John Nunziata also ran. Chrétien was the only leadership contender to have previously served in government, as his four challengers were all elected in 1984 or after. Chrétien took 57 percent of the vote, winning easily on the first ballot. Martin finished second with just over a quarter of the delegates. Many Turner loyalists backed Martin, and thus began not only the rocky relationship between Chrétien and Martin, but the continuation of the party's divisions. This all but guaranteed more than a decade of Liberal Party infighting.

Despite what Brooke Jeffrey calls the "divided loyalties" of Liberals, Chrétien won the 1993 election taking 177 of 295 seats with 41.2 percent of the vote. The Tories were reduced to two seats and the Bloc Quebecois became the Official Opposition. The Reform Party emerged as the dominant party of the West. It is often said that Chrétien won because the Right was divided, but after nine years of Tory rule that included bitter constitutional debates, numerous political scandals, and the leadership of the unlikeable Mulroney, the country was ready for change. The Liberals mostly won because they captured Ontario, taking 98 of 99 seats, although they did increase their seat count in the west, taking 27 seats west of Ontario (their best showing in the West since Trudeau won 27 seats in 1968, and three times as many as the Liberals had won in the previous three elections combined).

The Liberals returned to power, but they were not necessarily one big happy family again. In the 1990 leadership race, Chrétien had the support of more than 30 MPs and Martin had the backing of just seven. None of the MPs who supported Martin – Maurizio Bevilacqua, Jesse Flis, Albina Guarnieri, Jean Lapierre, Jim Peterson, Gilles Rocheleau, and Joe Volpe – ever rose to a position of prominence within the Chrétien government although Martin himself was appointed finance minister.

The Chrétien years are generally considered to be boon years for the Liberals. They won three elections and the economy grew in the late 1990s. The Chrétien-Martin team shrank government and delivered balanced budgets. The budget cuts nearly cost the government its majority, with Atlantic Canada turning its back on the party. In 1997, after opportunistically calling an early election just three-and-half years into his mandate, Chrétien won the narrowest of majorities: 155 of 301 seats.

Three years and another early election later, Chrétien increased his majority to 177 seats, in part because of the ruthless campaign he ran against Stockwell Day, who had only just became the leader of the Canadian Alliance Party months before the general election call.

The Chrétien years were marked by a decade of scandal including the broken promise of scrapping the GST, the APEC and Somalia inquiries, Shawinigate, and Jane Stewart's billion-dollar HRDC boondoggle, just to name a few of the most egregious examples. After Chrétien left the political arena, the biggest scandal of the decade of Liberal rule was uncovered. Andrew Coyne called it Adscam, but it was widely known as the Sponsorship Scandal, in which Liberal Party operatives were awarded lucrative government contracts to blanket the Canada wordmark all over Quebec as a pro-federalism initiative that did as much to bolster the party's fortunes in the province as it did to endear Quebecers to the larger country.

It is baffling to many that Chrétien maintained his grasp on power during those scandalous years, but the divided right and a record of good-enough governance kept the Liberals in power. Paul Martin and Jean Chrétien made a terrific team when it came to the fiscal files of the country. Although Canada benefited from the fruits of North American free trade, Martin delivered five consecutive surplus budgets, while lowering taxes. Martin and Chrétien reduced the national debt from about two-third of Gross Domestic Product to only half. Neither inflation nor unemployment were worrying the general public. After decades of profligate spending, higher taxes, and rising debt, the team of Martin and Chrétien seemed to have Ottawa's fiscal house in order and provided, at the very least, competent management of the economy.

But the Chrétien-Martin team was not getting along behind the scenes. Martin, just four years younger than Chrétien, was becoming impatient with his boss and was beginning to fret that, like his father, he would not himself become prime minister. Martin's allies and operatives were slowly taking over the Liberal constituency associations, stacking delegates to conventions, and had the numbers to prevent Chrétien's allies from amending leadership review rules. This was the culmination of two previous attempts before the 1997 and 2000 federal elections to convince Chrétien to step aside, and each had their set of loyalists within caucus and the party apparatus that were often in open conflict. The two reportedly did not get along well and in June 2002, as Martin was both trying to press Chrétien to step aside and consider his own next move, the finance minister was booted out of cabinet, replaced by John Manley. Chrétien maintained that Martin quit, while Martin insisted he was fired by Chrétien. The Prime Minister ordered all cabinet ministers to cease their unofficial leadership campaigns and suggested he might stick around and run again. He did not.

By August, Chrétien said he was going to step down – eventually, setting a 2004 deadline for leaving office, about 18 months after his late-summer announcement.

The leadership campaigns could begin in earnest, as Martin had a seemingly insurmountable lead and his loyalists had rewritten the rules to make a membership sales drive by a challenger difficult. Other party heavyweights such as Finance minister John Manley, former Industry and Health minister Allan Rock, former Newfoundland premier Brian Tobin, and former New Brunswick premier Frank McKenna, all decided against a Quixotic run against Martin, who faced only former deputy prime minister and Heritage minister Sheila Copps. Martin would take 94 percent of the vote at the September 21, 2003 leadership convention, while Copps would garner just six percent of the delegates' votes. Martin became leader of the party in November and was sworn in as prime minister a month later.

The polls suggested that Martin would win a majority government, rejuvenating the Liberals who were still favoured by a plurality of voters but whose support had dipped into the mid-30s according to most polls. At the very least, Martin would strengthen the party by ending the intra-party squabbling.

At about the time Martin became Liberal Party leader and Canada's prime minister, Stephen Harper, an MP and former head of the conservative activist group the National Citizen's Coalition, had helped unite the center-right Canadian Alliance and Progressive Conservative parties of Canada.

The Conservative Party, under a supposedly right-wing Harper, was given no chance of defeating the once again popular Liberals. Indeed, pundits were talking about record-breaking majorities and Harper was described as a caretaker leader of the new Conservatives until the party had a chance to win elections.

However, on February 9, 2004, Auditor General Sheila Fraser issued a report that showed sponsorship contracts that sought to increase support for the federal government in Quebec were missing about $100 million out of $250 million in program spending. Little or no work was being done by associates of the Liberal Party, and Judge John Gomery was eventually appointed by Martin to lead a formal inquiry of the Sponsorship Scandal.

While the Gomery inquiry had yet to sit and hear the lurid details of the Sponsorship Scandal, the stench of corruption following Fraser's report earlier that year hurt the Liberals. Not only did Paul Martin not increase the party's seats in parliament, but its support fell more than four percentage points from the 2000 election. The Liberals, who had 168 seats when the election was called, won just 135, enough to hold on to government, but only a minority. The Conservative party won just under 30 percent of the vote, about five points higher than the Canadian Alliance in 2000 but nine points less than the combined CA-PC support from the previous election. The Conservatives won 99 seats, a moderate improvement, while the Bloc Quebecois took 54 and the NDP 19.

As impressive as Paul Martin had appeared as finance minister under Chrétien, he looked utterly incompetent when he became the head of government himself. His first few months on the job finishing Chrétien's mandate were preoccupied with distancing himself and his Liberal government from the findings in Sheila Fraser's report on the Sponsorship Scandal, and when he finally won his own mandate he had the politically tricky job of navigating parliament's turbulent waters with a minority government. The last minority government in Canada was a quarter century earlier, and it was the brief tenure of Joe Clark. Having spent nearly 15 years seeking the Liberal leadership, he did not want to see it disappear so soon after becoming prime minister.

The Gomery hearings were under way, and resulting testimony lent credence to the suggestion of corruption, with testimony of "bags of cash" being exchanged by Liberal Party operatives. While Gomery exonerated Martin of any responsibility for the scandal, it tainted the party, especially in Quebec.

Martin also lacked focus on his numerous policy priorities; a Conservative press release identified more than 50 items Martin had described as priority while *The Economist* famously called him Mr. Dithers.

He was seen to be desperately buying favours to keep his government alive.

A poorly thought out aid plan for Sudan failed to win budget support from former Liberal MP David Kilgour. In the spring of 2005, Martinin famously welcomed former Conservative leadership candidate and then Tory MP Belinda Stronach into cabinet in order to secure the necessary votes to maintain government. It was seen as crass political opportunism for both Martin and Stronach.

Same-sex marriage legislation passed in parliament in June 2005 with the support of the NDP, Bloc Quebecois and most Liberals. The new law was controversial and divided the Liberal Party from parts of its immigrant base. Older Catholic Italian and Portuguese voters, as well as more recent immigrants, were unhappy with the new law and Martin's partial whipped vote (permitting backbenchers to vote their consciences, but not cabinet ministers).

The polls were heading south for the Liberals, and quickly. In November 2005, after Gomery released the first part of his findings into the Sponsorship Scandal, the opposition parties voted non-confidence in the government and forced the second election in 18 months. Martin asked the Governor General, Michaelle Jean for an unusually long eight-week campaign that was roughly divided in the middle by the Christmas break.

The Harper Conservatives ran a disciplined campaign focusing on a handful of issues, including a cut in the Goods and Services Tax and replacing the Liberals' daycare scheme with a child care credit of $100 per month. The Tories and NDP also hammered the Liberals over the Sponsorship Scandal, and the Martin campaign made numerous missteps during the campaign. They were reduced to fear-mongering, reprising their 2004 attack that Harper had a "hidden agenda" to ban abortion. The Liberals also ran a series of ineffective attack ads, including the infamous "soldiers in the streets" commercial that said: "Stephen Harper actually announced he wants to increase military presence in our cities. Canadian cities. Soldiers with guns. In our cities. In Canada." About Harper's promise to have a one-time vote to reconsider legalization of same-sex marriage, Martin said it was time to gut the notwithstanding clause of the Constitution. It all appeared desperate. And it was.

On January 23, 2006, the Liberals lost. With 36.3 percent of the vote, Harper's Conservatives won a small minority: 124 seats compared to the 103 for the Liberals, who won just 30.2 percent of the vote. The NDP gained 10 seats to finish with 29 and the BQ lost a couple. For the first time in 18 years, the Liberals lost an election. But it was the second election in a row in which the party lost both seats and popular support. Paul Martin resigned as leader. And the 2006 leadership race featured a crowded field for a position that many in the party still considered a prize.

Eleven candidates threw their hat into the ring, although three would drop out before the convention. Early frontrunners included Michael Ignatieff, a high-profile academic and first-term MP, and his old college buddy Bob Rae, the former NDP premier of Ontario (1990-1995) who joined the Liberal Party in 2006. In his book *Fire and Ashes: Success and Failure in Politics*, Ignatieff described being wooed to return to Canada by Alfred Apps, a former Paul Martin organizer, and Ian Davey, son of Keith "The Rainmaker" Davey, while Martin was still prime minister. They suggested that as a public intellectual with experience in the media, he could lead the party to its former glory. Many in the party wanted to prevent Rae, who as leader of the Ontario NDP was seen as too far-left for the Liberal leadership, from winning, even though his brother John was a long-time Chrétien adviser.

The race also featured Scott Brison, an openly homosexual MP who was a Liberal after bolting the Progressive Conservatives following their merger with the Canadian Alliance (and was previously a candidate for the PC leadership race in 2003); Stephane Dion, who served as Martin's environment minister and Chrétien's intergovernmental affairs minister; Ken Dryden, a Hall of Fame goaltender with the Montreal Canadians dynasty of the 1970s, and Martin's social development minister; Martha Hall Findlay, a Toronto lawyer and former candidate for the Liberal Party in Newmarket (she lost to Belinda Stronach in 2004); Gerard Kennedy, a former Ontario Education Minister; Joe Volpe, an MP first elected in 1988 and long-time Martin loyalist who served in his cabinet as Minister of Citizenship and Immigration.

On the first ballot of the convention held in Montreal on the final weekend of November, Ignatieff won slightly less than 30 percent, while Rae garnered just over 20 percent. Dion and Kennedy won 17.8 and 17.7 percent respectively. Three candidates dropped off the first ballot and on the second ballot Ignatieff lacked momentum, gaining the fewest delegates of the three frontrunners and just slightly more than Kennedy. On the third ballot, Dryden was forced to drop off but Kennedy surprised delegates and observers alike by endorsing Dion.

Dion, the only candidate from Quebec in the race, catapulted from third to first, and after Rae was dropped, won on the fourth ballot with nearly 55 percent of the delegates' vote. Some observers saw the influence of Jean Chrétien pulling strings for Dion. At the very least, Dion's victory continued the Liberal tradition of alternating between English and French leaders.

Dion was hampered by a Liberal Party that could no longer raise money in large chunks from the business community due to finance reform laws passed by the Chrétien government and tightened by Harper's. He was crippled early by being defined by the Conservatives as a tax-and-spend liberal, more interested in pumping money into government programs than reducing the tax burden of Canadians. They also ran attack ads painting Dion as weak, and a bit of wimp. The initial bump in polls for the Liberals quickly disappeared.

But Dion was his own worst enemy, hurt by a cluelessness about politics unusual for someone who had spent nearly a decade sitting at the cabinet table. In the 2008 he campaigned on carbon pricing which the Tories justifiably painted as a euphemism for a carbon tax that would increase the cost of everything people wanted to do, from drive cars to heat their homes. Not since Michael Dukakis got shellacked in the 1988 U.S. presidential election had a prominent politician run on a tax increase, even if Dion thought he could slip his tax past voters by not calling it a tax.

Dion also angered some Liberals by not running a candidate in Central Nova. Dion hoped to increase the chances of Green Party leader Elizabeth May against the Conservative Peter MacKay, then the minister of national defense. But the gesture made it look like the party was not only in cahoots with the Greens – May bafflingly called Dion the best candidate for prime minister – but that they were not serious about winning back government if it wasn't going to run a full slate of candidates.

The *Vancouver Province* reported that with party disagreement over Dion's coziness with May, Jewan Bassra, co-chair of Dion's leadership campaign, said, "If the Green and Dion's Liberal party have the same goal and same vision, I don't see a problem." This May-Dion cooperation would help Harper paint the Liberals as a danger to the economy, willing to experiment with risky environmental policies at a time of global economic uncertainty; (the 2008 financial crisis was making headlines south of the border but was hardly an issue during the Canadian election campaign. But it also undermined Dion's authority within the party by seemingly putting the interests of another party, at least on par, if not ahead, of the Liberals'.

Under Dion, the Liberals did even worse at the ballot box. On October 14, 2008, the Liberals were reduced to 77 seats, their poorest showing since Turner's 40 in 1984. Their 26.6 percent share of the popular vote was their lowest percentage ever. The Bloc ended up with 49 seats and the NDP 37 (their second-best showing behind the 1988 free trade election). It is tricky determining where exactly voters switch their support to, but it seemed reasonable that as since the Liberals were losing 400,000-800,000 voters each election compared to the previous election, that the Grits were bleeding support on the right to the Conservatives and the left to the NDP. The Conservatives were still shy of a majority, winning 143 of 307 seats.

Dion announced shortly after his election defeat that he would step aside as leader. Bob Rae and Michael Ignatieff were considered the frontrunners. Dominic Leblanc, the son of a former governor general and an MP since 2000, was reportedly pondering entering the race.

But the Conservatives gave the Liberals new life with their economic update in late November. In it the government announced plans to cut government spending, temporarily take away the ability of civil servants to strike until 2011 so the government could implement its spending restraint, and sell-off Crown assets. But Finance Minister Jim Flaherty also got rid of the $1.95 per-vote subsidy that political parties received. In naked self-interest, the opposition parties banded together to stop the government from ending their taxpayer subsidy, and a formal coalition of the Liberals and NDP, supported in principle by the Bloc Quebecois, was announced. Dion, who was ready to step aside, would be the prime minister.

Conservatives attacked the unholy coalition of opportunists, socialists, and separatists. Prime Minister Stephen Harper said they were undoing the will of the people as demonstrated in the election just months earlier. Harper described the Liberals, NDP, and Bloc as the election losers and said they had no right to form the government. The prime minister said they did not "have a legitimate mandate to govern" and called it an "undemocratic seizure of power." Revenue Minister Jean-Pierre Blackburn went further, calling it "a kind of *coup d'etat.*"

While the constitutionality of coalition governments is well-established, the NDP-Liberal coalition faced obstacles. At the federal level, Canada has had only one coalition government, Robert Borden's Unity Government that welcomed Liberals into the government during World War I. Furthermore, politically it was problematic. The only thing worse than the optics of a government led by a leader that only one-in-four Canadians voted for just months earlier was the image of the three party leaders together, including BQ leader Gilles Duceppe. Canadians could not have liked the idea of the separatist party even unofficially propping up a government. Leger Marketing found that six in ten Canadians concerned with the involvement of the BQ in the coalition.

Polls showed the public uneasy about the opposition trying to topple the government just two months after the federal election. Despite finding disagreement with the Conservative government in general, Angus Reid found that 41 percent of Canadians were opposed to the coalition's toppling of the government while 36 percent supported the move. An Ipsos-Reid poll found 56 percent of Canadians preferred returning to the polls than handing the reins of power to the coalition. Ekos Research found just 28 percent support for the coalition with a plurality (37 thirty-seven percent) favouring proroguing parliament and one-in-five (19 percent) preferring another election, a clear majority for alternatives to the coalition's power grab.

Harper's decision to prorogue parliament bought him time to create a new stimulus budget that turned on the spigot of government spending, which consequently won the support of the Liberal Party. The so-called coup attempt failed and the Liberals would expedite their leadership contest.

Leblanc dropped out of the race and after initially calling for an expedited leadership contest and a quick one-member, one-vote vote in January, Rae would cede the race to Ignatieff. All this happened by December 9, indicating the hastened pace of the political maneuvering at the time. On December 10, the Liberal caucus named Ignatieff interim leader and the party's biennial convention in Vancouver, held April 30 - May 2, 2009, confirmed the former Harvard academic as Liberal leader, with 97 percent of delegates endorsing his leadership.

Like they had done with Dion, the Conservatives sought to define the new Liberal leader through attack ads. Noting Ignatieff was away from the country for 34 years, they said that he was "just visiting" and "not in it for you." The Conservatives painted Ignatieff as an arrogant and out-of-touch egghead who was merely fulfilling the academic's dream of dabbling in politics to try out his theories. In his memoirs, *Fire and Ashes*, Ignatieff admits he was unable to make the transition to politics with its soundbites and need to pander. But he also implicitly admitted that the Tories were correct; he said he had returned to Canada for a political career to fulfill the family promise of public service and to climb political heights that his deceased father, diplomat George Ignatieff, had failed to reach. As if to add icing to the Tory cake, he returned to Harvard shortly after retiring from politics, proving that he was, indeed, just visiting Canada.

Ignatieff was leader for just two years. He was not a natural politician. Neither parliament nor the (permanent) campaign trail is a lecture hall. Then *Maclean's* columnist Andrew Coyne said that all the positions that Ignatieff the public intellectual took that made him interesting as a potential Liberal leader were tossed aside as he appropriated all the standard Liberal beliefs when he became the party's standard-bearer. In February 2011, the opposition brought down Harper's minority government over the budget. The Conservatives mentioned the c-word of Canadian politics – coalition – and Ignatieff offered a discourse on its legitimacy while professing to eschew the possibility if the election did not produce a majority government. It was a moot point.

On May 2, the Conservatives won a majority, 166 of 303 seats, with 39.6 percent of the vote. The NDP leap-frogged over the Liberals to become the official opposition for the first time in their party history. Taking fully a third of the vote, they won 103 seats. The Liberals fell to third-party status for the first time in their history, winning just 34 seats and 18.9 percent of the vote, both historical lows for the Grits. With most of Quebec electing NDP MPs, the Bloc was reduced to four seats, and the Green Party won its first ever seat.

The next day, Ignatieff announced that he would resign as leader of the Liberal Party. The party had its worst showing ever and pundits wondered whether it would survive, possibly merging with the NDP.

Between March 1876 and March 2006, every man – and they were all men – who became leader of the Liberal Party of Canada, was also, at some point, prime minister of Canada, except Edward Blake, the second leader of the party who lost the 1982 and 1887 federal elections to John A. Macdonald's Conservatives. John Turner was the only other Liberal leader not to win an election (although he completed Pierre Trudeau's fourth term). Of the five longest serving prime ministers (up to 2015), four are Liberals: William Lyon Mackenzie King, Pierre Trudeau, Wilfrid Laurier, and Jean Chrétien all served as prime minister for longer than 10 years. The only Tory was Canada's first prime minister, Sir John A. Macdonald.

The Liberals were not only Canada's most successful party, but they were the most dominant party in the developed world, governing for 69 years in the 20th century and earning the nickname the "natural governing party." John Crosbie, a minister in both the Clark and Mulroney governments, used to say that Canadians only elected Tories when they got sick of the Liberals and needed a break.

All that changed, or seemed to, in 2006. Two interim and two full-time leaders saw the party disintegrate from Chrétien's trifecta of majorities to Paul Martin's shrunken minority, to Official Opposition, and eventually third-party status.

When Stephen Harper became the leader of the united Conservative Party in 2003, only one Liberal – Edward Blake – had ever become leader and not served as prime minister. Once Harper achieved his majority in 2011, four Liberal leaders, if you want to include interim leader Bill Graham, served as head of the party without becoming the head of government.

Bob Rae would join that list of losers after the 2011 federal election when the Liberals couldn't show Michael Ignatieff out of the door fast enough. The party, in crisis, was looking for another savior.

Chapter 3: Trudeau the Younger

Justin Trudeau was born on December 25, 1971, three years into his father's first term as prime minister, and the first of three sons Pierre would have with Margaret Trudeau before the marriage quickly deteriorated (the couple divorced in 1984). The father made time for his sons, including having meetings at 24 Sussex with Justin in a baby seat on the table. Both Margaret and Justin recall in their memoirs time spent outdoors, something Pierre insisted the boys spend a lot of time doing. Justin was also at his father's side during prime ministerial trips abroad, and met world leaders both during his travels and at his home when they visited Canada.

After going to the same elite high school as his father, Collège Jean-de-Brébeuf, Justin Trudeau completed his Bachelor of Arts in literature at McGill, where he also began his Bachelor of Education, but he moved west and finished it at the University of British Columbia in 1998. He became a teacher, and while his modern critics mock his qualifications as a few years of being a drama teacher, in fact he taught elementary school math and high school French, English, and drama, over the next three years as a supply teacher and maternity-leave replacement at Sir Winston Churchill Secondary School and the elite private school, West Point Grey Academy, in Vancouver. At this time, he also dealt with two tragedies in his life: the deaths of his brother Michel in 1998 in an avalanche accident and his father to prostate cancer in 2000.

In 2000, at the age of 28, Trudeau, who grew up with the media around his father and home, was thrust into its spotlight. He delivered the eulogy at his father's state funeral at Notre-Dame Basilica in Montreal, and it instantly led to speculation of a political career in the young Trudeau's future.

The eulogy was a magnificent performance. He began with the first words of Mark Antony's speech in Shakespeare's *Julius Caesar*: "Friends, Romans, Countrymen." He told the story of visiting Alert in the Northwest Territories when he was six and his father arranging for him to see Santa Claus working in one the buildings at the settlement where they were staying. Justin Trudeau eulogized, "And that's when I understood just how powerful and wonderful my father was." After delivering most of his funeral oration in English, he ended in French: "*Je t'aime, papa*" – "I love you, dad."

Tracy Whalen, an associate professor in the Department of Rhetoric, Writing, and Communications at the University of Winnipeg, wrote an academic treatment of the eulogy – "'Je t'aime, Papa': Theatricality and the Fifth Canon of Rhetoric in Justin Trudeau's Eulogy for his Father, Pierre Elliott Trudeau" – in which she describes the dramatic flair of Trudeau: "After this opening quotation from Julius Caesar, he paused again, bit his lower lip and sustained that pose, a gesture that was repeated throughout the oration. The delivery was punctuated by head nods, hand gestures (a finger pointed to the ceiling, for instance), eyes closing tight, and moments when Justin's tongue thrust out between his teeth, a sign of excessive effort to carefully and forcefully enunciate words."

It worked. Much of the media fawned over young Trudeau, including typically sane writers like Christie Blatchford who wept at his performance. Political pundits started mentioning Trudeau as a future candidate for elected office. The CBC would later include the eulogy among the list of the most important events of the previous 50 years. The mythologizing of Trudeau the Younger had begun.

A rare voice of dissent came from Peter Worthington of the *Toronto Sun*. He addressed the media's reaction to Pierre's death and Justin's eulogy, noting that the emotional response to Trudeau echoed the reaction to Princess Diana's a few years earlier. Worthington said, "Those now suggesting that as a result of his eulogy, Justin is a possible future PM (!) is almost as embarrassing as advocating sainthood for Diana after her death - a wanton whose self-indulgence hurt those around her and whose self-discipline was non-existent." Worthington called the eulogy a "performance" as much as "genuine grief," a performance delivered by "a drama teacher" and the son of "a consummate actor, ham, show-off, poseur, [and] exhibitionist." It was, said Worthington, "a staged, calculated, neo-political speech."

Eulogies are about the dead, but Justin focused on himself. Jay Scott pointed out, "Justin used the word 'I' and 'my' nineteen times in the first three minutes of the speech." To some extent, talking about one's father will include personal stories, but Trudeau delivered a dramatic, grinning, smirking performance that was just as much about himself as the man he was eulogizing.

Tired of teaching, in 2002 Justin Trudeau began an engineering degree at l'ÉcolePolytechnique de Montréal, but quit the following year. In 2005, became a Masters student at McGill in the Environmental Geography program. At the same time he became involved with Katimavik, a youth volunteer service that had started as a government program by the Trudeau government in the 1970s. He campaigned against a zinc mine in the Northwest Territories, raised avalanche safety awareness, and in 2007, had a bit part in the CBC miniseries, *The Great War*.

Trudeau also toured the country making speeches. Doing speeches can be lucrative for a celebrity, even (then) a minor one whose fame was entirely attached to his last name and whose own accomplishments did not exactly merit hefty speaking fees.

During his 2013 leadership bid, Justin Trudeau revealed the details of his public speaking engagements from 2006 through 2009, for which he pocketed $1.3 million – about than $325,000 a year – for 112 speeches. (He continued making paid speaking engagements as an MP, taking $277,000 in speaking fees from 17 groups including charities, non-governmental organizations, and government bodies like school boards, colleges, and municipalities, but said he stopped the practice when he finally launched his leadership campaign.)

He was typically paid $7,500 to $10,000 per speech. The first speech he gave was on January 14, 2006 at the University of British Columbia, for which he was paid $5,000. Five days later, he was at the University of Guelph to collect a $7,500 cheque for a speaking engagement there. Later that month he was a speaker at Wilson Young & Associates Inc., a consultancy that does business with, among other clients, governments at various levels. The next month he addressed Mastercard Canada, the next month the Toronto District School Board and in April, at separate events, the Toronto School Administrators Association and the Ontario Catholic School Trustees Association. In May, he had his first $10,000 speaking engagement, the Elementary Teachers Federation of Ontario. Later that month he was back at both the Toronto District School Board and Toronto School Administrators Association for another round of speeches. He often spoke about education, using his brief three years as a teacher as a credential to tell professional educators how to do their jobs.

Sometimes he would speak twice in one day to different groups. On May 10, 2006 he talked to the Toronto school board and the Professional Administrators of Volunteer Resources, and made a cool $12,500 between the pair of engagements. Later that week he made two more speeches in Toronto. Over four days and four speeches he earned $30,000. If you include his May 3 talk, in two weeks he made almost as much in a half-month ($40,000) as the median full-time income in Canada that year ($41,401).

It isn't fair to say that he was paid $40,000 for a few hours of speaking and glad-handing. Speeches take time to prepare and speakers are also being compensated for the time it takes to travel and be away from other endeavours. (Usually groups had to pick up his travel tab, too.)

While it is easy to criticize Trudeau, the son of privilege and wealth, for making a living taking speaking fees from charities and NGOs – organizations whose goals he ostensibly supported – it could be argued that he was also building a brand, engaging future supporters and voters, and honing skills like public speaking, that could help a future politician.

In his memoirs, *Common Ground*, Justin Trudeau claims to have eschewed party politics growing up. "I was never a Young Liberal, and I never went to conventions or other Liberal events. That world simply did not appeal to me." He said that he was approached about running for elected office shortly after his father's death but doesn't even remember the details. All that changed by 2006. At first he became involved in the Liberal Party's Renewal Commission (in the aftermath of the party being out of power for the first time in 13 years) leading efforts to engage youth. Trudeau writes in his memoirs, "I did wonder whether, given my growing experience as a public speaker on youth and the environment with a message about citizen engagement, I might have something to offer a Liberal Party in renewal."

Later that year he became involved in the party's leadership race to replace Paul Martin, endorsing Gerard Kennedy, a former Ontario education minister, in his bid to become the next Grit leader. Trudeau officially introduced Kennedy to the convention and he joined him in supporting Stephane Dion after the second ballot when the former Ontario cabinet minister chose to exit the race before being dropped from the ballot.

It was becoming obvious that Trudeau's next career would be elected politics. He selected the Montreal riding of Papineau where he fought a contested nomination. He defeated a Montreal city councilor, Mary Deros, and a local Italian newspaper publisher, Basilio Giordano, and it wasn't close. Trudeau had 690 votes, Deros 350, and Giordano 45.

Trudeau often boasts that he could have picked an easier riding, like Outremont, which had a by-election in 2007 (ultimately won by future NDP leader Thomas Mulcair) and was considered a "safe" Liberal seat. Although Papineau was represented by Bloc Quebecois MP Vivian Barbot, her two-year stint as the riding's MP were the only two years which it did not have a Liberal MP going back to 1957. In the 2008 general election, Trudeau won handily with 38.4 percent of the vote, a ten-point victory over the NDP, with the incumbent falling to third.

Trudeau was unlike any other rookie MP. Many newly elected MPs personally dream of becoming leader, but few are widely assumed to be on such a track.

For Trudeau, the expectation among colleagues and pundits was that some-day, sooner rather than later, he would run for the Liberal Party leadership.

Althia Raj says in her fawning biography, *The Contender*, "Justin Trudeau's c.v. does not read like those of most politicians: camp counsellor, white water rafting instructor, bungee jumping coach, snowboarding instructor, bouncer, high school teacher, radio host, engineer school dropout, grad school dropout, not-for-profit administrator, public speaker, member of parliament." That certainly isn't leadership material, unless one has the pedigree of being a former prime minister's son.

Trudeau would not challenge Michael Ignatieff's leadership ambitions in 2009, instead biding his time. He was the co-chair of the national convention in Vancouver in April. He was named Liberal critic for multiculturalism and youth in October 2009. The next September, he was named youth, citizenship, and immigration critic. When Rae became leader, he appointed Trudeau the party's critic for post-secondary education, youth and amateur sport. Shortly thereafter, he would announce his intentions to run for the Liberal Party leadership.

Chapter 4: Looking for a Saviour

Michael Ignatieff, the Upper Canada College graduate and international intellectual, led his party to the worst defeat in its history on May 2, 2011. The next day he said he would resign, and on May 11 he sent his letter of resignation to the Liberal Party of Canada's National Board of Directors. The party's constitution required a leadership vote within five months, but after setting a date for a leadership convention for late October, the party amended the provision to allow themselves time to rebuild. The thinking was that with a majority government, they did not need to rush into a leadership campaign. The following June, the party leadership voted for April 14, 2013, but stated that the official kickoff for the leadership campaign would be November 14, 2012.

The National Board consulted with the caucus about an interim leader. The best interim leader would be Bob Rae or Marc Garneau. Both were bilingual and had broad support within caucus. The board wanted the interim leader to agree to not run for the permanent leadership – although both harboured leadership ambitions – nor implement major changes to the party, including negotiating a merger with the NDP. The caucus voted on May 25 for Rae after he reluctantly agreed not to seek the permanent leadership.

In September 2011, Leger Marketing polled Liberal supporters and found that Justin Trudeau and Bob Rae had about the same level of support. When Forum Research began asking Liberal voters who they wanted as leader, they did not even include Trudeau among the possibilities (although it did list Bank of Canada president Mark Carney and Calgary mayor Naheed Nenshi, two individuals who were never likely to enter the race). Forum Research found that Rae had about four times the support that the second most popular "candidate" (Carney) had, 47 percent to 12 percent. A month later, Forum Research found Rae had a 10-point lead over Trudeau, 40-30. Two months later, Trudeau narrowed the gap to 30-24, with about one-in-five supporters saying that they didn't know who they were backing; a raft of unlikely candidates sharing the remaining quarter of respondents.

On March 31, 2012, Ottawa witnessed a political battle quite unlike any other. For weeks, Justin Trudeau, the Liberal MP from Papineau, and Patrick Brazeau, the Conservative senator from Repentigny, Quebec, were training and trash-talking for a charity boxing contest.

The Fight for the Cure to raise money for cancer research occurs every year in the capital and features local minor celebrities such as authors, chefs, and local entrepreneurs, but it never gathered as much attention as when these two political brawlers were set to enter the ring. The *National Post* reported Brazeau was a three-to-one favourite; although this was never sourced to a sports book, it quickly became the conventional wisdom. Brazeau was favoured, perhaps because of his stockiness, despite the fact that Trudeau had boxed when growing up. According to the documentary *God Save Justin Trudeau* the Liberal MP said that he had boxed all his life and that he had always wanted to get into the ring. He was also caught on tape telling his wife Sophie Gregoire, "I was put on this planet to do this." She counselled him to be more humble.

After two months of hype, the contestants finally faced each other in the ring. Brazeau came out swinging hard but quickly tired. Trudeau used his height advantage to avoid the punches. Once the Tory senator was clearly winded, Trudeau started to put a beat down on him, and the MP from Papineau won a Technical Knockout in the third round when the referee declared it unsafe for Brazeau to continue.

The Huffington Post's Althia Raj's biography of Trudeau uses the boxing match as a metaphor for Trudeau's scrappy politics, a tale weaved throughout her ebook, *The Contender: The Justin Trudeau Story,* as do the documentarians behind *God Save Justin Trudeau.* They both stress that he is underestimated but should never be considered an underdog. The documentarians catch Trudeau confidently bragging, "I fight and I win." While the political messaging is obvious, Trudeau himself repeatedly denies making up with mind about running for leader at that time; for now, he's focused on beating Brazeau.

But was he really? His boxing jacket said, "The Canadian Kid." He talked about how the contest was not only against Brazeau, but all Conservatives. He is talking politics and there are references to "real Canadian values" – presumably Conservatives' values are not authentically Canadian – and complaints about Tories being out of touch with real Canadians. At one point he tells the *God Save Justin Trudeau* filmmakers "every fight for me is a fight for values." It buggers credibility to claim Trudeau did not have one eye on another contest or two: the Liberal leadership and the 2015 federal election.

Considering the attention Trudeau has always received, it is not accurate to say the boxing match thrust the 40-year-old, second-term MP into the spotlight. But it did add to his political stardom. The young MP with nice hair and a flair for speechifying, now had a win under his belt. It was arguably a meaningless victory in the grand scheme of things but it was all his own. Trudeau wasn't able to beat up Brazeau because of his own famous last name. Trudeau, and his handlers and fans, would use the boxing match to vividly illustrate what Justin Trudeau could accomplish with hard work and dedication.

The victory also contributed to Trudeau's underdog narrative. From winning in a riding that was ostensibly difficult for him to do, so to beating the buff senator that was going to wipe the floor with him, Trudeau overcomes the odds. Or so the story has it.

On the Liberal leadership front, he was emerged as the favourite.

By spring 2012, there was talk that the National Board of the Liberal Party would release Rae from his signed agreement not to run for the permanent leadership, but on June 13, 2012, Rae announced that he would not be a candidate and would remain interim leader until the convention the next April.

The next poll by Forum Research released days later had Trudeau with the support of a third of Liberal voters, more than twice the backing of the next two (theoretical) candidates combined: Liberal MP David McGuinty, the brother of Ontario premier Dalton McGuinty, and former industry and finance minister John Manley. Neither of them would end up throwing their hat into the ring.

Over the summer only one candidate would formally enter the race. Deborah Coyne, an academic and constitutional expert, lost to Jack Layton in Toronto Danforth in her only foray into elected politics in 2006. She garnered a fair amount of attention for two reasons. She was the first candidate to officially launch a leadership bid (announcing 23 detailed policies on her website) and she had her own Trudeau connection. She had advised Newfoundland premier Clyde Wells during his opposition to Meech Lake and she had dated Pierre Trudeau during the constitutional debates of the early 1990s. In 1991 she had given birth to his only daughter, Sarah Coyne. The papers were atwitter with the possible familial connection: Justin, Pierre's son, facing off against the mother of Pierre's only daughter.

Despite being the only declared candidate, the media was focusing on the man who had earlier eschewed any interest in the job: Justin Trudeau.

On October 2, Trudeau announced that he was seeking the Liberal Party leadership.

Trudeau and Coyne had the race to themselves for more than a month. Coyne's policy pronouncements were no match for the flamboyant, slick-talking son of a former prime minister. It certainly helped that many in the media were nostalgic for the first Trudeaumania and eager to help along its second incarnation. Trudeau offered platitudes about engaging citizens, helping the middle class, and uttered cliches about Canadian values, and no one was going to call him out on it.

In November there was an avalanche of new candidates. On November 7, David Bertschi, an Ottawa lawyer and failed 2011 Liberal candidate for Ottawa-Orléans, announced that he was seeking the Liberal Party leadership. On November 14, the official start to the leadership race, Martha Hall Findlay, a former one-term MP for Willowdale defeated in the 2011 election and failed 2006 leadership candidate, announced that she would try again for the leader's job. On the same day, Karen McCrimmon, a retired Canadian Forces Lieutenant colonel who served in the Gulf War, Yugoslavia, and Afghanistan, and whose only political experience was losing in the riding of Carleton-Mississippi Mills in 2011, also entered the race. On November 26, Joyce Murray, who the year earlier was re-elected to a second term representing Vancouver Quadra, entered the race as the unite-the-left leadership candidate. Two days later, Trudeau's most serious challenger, former astronaut Marc Garneau, a second-term MP from Westmount–Ville-Marie, entered the contest. Soon they were joined by George Takach, a technology lawyer from Toronto and in January, former federal justice minister Martin Cauchon who had last sat in parliament in 2004 and had lost in his attempt to return in 2011.

It was less a leadership race than a coronation. The big names such as Ontario Premier Dalton McGuinty, former New Brunswick premier Frank McKenna, and MPs such as Scott Brison, Dominic LeBlanc, and David McGuinty, all decided not to challenge Trudeau for the crown, if they ever gave serious thought to entering in the first place. Trudeau's challengers were a pair of lawyers, a retired member of the military, and an academic whose combined elected political experience was three election losses, a former MP who had lost three of her last four elections (Findlay also lost as the Liberal candidate against Belinda Stronach in Newmarket-Aurora in 2004), a former MP who lost his last two elections, and two MPs that were first elected to parliament at the same time he was. Garneau was the only candidate to win the support of a sitting Liberal MP, and he could only get three of them to back him.

Trudeau had more endorsements than all other candidates combined. Twenty-four sitting MPs, more than two-thirds of the caucus, backed Trudeau, including Scott Brison, Irwin Cotler, Ralph Goodale, Dominic LeBlanc, and John McCallum. There were also 18 senators supporting his leadership bid, including party hacks like former defense secretary Art Eggleton, defeated

Grit MP Mac Harb, Jean Chrétien's director of communications Jim Munson, and backroom legend David Smith. He also had the support of 15 former MPs including Sheila Copps, Mark Holland, Dan McTeague, and Paul Szabo (two notable social liberals and two social conservatives). He was also backed by more than a dozen prominent provincial Liberals including Ontario Finance Minister Dwight Duncan, Manitoba Liberal Leader Jon Gerrard, Nova Scotia Liberal Leader Stephen McNeil, and former Ontario premier David Peterson. He also attracted the support of Gerald Butts, president and CEO of World Wildlife Fund Canada and former Principal Secretary to Ontario Premier Dalton McGuinty, child-rights activist Craig Kielburger, Mississauga mayor Hazel McCallion, and *Cirque du Soleil* founder Guy Laliberté.

The leadership race was a bit of a farce. The polls and general mood indicated that Trudeau's path to the leadership would be a cakewalk. In three Forum Research polls of Liberal Party supporters (among the general public, not paid-up members who would be voting for leader) in December and January, Trudeau never polled under 60 percent, while his next nearest competitor, Garneau, fell from 20 percent to six. Martha Hall Findlay, widely believed to be among the second-tier of candidates, had three percent. Everyone else polled worse.

Bertschi, Takach, and, eventually, Garneau, would all drop out.

The party held debates in Vancouver, Winnipeg, Mississauga, Halifax, and Montreal. Chantal Hebert of the *Toronto Star* asked, "Sure, he beat a Conservative senator in the boxing ring, but can Justin Trudeau take a debate punch from fellow Liberal leadership candidates?" He didn't have to find out. Perhaps because he was Liberal royalty, or perhaps they didn't want to weaken the presumptive winner and future leader, these debates were not really the forum to strike blows against Trudeau. There was some debate about uniting the left, which was the essence of Murray's campaign and was opposed by Trudeau. Murray proposed a one-time cooperation among the Liberals, NDP, and Greens to run a single candidate against the Conservatives. Trudeau said that Murray's plan would result in "Thomas Mulcair as prime minister of this country and that's not what I'm interested in."

After the debate in Mississauga, Bertschi justified not going after the front-runner saying that Trudeau would play an important role in rebuilding of the Liberal Party.

During the Feb. 16 debate in Mississauga, Findlay challenged Trudeau on whether he could speak for the middle class, considering his personal wealth and circumstances. She was booed by the audience. She said Liberals shouldn't be dividing Canadians by class, and was booed some more. Trudeau defended himself saying that he got into politics to serve the public, people not like himself.

The format of that debate was one-on-one and three-way debates, and shortly after the Findlay-Trudeau exchange, Garneau used part of his time, about another question, to defend Trudeau: "Anybody in this country who wants to run for the leadership of this country should not be looked down upon in any way, whatsoever, regardless of their financial income." He was cheered by the Toronto-area crowd.

But Garneau could still ask fair questions of Trudeau. He looked at him and asked: "What in your résumé qualifies you to be the leader of the country?" The crowd wasn't pleased, but the question gave Trudeau the chance to wax platitudes: "Leadership is about drawing people in, and about involving Canadians in the kinds of conversations we have, and you can't lead from a podium in a press conference, you can't win over Canadians with a five-point plan, you have to connect with them. And we have to make room for Canadians in the debate that we have coming forward." Garneau challenged Trudeau, saying that he was speaking "in generalities." More hisses from the audience. Garneau asked again, "What is it in your résumé that qualifies you to be the future prime minister of Canada?" Trudeau responded: "I fought extremely hard to earn a nomination in Papineau that involved going up against strong Liberals and convincing people to come together under my leadership." After the debate, Garneau told reporters that Trudeau was "short on details" of how he would help middle class voters. Earlier that week, Garneau criticized Trudeau's campaign which was strong on clichés but weak on policy: "As Liberals we cannot afford to wait until after the leadership race to find out what we signed up for ... Justin has stated that now is not the time to tell Liberals, to tell Canadians, where he stands and what his plan is for the country. He has said he will do this after the leadership race, sometime before the next election in 2015. In my opinion, this is the same as asking Canadians to buy a new car without test-driving it." Garneau couldn't be more blunt: "He has told Canadians that we need a bold plan and a clear vision without defining either. On Justin's two clear priorities, the middle class and youth engagement he has said nothing." A month later Garneau withdrew from the race and he endorsed Trudeau.

Answering for Trudeau, the CBC's Susana Mas rounded up the specifics of Trudeau's campaign by summing up an interview he gave several months later: "He is against the proposed Northern Gateway pipeline, that he's in favour of decriminalizing marijuana, that he would reverse the federal government's decision to raise the age of eligibility from 65 to 67, and that he would not raise the GST." On such lofty visions leaderships are made.

If there was a debate within the leadership race, it was over Murray's idea that the left-of-center parties should cooperate to dislodge the Tories from power. Trudeau summarized his view: "I don't think we'd ever come to the point of a coalition being necessary. I am running to win for the leadership of the Liberal Party and to win the prime ministership of the country. I do not think we're ever going to have to build any sort of coalition."

Of the fifth and final debate in Montreal, the Canadian Press reported that it "was a mostly sedate affair that only saw some sparks fly toward the end over the issue of strategic voting." By the Montreal debate, two weeks before the voting for leadership began and three weeks before the convention that would announce the winner, it was a foregone conclusion that Trudeau would win.

When the first-ballot results were announced, it wasn't even close. Justin Trudeau won 81,389 votes as 78.8 percent of Liberal members and supporters who cast a ballot marked his name. Under the point allocation system that weighted votes by riding, he did even better, with 80.09 percent. Joyce Murray was a distant second with 12,148 votes (11.76 percent). Martha Hall Findlay finished third with 6.37 percent of the total, and Cauchon was fourth with less than 1.6 percent.

The party had spoken loudly and clearly. It seemed as if destiny was being fulfilled, for both the Liberal Party of Canada and for its new leader, Justin Trudeau, son of the 15th prime minister and the man the party hoped would follow in his footsteps.

At the Westin Hotel in Ottawa, Trudeau gave his victory speech, urging the party faithful to unite behind him. He said that infighting had hurt the party in the past:" Canadians turned away from us because we turned away from them, because Liberals became more focused on fighting with each other than fighting for Canadians." He continued:"Well, I don't care if you thought my father was great or arrogant. It doesn't matter to me if you were a Chrétien-Liberal, a Turner-Liberal, a Martin-Liberal or any other kind of Liberal.The era of hyphenated Liberals ends right here, tonight."

But it wasn't all forward looking. There was a new Trudeaumania.

Part II: Justin Trudeau's Leadership

Chapter 5: Justin Trudeau, Part-time MP, Part-time Speaker

Justin Trudeau made a lot of money making speeches and it wasn't a job he would relinquish easily even once he was elected to parliament. Technically, this is not breaking any rules. The House of Commons requires that MPs publicly report any source of income over $10,000 to the Office of the Conflict of Interest and Ethics Commissioner, although not the dollar amount. The Huffington Post analyzed the public registry and found that more than about 40 percent of MPs – 121 of them in 2013 – declared additional income aside from their $160,200 base salary, with income sources including rental properties and music royalties. In most cases it is not a second job they are practicing but income that is attained with little or no work on the part of the MP, such as ownership stakes in restaurants, productive farmland, or sitting on the boards of companies. Elizabeth May earned an additional salary as party leader while Conservative MP Mark Adler continued to make money from his 50percent ownership stake in the Economic Club of Canada, a forum for high-profile speakers, and Liberal MP Scott Brison earned money as chairman of SeaFort Capital Inc., a private investment venture, which he partly owns.

More than a year before becoming MP, Trudeau criticized the idea of taking outside jobs as a Member of Parliament: "You don't get to be an MP and also be on multiple directorships." He said he would step down from his various directorships if elected MP: "It's just par for the course. You represent your constituents. You don't represent any other organizations." There is a difference between being a director and flying around the country taking money to deliver speeches, especially when it comes to who an MP represents. But there is also the question of doing one's job.

After Trudeau became leader he stopped doing speaking gigs, but it was in his first few months as leader that it became public that he had accepted paid speaking appearances as MP. He admitted that he had done "hundreds" of speaking engagements after being elected in 2008, but he had only been only paid for 17 of them, although he had made the tidy sum of $277,000 for those appearances. He defended taking speaking fees by saying, "While speaking as an MP, I've never charged anyone a single penny." He claimed, "Any work that I did when hired by charities to make a fundraiser successful was completely separate from my role and identity as an MP." It's not obvious that the distinction is all that easy to maintain. Certainly his profile as MP made him more attractive as a speaker and no doubt he was introduced as the Member of Parliament for Papineau. It is worth noting that he made an average of $16,294 per speaking engagement after being elected, and that while he was only once paid a $20,000 speaking fee before becoming MP, he did so ten times after being elected. At the very least, being an MP made it easier to charge more.

Trudeau was criticized by some Conservative and NDP MPs for charging charities for appearances, but he said that that's the way charities and professional speaking work, ignoring the fact that he was no longer a professional speaker but a parliamentarian. During a speech at the Operating Engineers Training Institute of Ontario in Oakville, Trudeau lumped himself in with "professional fundraisers" and poked fun at his critics: "Just because no one would hire many of my colleagues to actually come and be a draw at an event doesn't mean they're not good parliamentarians."

Trudeau insisted that he only charged charities because he was a draw for their events which in turn raised money for their work. But according to the list of all his prior speaking engagements that he released during his leadership campaign, he spoke to unions (Ontario Public Service Employees' Union), trade organizations (Certified Management Accountants of Ontario), and school boards (the Algonquin & Lakeshore Catholic District School Board and Waterloo Catholic District School Board) and schools (Kincardine District Secondary School). He also spoke at an event hosted by the Rogers Media-owned Marketing Magazine shortly after being elected, and addressed the Ontario Library Association and Credit Institute of Canada. Despite his claim that he was only helping charities raise money by appearing at their fundraisers at great expense (they also had to cover transportation and other related travel expenses), a majority of the remunerated speaking engagements he had after becoming an MP had nothing to do with charity, even if some of them may have had charitable status or non-profit status (such as schools).

One charity, the Grace Foundation, which works with seniors in Saint John, New Brunswick, complained that they had lost money on the fundraiser at which Trudeau was the star attraction in 2012 and for which he charged them his by now usual $20,000 fee. The Grace Foundation reportedly asked Trudeau for a refund, and when the news became public the negative publicity led to a media brouhaha. Trudeau said, "I have decided to reach out to all the organizations that hired me as a professional speaker while I was a member of parliament to engage with them to find a satisfactory solution. I am open to exploring all options with them to ensure that they are satisfied with the outcome." This was widely reported as Trudeau being willing to pay back organizations unhappy with his performance. Trudeau spokesperson Kate Purchase later told the media that no group asked for their money back, including, ultimately, the Grace Foundation.

NDP ethics critic Charlie Angus said that it was inappropriate for Trudeau to charge charities for speaking engagements. He told the CBC, "It was completely unethical for a member of parliament to be charging fees, especially outrageous fees, to charities and schools." In the House of Commons, Angus said that it was one thing for a doctor to occasionally practice medicine to maintain the license, but added, "What we don't make allowance for is people skipping votes, having terrible attendance records and running a side business." Angus said, "I speak at numerous events. I believe it's part of my job as an MP."

Canadians seemed to agree. A Forum Research poll in March 2013 found that 76 percent of people did not want MPs earning speaking fees and 57 percent of Canadians wanted Trudeau to return the speaking fees he collected from charities and non-profits.

Trudeau also said in his Oakville speech that he would never use his MP budget to travel to speaking appearances, and that he kept his MP and professional speechifying separate. He reiterated that message a few days later on CTV's *Question Period*. Host Kevin Newman asked the Liberal leader, "Have you, did you, while you were an MP, use any of the House of Commons travel fund to be able to do any of these speaking engagements?" Trudeau responded: "Absolutely not. From the very first day I arrived as an elected MP in 2008, I checked with the ethics commissioner, we were clear before, during and after. It was always entirely, entirely separate for me. There was no overlap. There should be no overlap. And I never spoke as an MP either. I always spoke as an environmental education advocate, which I've been for a long time, and as a former teacher." On another occasion he insisted, "I absolutely never used any house or parliamentary resources in any speaking engagements, in any of my professional work."

Later that year, on December 5, Audrey O'Brien, clerk of the House of Commons, informed Trudeau that he had expensed parliament – that is, charged taxpayers – $672 for a car service he had used to travel from Ottawa to Kingston in April 2012 to talk at Queen's University about youth engagement and education, for which he was paid $12,000 by the school. Trudeau claimed that it was accident and repaid the full amount in January. In a statement released by his office, Trudeau explained: "Due to human error, the invoice was batched with a number of other invoices relating to my parliamentary duties, which involved the same transportation company used for my regular travel between Ottawa and Montreal, totalling $2085.71." He added, "Shortly after being advised of this error, I wrote a personal cheque for the improper claim of $672.00 and asked that it be delivered to the Receiver General of Canada immediately." The error, he said, led to a review of more of his expenses which found that two other items had been incorrectly submitted, per diems from November 2009 for $83.55 and May 2010 for $84.50, which were also paid back. Trudeau said, "As a member of parliament, I take full, personal responsibility for the financial administration of my office, including these errors." NDP leader Thomas Mulcair said that Trudeau only apologized for mistake after it was revealed publicly. Conservative MP Candice Bergen said, "Justin Trudeau's willingness to take hundreds of thousands of dollars from charity and now taxpayers raises serious questions of his judgment."

Trudeau did not appear to break any rules, but continuing to accept speaking gigs after becoming MP showed poor judgement, a serious shortcoming for a person who wants to be prime minister.

Chapter 6: Open Nominations

There is theory and then there's practice. Nearly every would-be leader in any party promises more open nominations. The party membership likes the idea that they will be able to choose their own candidates at the riding level with no or minimal interference from party central. Paul Martin and Stephen Harper both promised more open nominations when they ran to become the leaders of their respective parties, but they too would meddle when there was a favoured candidate to be parachuted into a riding or a local favourite from the community that the party headquarters wanted to carry the team's colours. No one should be surprised that Trudeau would break his promise of ensuring open nominations.

Trudeau ran for leadership calling for open nominations in every riding. It was so important that it was an idea that needed a proper name with capital letters: Open Nominations. Even sitting MPs would face nomination fights. The Liberal Party website has a section called "Open Nominations." It states, "Our Leader Justin Trudeau is committed to open nominations in all 338 ridings from coast to coast to coast." That's signed by Katie Telford and Dan Gagnier, National Campaign Co-Chairs.

It's not quite as simple. Before a Liberal can become an official candidate, they must be vetted by the Green Light Committee. That is a subcommittee of the National Election Readiness Committee and its job is to evaluate the fitness of individuals who want to run for the Liberals in a federal election contest. It would do background checks, investigate the financial affairs of applicants, examine any ethical concerns, look at the "history of contribution to the community and/or participation in public life," and ascertain the candidate's history within the party and whether he or she subscribes to the "policies and values" of the Liberal Party. If the candidate passes muster, the committee green lights the "Potential Nomination Contestant" and he or she becomes a "Qualified Nomination Contestant." The fine print is that "any approval shall not be construed as in any way precluding the Leader from subsequently expressing an intention ... that it will not be his or her intention to endorse such person" as the official candidate. Under both Liberal Party rules and federal law, the party leader must sign papers for every candidate running under the party banner.

The idea that there are open nominations decided by riding members is completely false. First candidates must pass muster with party headquarters and the leader.

But it might be surprising that for someone who has made the open nominations a centerpiece of his leadership, Trudeau has come under an unusual amount of fire for breaking his promise with a number of high profile conflicts leading to charges that open nominations are a complete joke.

Most political parties will clear the way for their star candidates. It has happened several times for Trudeau's favoured candidates.

Bill Blair was the former chief of police in Toronto, presiding over the force when it arrested and detained more than 1000 people during the 2010 G-20 summit in Toronto. Blair defended the police actions, including arresting peaceful protesters for not showing identification within five meters of a perimeter set up around the meeting of world leaders, because as the police chief said, he was "trying to keep the criminals out." There were calls for his resignation and the Liberal McGuinty government in Ontario attempted to clarify the extraordinary powers the police had during the international gabfest, but Blair remained adamant that he had acted properly. Within days of his retirement in April 2015, Blair announced that he was going to run for the Liberal nomination in Scarborough Southwest to face NDP MP Dan Harris. Claiming that both the Liberals and Conservatives had courted him as a candidate, Blair, the police chief who defended arresting peaceful protesters, said, "Frankly, Mr. Trudeau and the Liberals put forward values that I felt most closely aligned with."

According to the *Scarborough Mirror*, a local weekly paper, more than a half dozen candidates were seeking the nomination. Already green-lit were Michael Kempa, a University of Ottawa criminology professor, Tim Weber, a former CTV news anchor, and Marlène Thélusma Rémy, a Haitian-born social science professor at Collège Boréal in Toronto, all of whom were signing up members for nearly a year before the riding nomination. Also green-lit were Muhammad Bukhari, a Bangladeshi-born journalist and local community organizer, and Michele Serrano, an accountant and immigration consultant. Three other candidates were awaiting their green light: Chayanika Dutta, Alamgir Hussain, and Shamsul Islam. The *Mirror* quoted former MP Michelle Simson in

February saying that she opposed waiting for the riding to hold its nomination meeting until Blair was ready to run following his anticipated retirement in April: "I do not support holding the nomination open. It is very unfair to the existing candidates. Their lives are essentially on hold."

Trudeau's team did not disqualify any of the higher profile candidates who had been working for nearly nine months on their nominations by the time Blair threw his hat into the ring. But Trudeau did appear beside Blair in announcing a campaign platform plank about a fund for police who are killed or injured on the job. The message was clear: Bill Blair was the leader's favoured candidate.

Weber initially welcomed Blair to the nomination race, but days later withdrew and became his campaign co-chair. Several weeks later Kempa withdrew, saying, "Immediately following Mr. Blair's expression of interest to join the contest, it was made clear – through joint appearances with the leader, and appearances with other nominated candidates – that the former chief is the Liberal Party's preferred choice."

Despite having a year's advantage signing up new members to support their nominations, it was clear that they either couldn't win or the party didn't want them to.

Trudeau did not need to fix the contest in Scarborough Southwest because he signaled his preference and everyone that needed to fell into line with the party.

It doesn't always go so smoothly.

Andrew Leslie retired from the Canadian Armed Forces in 2011 as a Lieutenant-General who served in several senior jobs such as Chief of Transformation and Chief of the Land Staff. His military and political pedigree is impressive. He is the son of Brigadier General Edward Leslie and grandson of both General Andrew McNaughton and Brooke Claxton, each of whom served as Minister of National Defence under Liberal prime ministers William Lyon Mackenzie King and Louis St. Laurent respectively (Claxton also served as King's Minister of National Health and Welfare.) The Conservatives wanted Leslie to run either the Royal Canadian Mounted Police or one of the national museums, but he had his eye on politics.

In September 2013 Leslie became co-chair of Liberal International Affairs Council of Advisors, advising Trudeau on foreign and defense issues, and later he announced that he would seek the Liberal nomination in Ottawa-Orléans. On December 7, 2014 he was acclaimed the Liberal candidate despite never living in the riding and not speaking French in the largely Francophone area.

It was anything but a smooth ride for the Liberals getting their star candidate the nomination.

Former leadership contender and Ottawa lawyer David Bertschi also wanted to run again in Ottawa-Orléans after losing to incumbent Royal Galipeau in 2011. Despite receiving Green Light Committee approval for his nomination six months earlier, he learned that he was disqualified in November 2014. Jeremy Broadhurst, the Liberal party's national director, told Huffington Post that "new information regarding a number of areas of concern had been brought to light in recent weeks." Although the committee does not formally announce reasons for non-approval or disqualification, the Huffington Post reported party officials claims that Bertschi had failed to repay old campaign debts and had not disclosed a defamation case against the American gossip website TheDirty.com. Bertschi supporters wrote an open letter to Trudeau in November accusing the Liberal Party of sidelining their candidate in favour of Leslie, the star recruit: "We understand that you have a preferred candidate, it has been clear since day one." They accused Trudeau of providing campaign staff for Leslie's nomination and helping raise his profile by appearing publicly with him. They also suggested that the local riding association had delayed the nomination meeting to give Leslie more time to sell memberships to have a better chance of beating Bertschi. His supporters said that they were looking forward to the contest despite the "uphill battle" of fighting the party's favoured candidate, but after the green light was rescinded the work of more than 120 volunteers who put in 13,000 hours of work, was victim to "the world of backroom politics." They urged Trudeau to "let us vote" in the riding nomination to see who would win the contest. Bertschi filed an appeal with the party, but it was unsuccessful.

The *Ottawa Citizen* referred to the meeting in which Leslie was acclaimed as "chaotic" and local television had footage of a woman tearing up her Liberal membership card in protest. The *Citizen* reported, "The event dissolved into a divisive shouting match, with Ottawa police needed to break up a scuffle in the hall." Bertschi supporters seemed surprised that Leslie was acclaimed without a fight and interrupted his speech with cries of "shame, shame." Leslie responded, "Today, we are a team, we are a family. Yes, there has been some tensions in the family. This is natural. It's actually healthy. It shows that there is passion, there is fire."

In early 2015 Bertschi filed a pair of lawsuits against senior Liberals including Trudeau, national director Jeremy Broadhurst and campaign directors Katie Telford and Dan Gagnier. Two Trudeau staffers, principal adviser Gerald Butts and chief of staff Cyrus Reporter were also named in the second lawsuit. The first lawsuit claims defamation in leaking false information to the media about his disqualification and the second suit alleges gross negligence and breach of contract in disqualifying his candidacy after initially approving it. In court documents he claims that senior Liberals breached contractual and fiduciary duties to treat all Liberal Party members fairly by "providing staff, resources, and funding to Leslie." In the documents Bertschi refers to Leslie as "The Chosen One." Bertschi told the *Ottawa Citizen*, "the failure of the Trudeau leadership group to properly and adequately maintain their statements of fair and open nominations are, I think, pretty self-evident from this pleading." He even accused Trudeau of making "a purely political decision" along with his "coterie" and said outright that the decision to disqualify him and promote Leslie was not made by the Green Light Committee.

Another potential candidate, Christine Innes, sued Trudeau for defamation after she was disqualified from seeking the nomination in Trinity-Spadina.

Innes, the wife of former MP Tony Ianno who herself twice ran and lost against NDP Olivia Chow in Trinity-Spadina, wanted to contest the June 30 by-election in the open seat after Chow exited federal politics to run for mayor of Toronto. On March 13, she was informed that she would not be allowed to run in the by-election or seek the nomination for the party in any seat in 2015. Later, the Liberals would announce that Toronto City Councillor Adam Vaughan would run in the by-election, a deal which was struck, the official story goes, on the day of former federal finance minister Jim Flaherty's funeral on April 16. It is possible that talks to convince Vaughan to run for the Liberals in Chow's abandoned seat had occurred well before then and that the Liberal Party was clearing his uncontested run for the nomination, perhaps as part of a deal to convince him to leave the cozy confines of municipal politics.

Later Justin Trudeau and top Liberals would claim that Ianno had "bullied and intimidated" young Liberals, threatening their future in the party if they did not help Innes. Innes was reportedly also gearing up for a challenge to another former star candidate, Toronto Centre MP Chrystia Freeland, in 2015 in the redrawn riding of University-Rosedale that would encompass parts of Trinity-Spadina and Toronto Centre. *Toronto Life* reported, "Immediately after Innes' situation became known to the press, there was speculation that Liberal leader Justin Trudeau's real motive in preventing her from running was making sure she wouldn't oppose Chrystia Freeland–MP for Toronto Centre and a rising star in the party–in the next election." This seemed a violation of Trudeau's vow not to become involved in local nomination races, even though he would establish a pattern of highlighting favoured candidates in the media; only a foolish riding association would dare defeat the leader's hand-picked candidates.

In April, Innes filed a defamation suit against Trudeau and Liberal National Election Readiness Co-Chair for Ontario David MacNaughton, asking for $1.5 million, or about nine years worth of salary for an MP. Innes claimed that accusations of bullying and intimidation against her husband were a defamatory "smokescreen" that "deliberately sacrificed Innes' reputation" to "shield Trudeau from public outcry for breaching his public vow of non-interference in local riding nominations." She said that the real reason the party nixed her candidacy was that she refused to refrain from challenging Freeland in her new riding the following year rather than agree to run in the new riding of Spadina-Fort York. Innes called out Trudeau's Open Nominations pledge in her statement of claim, which said, "The promise of 'open, transparent and fair' nominations was an essential part of Trudeau's image as a progressive leader of the LPC," but "when it came to the redistributed ridings in downtown Toronto, however, this promise proved to be inconvenient." It continued, "The defendants and other senior LPC leaders were bothered that Innes could win that local nomination over their preferred candidate. They did not want this to happen; on the other hand, they could not be seen to be meddling in local riding politics." It also stated, just three days after Innes turned down a "backroom deal" to run in a different riding, "The defendants launched a full-scale character attack on her."

In Trudeau's statement of defense, he claims that Innes was repeatedly warned by his personal adviser Gerald Butts, Toronto MP Carolyn Bennett and MacNaughton that her campaign team's aggressive tactics were beyond the pale and had to cease. The Trudeau statement said that Innes denied the allegation and dismissed the concerns of those Liberals. It also said that he and MacNaughton were "of the settled view" that "Innes bears ultimate responsibility for the conduct of her campaign team." At the same time national director Jeremy Broadhurst issued a statement saying, "We stand behind the campaign's decision to red light Ms. Innes' nomination and the party has no intention of being pressured into revisiting that decision."

The defendants turned down an offer from Innes to drop the suit in return for a public apology, the right to run in whichever riding she wanted, and a donation to several specific charities.

There were several other lower profile controversies.

In the southwestern Ontario riding of Brantford-Brant, riding executives complained that the spirit of Open Nominations had been violated. Danielle Takacs, who worked for the Ontario Catholic School Trustees Association in Toronto and was a long-time Liberal volunteer, was acclaimed, but local association president Edward Chrzanowski sent an email to riding Liberals urging them to express concerns to the federal Liberal executive over the nomination process and the way the Ontario Liberal organizers had set up the meeting in August 2014. Chrzanowski said there was "an unreasonably short deadline" so "no other candidates were able to come forward." Several interested individuals were given just hours notice before the application deadline to run for the nomination. Chrzanowski said that Brantford-Brant Liberals were "left with an acclaimed candidate through a questionable and most unusual process." He said that members should have stood up "for democracy in protest by not attending the meeting." Within a few weeks, the CBC reported, two members of the riding association board resigned and Chrzanowski was thinking of not only resigning but not voting Liberal. He said, "We had other candidates. They were not allowed to submit." Board member Bryan Kerman said that the meeting at which Takacs was acclaimed, "goes explicitly against what [Justin Trudeau] has said in terms of free, open, transparent nominations. We've had something that was distinctly closed and very, very opaque." The CBC reported that Takacs "wouldn't say whether she thought the process was fair and open."

Some Liberals threatened to quit the party after they said that the nomination process was manipulated to install one of the "stars" Trudeau had brought to the party, Harjit Sajjan, as the candidate in Vancouver South.

In Vancouver South, thousands of members of the Sikh community left a Liberal nominating meeting to protest the acclamation of the World Sikh Organization-backed Harjit Singh Sajjan following businessman's Barj Dhahan's withdrawal from the race. Rajinder Singh Bhela, a longtime party member and former general secretary of Vancouver's largest Sikh temple, the Ross Street Temple, said that the Liberals were "hijacked by the WSO," which Kashmir Dhaliwal, ex-president of the Khalsa Diwan Society, called an "extremist" and "fundamentalist" group which the "Liberal Party, especially Justin, is in bed with." The riding was held previously by Liberal MP Ujjal Dosanjh who lost to Conservative Wai Young in 2011, so it is considered a swing riding. Sajjan, a decorated soldier for his service in Bosnia and Afghanistan (serving twice as a special adviser in Afghanistan), was featured at the Montreal biennial convention as a speaker. The CBC said Dhahan "was persuaded by the party leadership to withdraw" and that the erstwhile candidate "declined to discuss his reasons with CBC News, except to confirm that he withdrew reluctantly." Jagdeep Sanghera, who had served two separate terms as chairman of the Liberal executive in Vancouver South, said, "The democratic process was ignored." Dhahan accompanied Prime Minister Stephen Harper for a trade mission to India, which some speculated led to pressure to withdraw. Sanghera accused former World Sikh Organization president Prem Vinning, a long-time Liberal organizer in the province, of pulling strings to push Dhahan out of the way for Sajjan. Sanghera also said that the 4,000 Sikhs who became

Liberal members to support Dhahan would "tear up the memberships and walk away" from the party. "We will not support the Liberal team in the next election," he threatened.

The CBC reported, "Justin Trudeau said he was satisfied with the nomination process in Vancouver South." Trudeau dismissed the controversy: "In various situations across the country, there have been issues with different candidates and some people have chosen to withdraw." He suggested that those who weren't part of the winning side were sore loser. "There are winners and there are people who don't win. And, from time to time, the people who didn't succeed through the process will have complaints, and that's just part and parcel of it. But the open nominations – letting the communities have the final word on who will be their next Liberal candidate – have been a tremendous success and I'm very proud of it." While there is no indication of party headquarter pressure, Trudeau's suggestion that those who were on the losing end of a nominating meeting had sour grapes ignores the fact that they did not lose a nomination but felt that their candidate was pressured to quit. The Liberal leader cannot just flippantly dismiss as grassroots level politics allegations that local communities did not, in fact, have the final word on who was their Liberal candidate.

Two other Vancouver nomination races saw party interference.

In Vancouver East, Jodie Emery, a marijuana advocate, and wife of the Prince of Pot Marc Emery, expressed interest in challenging incumbent Libby Davies, although she admitted little chance of beating the veteran NDP member of parliament. Davies decided against running for re-election and on January 16, 2015 the Liberals informed Emery that she would not be green-lit to run. Their email did not give any reason, but Emery said that her high-profile would have been a distraction during the federal campaign, especially in a contested riding. She expressed disappointment but understood the decision. At the same time, she questioned the Liberal Party's commitment to open nominations and local democracy.

In Vancouver-Granville, would-be candidates were discouraged from challenging aboriginal leader Jody Wilson-Raybould, Trudeau's hand-picked candidate for the riding. Wilson-Raybould, whose father asked Pierre Trudeau to include a section about aboriginal rights in the 1982 Constitution Act, was a co-chair of the 2014 biennial convention in Montreal and, as regional Assembly of First Nations chief for British Columbia, a fierce critic of Conservative aboriginal policy. The *Vancouver Sun* reported that after Trudeau met Wilson-Raybould during land-claim meetings she chaired, he asked her to run for the Liberals despite the fact that she did not live in the riding. The paper also reported, "Several longtime Liberals expressed interest in contesting the nomination, but the party used "moral suasion" – according to one party member – to persuade them to not challenge Trudeau's choice." Sam Wyatt, who had previously sat on the Vancouver Granville riding association board, said, "There's no question that Jody was the leader's pick and that he'd like her to win, and I would like to see her win," but that it would have been better for the party for her to win a contested nomination. Vancouver Crown prosecutor Alex Burton and businessman Taleeb Noormohamed had both been reported interested in running but neither ultimately challenged Wilson-Raybould.

In Edmonton-Mill Woods, Varinder Bhullar was banned from running for the nomination when their audit determined that he had broken party rules by signing up individuals who did not pay for their own memberships. The Huffington Post reported that "party officials acknowledged that Edmonton–Mill Woods resident Varinder Bhullar was not their preferred candidate," but that the rule-breaking was the reason for red-lighting his campaign. An anonymous party source told Althia Raj bluntly, "The man cheated." Bhullar was given the green-light to run in March 2014, but told Huffington Post that Liberal national campaign co-chair Katie Telford revoked it in January 2015 in order to clear a path for the nomination of a star candidate, Edmonton city councilor Amarjeet Sohi. Bhullar was also informed that he was not allowed to appeal the decision. He claimed that a party poll found Sohi more likely to win the riding against Conservative MP Tim Uppal, who also served as Minister of State for Multiculturalism, and that they offered Bhullar the nomination in the solidly Conservative riding of Edmonton–Wetaskiwin. He also claimed that the party officials had offered him the vice presidency of the federal Liberals in Alberta and provided assistance to run for Sohi's vacated city council seat. Huffington Post reported the usual denials, but found local Liberals were unsure which side to believe. A former provincial Liberal candidate, Aman Gill, said, "Everyone is wondering what is real, what is the actual story." Sohi admitted that he had been approached by Trudeau the previous summer about running but wanted to remain focused on city council matters. He had later changed his mind and announced in early 2015 that he would enter the race, shortly after which Bhullar was disqualified. But he also admitted that he was told the previous November that the federal party was re-examining his nomination over membership irregularities and could be asked to withdraw. Bhullar told Huffington Post, "I didn't have anybody against me, so why would I cheat? There was no other candidate at all, until this candidate came in after I was kicked out, so I didn't need to cheat at all." Raj's unnamed source said, had Bhullar "not been caught cheating, he would still be a green-light candidate right now, in spite of the fact that we wouldn't be particularly pleased about his candidacy and we would greatly prefer the other guy to win." Interestingly, Northern Alberta election readiness chair Kevin Feehan said that he was unaware of the case because federal party officials took over the file. Local riding president Sital Nanuan said that he was unaware of any problems with Bhullar's campaign or the memberships he signed up.

On the east coast, former Tory MP Bill Casey announced that he would seek the Liberal nomination to win back his old seat of Cumberland-Colchester. The Halifax *Herald-Chronicle* reported that Susan MacQuarrie accused the local riding association of "sidelining" her in favour of the high profile, turncoat former MP. MacQuarrie, an investment adviser, told the party that she would run for the nomination in the spring of 2014, but in February 2015 chose not to file her nomination papers after Trudeau warmly embraced Casey to the Liberal fold. She also accused the riding executive of holding the nomination meeting in tiny Springhill, N.S. instead of the much larger Truro, where she had her base of support. MacQuarrie was careful not to imply that Team Trudeau had manipulated the nomination, but suggested that the local riding association had bent over backwards to help nominate his favoured candidate.

The Huffington Post's Althia Raj reported her anonymous Liberal Party source on the Bhullar fiasco said, "We said all along that open nominations means a) not every candidate has the right to run if they don't pass the process or even if they pass the process subsequent to that they are caught breaking the rules; or b) just because the contest is open doesn't mean people [in the Leader's office] are agnostic about who the winner is going to be." The source added that even "when things are not smooth ... democracy is better served by a transparent process even if it is messier."

The political website Pundit's Guide says that "open nominations" means different things to different audiences. For party activists, it is merely a process in "which the leader does not appoint the candidate, and the incumbent MPs are not protected from facing a contested nomination in their home riding." That seems fair, but to outsiders such as the media and general public, it implies much more: "the idea that anyone should be able to run to become the nominee of a political party" or "the idea that the party leadership will never secretly or otherwise have a preference as to the outcome or try to influence it."

But the Dauphin holds himself up as a new kind of politician, who doesn't play the old political games. When the Liberals are caught playing favourites and intervening in nominations, senior party officials argue, correctly perhaps, that no party is going to allow just anybody to run under their banner without being vetted, and that open nominations never meant that Team Trudeau couldn't find star candidates. But it would have been nice if he had been straightforward about these things early on and not pretended that open nominations are a brand new way of doing politics when in fact it is the same-old, same-old. Trudeau claims to eschew the dark arts of politics, but his team

THE DAUPHIN: THE TRUTH ABOUT JUSTIN TRUDEAU

has manipulated and micromanaged nomination meetings just as Jean Chrétien's and Stephen Harper's teams have. That might be politics, but Trudeau vowed not to be politics as usual.

Chapter 7: Dealing with Sexual Harassment

In November 2014, it was revealed that two NDP MPs had come forward with separate allegations of sexual harassment against a pair of Liberal MPs, Scott Andrews (Avalon) and Massimo Pacetti (Saint-Léonard–Saint-Michel). The Liberal MPs, both married with children, were promptly suspended from caucus by Justin Trudeau. The Liberal Party referred the allegations to House Speaker Andrew Scheer for an independent investigation, who said it was a matter to the board of internal economy that handles issues surrounding House business. For their part, Andrews and Pacetti maintained their innocence and claimed they would be exonerated. After an independent inquiry solicited by Trudeau and conducted by lawyer Cynthia Peterson which reported only to the Liberal leader, the two MPs were permanently kicked out of the party, banned from returning to caucus or running for the Liberals in the future. It was a tough response in a difficult situation, but Trudeau managed to handle the whole situation in about the worst way possible.

The two female MPs did not want the case made public, had not come forward with their identities (although one of them shared her story with several media outlets), and both sought to have the situation handled discreetly. The NDP went ballistic when Trudeau went public with the case, even though he did not reveal their identities nor share the specific nature of the harassment. NDP leader Thomas Mulcair said that Trudeau going public revictimized the two women, noting that they both wanted the allegations to remain private: "Anyone who went against that, of course, would be making them victims a second time."

There was almost no way in which the Liberal leader was going to come out of the delicate situation without some damage. Going public in the limited way he did led the NDP to complain about going against the wishes of the alleged victims, but if he did not do anything public, Trudeau risked looking apathetic to allegations of sexual harassment if the media caught wind of them.

Trudeau explained why he had acted decisively: "I am aware of how difficult it is for people to come forward. I believe strongly that those of us in positions of authority have a duty to act upon allegations of this nature. It's 2014 – we have a duty to protect and encourage individuals in these situations to come forward. The action must be fair but decisive. It must be sensitive to all affected parties but, recognizing how difficult it is to do so, it must give the benefit of the doubt to those who come forward." In another statement, Trudeau said he had "a duty to act." It should be noted that the allegations became public in the weeks after the CBC let *Q* host Jian Ghomeshi go following charges of sexual assault; in the American media, there was also a heightened sense of issues related to sexual harassment and sexual assault due to several high profile (and in some instances, fabricated) cases. There was no way that Trudeau would stand by and do nothing. But his handling of the sensitive situation might have been the worst possible approach.

The complainants, the CBC's Rex Murphy noted, "wished not to go on the record, not to be named, not formally to complain, and definitely not to go to the police." He said that nothing is gained by having the identities and the specific allegations remain veiled – even to Andrews and Pacetti, meaning they could hardly defend themselves – and that "matters of such high consequence" cannot be simultaneously both private and public. He said that while "everybody wants some vague action" nobody was willing to "go to the law."

Remarkably, the House of Commons has no rules against sexual harassment. Trudeau and a chorus of MPs from all parties said that it was time for parliament to write a sexual harassment policy, as if MPs need rules to know not to harass their colleagues and staffers. And the *Globe and Mail* reported that even with new rules, it was uncertain that the two female NDP MPs would file a formal complaint.

For several months, Andrews and Pacetti sat as independents, maintaining their innocence, but probably awaiting exoneration when they could rejoin their erstwhile colleagues. *Toronto Star* columnist Chantal Hebert predicted in November that it was unlikely either would ever rejoin the Liberal caucus. "Their banishment from the party fold stands to be permanent," she predicted less than two weeks after they were suspended from caucus. Four months later, both Andrews and Pacetti were expelled from the party following the submission of Peterson's confidential investigation to Justin Trudeau, and Trudeau alone. He considered the matter closed.

One of the NDP MPs told the media in November that she did not want her harasser to be ejected from caucus, but was unclear what she thought an appropriate ramification would be after alleging he had sex with her "without explicit consent" (although she offered him a condom). The board of internal economy never sanctioned either Pacetti or Andrews. It did not need to; both MPs had their reputations sullied to the point where they were probably unelectable. Indeed, both would soon say they would not seek re-election, although Andrews briefly reportedly flirted with the idea of suing Trudeau and the Liberal Party.

Once again, it was up to Rex Murphy to explain why Trudeau was wrong, this time in the *National Post*. Acknowledging that workplace employment rules are not bound by the niceties of the criminal justice system, Murphy noted the imbalance between the accusers and accused. The two Liberal MPs had their names tarnished "more or less irrevocably," while the accused remained anonymous, "shielded by Mr. Trudeau and NDP leader Thomas Mulcair." Trudeau allotted to himself the power to "hold the facts, make the judgments, and seal the file." The careers of Andrews and Pacetti were ruined by a "marsh gas of fact and rumour, hearsay, leaks, and speculation." The details of the inquiry that formally ended the two men's careers were "wrapped in secrecy" leading Murphy to observe, "Rarely has a matter of such substance involving members of parliament and the public's concept of justice been handled so closely, so arbitrarily, so tidily." Trudeau and the Liberals claimed that this was a workplace harassment issue dealt with privately, but Andrews and Pacetti are not employed by the Liberal Party of Canada, but rather the House of Commons with the voters as stakeholders, and the Dauphin had no right to subject principles of justice – such as the right of Andrews and Pacetti to face their accusers, know their alleged crime, mount a defense – for political convenience.

Justin Trudeau often brags about transparency and accountability, slamming the Harper Conservatives for their secrecy. But never has Prime Minister Stephen Harper ruined the lives of two MPs by acting secretly. That two of his own colleagues could be treated so shabbily to help establish the leader's bona fides when it comes to respecting women's rights, is a telling indictment of Trudeau's ability to discard any semblance of transparency when it is needed most. As Rex Murphy noted, a "great principle of natural justice" is "justice must not only be done but be seen to be done." And raising the stakes for this whole affair, Murphy said that it was more than a matter affecting parliamentarians. "It suggests that the entire process of justice as it applies to every citizen can be bypassed when the political parties see bypassing it as convenient."

But Tom Flanagan, a former Harper adviser, had another warning. If the secrecy surrounding the allegations was allowed to stand and the precedent set that expulsion was the appropriate punishment, Flanagan worried that in an environment where politicians accuse one another of committing metaphorical crimes, that the stakes were raised in which false accusations could become so politically advantageous to remove political opponents as to make it irresistible.

No doubt Trudeau was put in a difficult situation. But it is instructive that he acted against traditional principles of justice in dealing with the situation, taking the politically expedient route. If one looks beyond the issue of sexual harassment, the whole fiasco might be instructive in understanding Trudeau's priorities when dealing with future scandal. Not only voters, but also his Liberal colleagues, ought to beware of the priority that political convenience plays in Trudeau's decision-making.

Chapter 8: Trudeau the Opposer

The job of the opposition parties is, in some sense, to oppose. It's right there in their titles. But that does not mean that they are to have a knee-jerk reaction to whatever the government does. With the Conservatives in power, the Official Opposition NDP and third-party opposition Liberals should attempt to hold the government to account while offering constructive criticism that includes what policies they would like to see implemented instead. Justin Trudeau regularly attacks not only the Harper government, but also the Conservatives' motivations which are almost always attributed to crass politics. Trudeau's criticisms ring hollow considering that he seldom, if ever, offers an alternative policy or suggests what he would do differently.

Trudeau has blamed the lack of U.S. support for the Keystone XL pipeline project on the government's failure to address environmental concerns about climate change. Trudeau claimed that the Obama administration blocked the mutually beneficial pipeline because Canada lacked a plan to combat anthropomorphic global warming. But the Liberal leader did not once say what he would do about climate change. The Dauphin would talk about the supposed need for carbon pricing but did not indicate which of the various carbon pricing plans he preferred: a carbon tax or cap-and-trade, or a hybrid of the two. Considering the number of times Trudeau talked about the need for carbon pricing, one would think that he had given the issue some thought and at least leaned toward a direct tax or a tradeable permit system. But for years he would knock Ottawa for not having some sort of carbon pricing mechanism without once advocating for the plan he thought was best for Canada. Trudeau would eventually endorse a medicare-type system in which provinces would ultimately be responsible for climate change policy through whichever pricing mechanism they considered best. After charging Prime Minister Stephen Harper with failing to demonstrate leadership on the climate change file, Trudeau's approach is to leave it to the provinces.

Usually Trudeau's attacks on Harper condemn the Prime Minister's supposed political motivations.

While Justin Trudeau glad-hands at ethnic events because he genuinely claims interest in reaching out to visible minorities, immigrants, and other cultures, he does not assume a similar benevolence in the outreach of his political opponents. When Trudeau was lined up opposite Immigration Minister Jason Kenney as his official Liberal critic, he said that the Tory approach to talking to representatives of Canada's diverse mosaic was purely "utilitarian" and "transactional." He accused Kenney, who was famously nicknamed Curry-in-a-Hurry because of his seemingly non-stop attendance at various ethnic events – sometimes more than a dozen per weekend – of "buying off certain groups" with the attention he showered upon them.

Acknowledging that the Liberal Party, despite being the creators of official multiculturalism in Canada, sometimes took "some of its minority communities for granted," he said, "That's going to stop, definitely." The phrase should set off alarms. The view that some ethnic communities belong to the Liberal Party – "its minority communities"? – betrays the sense of entitlement that led to the party's decline in the late 1990s and early 2000s. No, ethnic groups do not belong to this or that party, but Trudeau is of the view that minority voters belong to the Grits.

Trudeau has said the same thing about Harper's foreign policy on Israel, that it is designed to win Jewish votes rather than support the Middle East's only democracy and Canada's long-time ally in the region. "My big disappointment with the Conservative government today is that they are making support for Israel a domestic political issue and not a position of principle." The Dauphin claimed both the Liberals and Tories are all "in favour of a friendship" with Israel, but somehow the Tories are pandering for votes and the Liberals are not.

Likewise, when Stephen Harper traveled to Ukraine to become the first G7 leader to visit the country after Russia sought to annex Crimea in March 2014, Trudeau criticized Harper's visit with interim Prime Minister Arseniy Yatsenyuk in Kyiv. A Harper spokesman said that the visit was an "expression of Canada's principled stand on Ukraine" but Trudeau dismissed it as a "three hour photo op." Trudeau then told Shalom Toronto, a Farsi-language paper in Toronto, that Harper was not much of an international traveler when compared to his own *Globe*-hopping adventures in his twenties, as if to somehow discredit the Prime Minister's official visit to a troubled ally.

Closer to home, the Conservatives announced in February 2015 that the federal government would appeal a Federal Court ruling that allowed a Pakistani woman to keep her face covered with a niqab while taking taking the oath of citizenship. Prime Minister Harper said in the House of Commons, "We don't allow people to cover their faces during citizenship ceremonies. And why would Canadians, contrary to our own values, embrace a practice at that time that is not transparent, that is not open and, frankly, is rooted in a culture that is anti-women. Mr. Speaker, that is unacceptable to Canadians, unacceptable to Canadian women." Justin Trudeau condemned the government's position and Harper's statement. He said, "I think this government is indeed doubling down on the politics of fear." During a March 9, 2015 speech at the McGill Institute for the Study of Canada in Toronto on "Canadian Liberty and the Politics of Fear," Trudeau said, "Canadians are being encouraged by their government to be fearful of one another." He called Harper out for using the Federal Court niqab case in "an attempt to play on people's fears and foster prejudice, directly toward the Muslim faith." The Dauphin charged, "Their instincts are now to be suspicious of people who do not share their beliefs, to harden divisions with people whose views differ from their own." He compared the "fears against Muslims today" to Canadian refugee policy that refused Jews entry in the 1930s and '40s. "Mr Harper and I disagree fundamentally about many things. None perhaps more so than this: leading this country should mean you bring Canadians together. You do not divide them against one another." He then condemned the Tories for using the Prime Minister's comments about the niqab in a fundraising pitch in "an indefensible perversion of Canadian values." To Trudeau, there was no honest difference of opinion on the appropriateness of permitting the niqab – a headdress that covers most of the face except the eyes – during a ceremony in which the identity of new citizens must be affirmed and officials must witness the oath being said. The Liberal leader was not interested in seriously debating the merits of the government policy and its reaction to the court that overturned government policy. No, to Trudeau, one side was motivated by anti-Muslim animus and a political desire to stir anti-Islamic sentiment among the public.

In 2013, Trudeau condemned Harper and Finance Minister Jim Flaherty for working toward a balanced budget by 2015 that would fulfill a 2011 campaign promise. Trudeau complained to Peter Mansbridge, "Mr. Harper and Mr. Flaherty have set up a specific target of, 'We have to eliminate the deficit for 2015 just before the election; perhaps we can offer all sorts of goodies to Canadians in a 2015 election campaign.' And that's a political target that they are adjusting the reality of everything else around." As 2015 neared, he and his Liberal team said that the Tories had created an artificial deadline to balance the budget with the government's only goal to tick off the box of a kept promise – as if that's a bad thing.

When Justin Trudeau was criticized by some Conservative MPs and cabinet ministers for taking speaking fees as MP for headlining charity fundraisers, he chastised them for not knowing how charitable events are run and insinuating that their attacks on him threatened the charity industry. He condescendingly explained that sometimes organizations hire high-profile speakers that bring larger crowds to their events. Despite the fact that he carried out this function as an MP, Trudeau described himself as a "professional fundraiser." He suggested that Tories did not understand fundraising techniques. He said in June 2013, "I mean, the Conservatives are so focused on attack and negativity that perhaps they're not thinking about the consequences in the charitable sector of what they're doing." In an outrageous non sequitur the Dauphin suggested that his Conservative critics opposed "caterers who provide the food to banquets halls who are raising money for charities," completely ignoring the difference between a company established to cook and deliver meals and an MP moonlighting as a speaker to make a little extra money on the side. For Trudeau, the first impulse was to attack his partisan opponents even though he would also acknowledge that Canadians expected more of him which is why he stopped doing paid speaking gigs when he became leader.

As an opposition leader Trudeau cannot be expected to agree with the government, but he can be expected to raise substantive points of disagreement. Instead, the Dauphin spent more than two years attacking Harper's political motivations without acknowledging that his own criticisms are intended to have the political consequence of diminishing the public view of Harper's leadership. He condemns Harper for his negativity and attacking style of politics while himself going negative in attacking the prime minister. No doubt Trudeau needed to turn the public against the government, but when he filled the air with little more than musings about legalizing pot and banning pro-lifers from the Liberal Party while doing nothing to offer substantive alternatives on the major issues of the day, his criticisms of the Conservative government leads to the obvious question: Canadians know what Trudeau opposes, but what does he support?

Part III – Trudeau on the Issues

Chapter 9: Justin Trudeau on the Middle Class

Central to Trudeau's stated political *raison d'etre* is helping the middle class, a group that he won't, or can't, define. What he is adamant about is that the middle class is falling behind, that its standard of living is getting worse, compared to middle class families a generation ago. In fact, this is a matter of debate among economists. So is the definition of middle class, but for a political leader who talks incessantly about this group of voters, it is odd that the Dauphin seems to have no idea whom he is talking about.

Justin Trudeau launched his leadership campaign on October 30, 2012 and on that day he authored a column for the *Toronto Star*: "Canadian middle class left out of the growth equation." It would be the defining issue for the young politician and rising star. He wrote, "Upward mobility through economic opportunity ... is under real threat," and Canada's political leaders were not addressing the issue. He wrote, "Those who think the middle class is thriving in this country should spend more time with their fellow citizens." Without evidence or explanation, he wrote that the middle class is being squeezed, but the economic stagnation does "not need to be explained to those who live it every day." Trudeau claimed that some "commentators have their doubts" about the middle class squeeze, pointing to statistics that show rising family incomes. But, wrote Trudeau, they are wrong. "A closer look shows that family incomes in the middle have risen for one primary reason: the unprecedented entry, en masse, of a new generation of well-educated, hard-working Canadian women into the workforce, which was a one-time event." Trudeau wrote, "The bottom line is that individual middle class wages have stagnated for decades." He then added income inequality into the mix as virtually all the growth in income over the "past 30 years ... accrued to a small number of wealthy Canadians," a trend he saw "accelerating." Meanwhile, "The middle class is carrying unprecedented debt levels and facing an increasingly inaccessible housing market, especially in cities like Toronto, Calgary and Vancouver." Trudeau claimed to have "Heard from too many people across this country who are questioning whether their kids and grandkids will achieve the same quality of life that we enjoy today." If income inequality continues to grow and middle class incomes continue to stagnate, Trudeau predicted widespread questioning of the "policies, and the very system, that values and encourages growth."

These are standard talking points from Liberals and the NDP, but are they true?

In April 2014, the *New York Times* reported their own study using data compiled by the Luxembourg Income Study comparing living standards in a variety of countries at numerous points on the income scale over time. It found that Canada's middle class was doing better than America's, ranking fourth (not first as some reported) in the world, behind Luxembourg, Norway, and Sweden. The study measured after-tax income, and found that from 2004 to 2010, real income (including transfers and taxes) rose for every centile examined. Yes, the rich got richer, with people at the 95th centile earning 10.8 percent more, but the poor (the 5th centile) saw their income grow more (14.5 percent.) The smallest increase for centiles examined between those two extremes was 9.1 percent. That is, every specific point along the income spectrum examined in the study saw its income rise by at least $1000 (inflation-adjusted) over the six-year period, for an increase around 10 percent.

The Canadian media reported the findings and the Conservatives were practically giddy. Jason Kenney said, "For the first time in history, Canadian middle class families are better off than those in the United States." That's good (for Canadians), but it isn't proof that Trudeau is incorrect about the pressures facing the middle class. It was theoretically possible that Americans are being squeezed and that the Canadian middle class is doing better than their American counterparts, while still struggling themselves.

A 2012 Environics poll found that 33 percent of Canadians were strongly satisfied with their standard of living and 52 percent were somewhat satisfied, which means that 85 percent of Canadians were satisfied with their standard of living. Just 14 percent were somewhat or very dissatisfied with their standard of living. Trudeau was correct to warn that many Canadians were worried about the prospects of their children. Environics found that while 52 percent said they are better off than their parents and another 23 percent said that they were doing about the same, only 25 percent think the next generation will be better off while 38 percent say they will be worse off (and 33 percent thought they will do about the same). Yet, the pessimistic predictions are lower than they were in 1990 (42 percent) and 1996 (56 percent).

It was not only the LIS data the *Times* used that shows the Canadian middle class improving their lot. In February 2014, Statistics Canada released a study that showed the median net worth of Canadian families increasing 43.5 percent from 2005 to 2012. Going back 18 years, the figures increased 80 percent. Stats Can calculated the inflation-adjusted worth of families once debts were paid and assets such as houses sold; it also took into account pensions funds owing. Countering the cliché that the rich get richer (at the expense of everyone else), Stats Can found that the middle class increased their share of Canada's net worth as the wealthiest 20 percent saw their share of the country's $8 trillion worth of personal wealth decrease by nearly two percentage points to 67.4 percent. Philip Cross, a former chief economic analyst with Statistics Canada and now a research fellow with the Macdonald-Laurier Institute, told the *Financial Post*, "This shows the middle class is not withering away," despite what some politicians claim.

According to Environics in 2012, 56 percent of Canadians call themselves middle class not including the 19 percent who labeled themselves lower middle class and 18 percent who said they were upper middle class. In total, 93 percent of Canadians viewed themselves as middle class. Just five percent said they were lower class while 1 percent said they were upper class. The proportion of people who earn more than $100,000 annually who called themselves middle class was similar to the proportion making $30,000-$60,000 and labelled themselves thusly. While it is unlikely that more than nine in ten Canadians are middle class, almost all Canadians view themselves as such.

The middle class didn't feel they were being squeezed, and the data suggests that they are right. Three Fraser Institute economists looked at the numbers and they didn't find that middle class incomes have stagnated. Their study, "Measuring Income Mobility," used Statistics Canada's Longitudinal Administrative Databank, and they found that most people moved among the various income quintiles. The majority of people in the lowest quintile (20 percent) of income earners, moved to a higher quintile; between 1990 and 2009, 87 percent who began in the lowest quintile moved to a higher quintile, with nearly a fifth of them moving all the way up to the highest quintile. In other words, there is a great deal of social mobility within Canada, rhetoric about the one percent versus everyone else notwithstanding. As for the notion that the rich-get-richer, in Canada, the poor get richer quicker. Using the same time period (1990 through 2009), those in the top quintile saw their incomes grow 23 percent while those in the bottom quintile saw their incomes grow 635 percent. The authors said that there is a pattern of "typical lifecycle of income" in which students and young adults beginning work make comparably less than those who have been employed for a decade or so, and that when those workers retire, they earn less income (but also have lower costs and less debt).

But what about middle income earners? By definition, the three middle quintiles are middle class (as, probably are many in the bottom and top quintiles, but for the sake of simplicity, only the three middle tiers will be used.) The second quintile, people making an average of $44,500, saw the second largest increases (170 percent) to almost catch up to the middle quintile. That middle quintile now earns an average of $47,500, up 58 percent in 2009 from 1990. Put in simple terms, there is now little difference between lower middle income and middle income earner. The fourth quintile saw its income increase 32 percent, to $60,100. The highest fifth of income earners now make more than $94,900.

Writing in the *Financial Post*, the Fraser Institute's Charles Lammam and Niels Veldhuis took Trudeau to task for his rhetoric that most of the gains of the economy went to the "super-rich." These figures, they wrote, suggest that, "We live in a dynamic society where the majority of us experience significant upward income mobility over the course of our lives." They concluded, "Thankfully the story of stagnating incomes in Canada is just that, a great fictional tale. The reality is that most Canadians, including those initially in the poorest group, have experienced marked increases in their income over the past two decades."

The *National Post*'s Andrew Coyne said, "The more the evidence piles up, the more it discredits the thesis ... of a struggling middle class." Coyne said that regardless of the metric (median incomes, real wages, household net worth), in constant, inflation-adjusted dollars, the middle class is doing well. He goes on to say, "In fact, pick any time frame except 30 years – 10, 20, 40, 50 – and the trend is up. The only one that produces relative stagnation is the one beginning in 1980," and that is because the early 1980s experienced one of the worst recessions since World War II, wiping out much of the gains of the 1970s.

Perhaps Justin Trudeau is cherry-picking dates or perhaps he was ignorant of these facts. But as McGill University economist William Watson has said, "Apart from his love for the middle class, Mr. Trudeau is known for favouring 'evidence-based policy.' I'm betting he won't show similar passion for fact-based politics." By any measure, Trudeau is simply wrong about the middle class.

If Trudeau stopped playing politics with his convenient but misleading starting point of 1980 and looked at middle class incomes since the early 1990s, he would see that the incomes of voters he is trying to woo are at the highest they have ever been.

Perhaps Trudeau appears wrong because he and the economists are not talking about the same people. The Dauphin has been asked numerous times what constitutes the middle class, and he doesn't have an answer. He says he wouldn't tax them, but without a specific income level, Canadians voters cannot know whether they would be included in his promise not to raise their taxes. Considering, as Environics found, that more than 90 percent of Canadians think of themselves as middle class, Trudeau's ambiguity allows him to pander to nearly every voter.

After being asked repeatedly, Trudeau eventually defined the middle class not by their income, but by what they do. They are, he said, "People who work for their income, not people who live off their assets and their savings." This is patently absurd. As more than one commentator observed, this definition would include millionaire bank CEOs who earn salaries (and work for them), but not retired Canadians who no longer earn a salary and draw upon their savings. So Trudeau refined his definition a few days later, claiming that the middle class are, "People who live paycheque to paycheque." Maxime Bernier, federal Minister of State for Small Business and Tourism, wondered, "Does that mean that Canadians who manage to put some money aside are not part of the middle class?"

Bernier charged Trudeau of not knowing what he is talking about when he talks about the middle class. In a Huffington Post column, published in both French and English, Bernier noted that Trudeau, "Has a track record when it comes to saying weird things about the middle class." Bernier should know what he's talking about on economics. He has a Bachelor of Commerce degree from the Université du Québec à Montreal and has held numerous positions in financial and banking companies including National Bank, the Securities Commission of Québec, and Standard Life of Canada. He was also vice president of the Montreal Economic Institute think tank. Bernier pointed to comments Trudeau made when he launched his leadership bid in October 2012: "The great economic success stories of the recent past are really stories of middle class growth ... China, India, South Korea and Brazil, to name a few, are growing rapidly because they have added hundreds of millions of people to the global middle class." Bernier said that the middle class does not bring about economic growth, as Trudeau suggested. "Justin Trudeau confuses cause and effect in terms of economic development." Bernier explained standard economic analysis when he said, "It is not because their middle classes have grown that China and India have become economic successes. It is rather because these countries have abandoned their socialist and interventionist policies and have liberalized their economies that they have experienced strong economic growth. It was then and only then, that millions of their citizens left the condition of extreme poverty they were in and were able to reach a standard of living which is that of the middle class." A rising tide, as John Kennedy was fond of noting, raised all boats; economic growth moves people out of poverty into the middle class. The Liberal leader gets his cause-and-effect wrong on the relationship between economic growth and the creation of a middle class.

Well after Trudeau's concerns about the middle class were refuted – shift the starting point of his narrative from 1980 to 1990 and the stagnation disappears – he was still hammering away about the economic anxiety Canadians felt.

At the 2014 biennial Liberal convention in Montreal Trudeau gave a speech that featured a fictional character, Nathalie, who along with her partner, had a household income of about $80,000 ($40,000 each.) He said that she worries about her debt, her ability to save for her retirement, and most importantly, "She's still worried. She's anxious about her future, probably even more so for her kids' future." Trudeau sees it as his job to make her worries go away. If Nathalie were real, he offered her little comfort. He gave boilerplate: "To me, a strong economy is one that makes sure every Canadian has a real and fair chance at success. It means a thriving middle class. One that provides growing incomes and job opportunities. One that provides a real chance at joining the middle class for struggling Canadians." He focused on ending partisan bickering and raising the tone of politics. But Nathalie cannot pay off debt, save for retirement, or invest in a child's education and future with promises by politicians to be kind to one another. For Trudeau, every economic interventionist plan, from carbon taxes to infrastructure spending, is justified by the assertion that it will help the middle class.

Nathalie would probably like to make a bit more money at her job, but if the Fraser Institute study and Environics poll are any indication, she is probably doing fine even if she worries about the future every once in a while. That is part of life, not a reason to vote for a Liberal who wants to jack up spending and have the provinces raise the price of energy through carbon taxes or cap-and-trade schemes.

Trudeau said, without a hint of irony, that, "The last thing Nathalie needs is for a politician to use the worry caused by these important questions for partisan purposes." Yet he has built his political career out of stoking fear about not just the dismal future for the middle class, but Prime Minister Stephen Harper's supposedly ominous brand of politics.

Trudeau's brand of middle class pandering is not everyone's cup of tea, including within his own party. During the leadership campaign, Martha Hall Findlay challenged Trudeau on how he could champion the middle class when he has never been part of it, considering his privileged upbringing – and, she could have added, trust fund-aided adulthood. More importantly, she criticized the putative leader for dividing Canadians by class. She preferred to talk about equality of opportunity rather than "narrow the conversation" about classes, and pander to one segment of society. After smirking through most of Hall Findlay's one-minute question, Trudeau responded that he has used the advantages he was given growing up, including great schools and the opportunity to travel, "in service to my community," including representing Papineau, "one of the most economically disadvantaged ridings" in the country.

Yet perhaps Hall was onto to something. Trudeau is a millionaire. Not only did he inherit a substantial fortune from his father (who had inherited it from his millionaire father), but he had a lucrative gig collecting sizable fees for speaking before he became an MP. The *Ottawa Citizen* reported in 2013 that according to documents provided by Trudeau to the paper, the Dauphin inherited $1.2 million from his father and earned another million from his professional speaking career over six years before becoming an MP. Trudeau told the *Citizen* that he "won the lottery" due to the fortune he inherited, but added, people are "shocked that I don't live in a castle." He explained the family downsized from a $1.6 million home in Outremont in 2010 for a $777,000 semi-detached, two-storey home near Mont Royal after he became an MP due to the decrease in salary from being a regular speaker that in one year netted him as much as $462,000. The family also had to forego the salary of his television host wife Sophie Grégoire, as she decided to stay home to raise the kids.

Despite his many advantages, Trudeau said that he worked as a teacher and river guide to make a living. He explained that he could not live off the family fortune; Pierre Trudeau set up his estate so that it would pay out a dividend of about $20,000 annually to Justin. The stipend allowed Justin to travel, go to school, and take lower paying jobs along the way. The *Citizen* reported, "Trudeau says his father had hoped the family money would allow him and his brother to pursue their interests – his in education and now politics, brother Alexandre ('Sacha') in filmmaking and journalism – without having to take the well-trod path of Montreal well-to-do into law or business." Trudeau himself said, "Whatever we wanted to do, we had enough to live a modest but decent life. And that was incredibly lucky."

To his credit, Trudeau has never claimed to be middle class. "I'm not middle class," he told the *Citizen*. "I don't pretend I am." He also says that people "like me" should not disproportionately benefit from certain Harper policies, like income-splitting. But Hall Findlay's point is still worth considering: can Trudeau really understand middle class struggles? Is the Dauphin a little out-of-touch with real middle class families? Do Trudeau's "lucky" circumstances perhaps lead him to condescend to the middle class as he panders to them? This large bloc of voters might look needy and anxious only relative to his privileged upbringing and adulthood.

While his biography might warp his understanding of middle class life, personal experience aside, the larger question is Trudeau's understanding of that large voting cohort.

As the economist William Watson has asked, "If our middle class is the world's richest, do we really need to elect Mr. Trudeau to help it out of the hole it evidently hasn't fallen into?" There is, Watson insists, no "moral urgency" to help the middle class. So why does Trudeau harp upon it so much? Is it possible that he repeats "middle class" as a mantra so that voters do not notice his fabulous wealth and possibly how completely out of touch he is with most Canadians? After all, two years after becoming leader, he invokes the middle class but has barely articulated actual policy to help it out of the doldrums he imagines them to be in.

Chapter 10: Justin Trudeau on Economics

Justin Trudeau fancies himself a big thinker and he considers the time he grew up near the center of power when his father was prime minister a qualification for the job of head of government. But on what is likely going to be one of the central issues in the 2015 federal election – who can best navigate the uncertain economic waters of the mid-2010s – Justin Trudeau offers little comfort. While he talks a lot about the middle class, he hasn't been forthcoming on what his economic agenda would look like. He has little experience with economic issues and his worldview, as expressed so far, should cause concern.

He has no formal training or job experience in anything related to economics or business. But has no shortage of opinions about economic matters, and he began voicing them long before becoming an MP.

On May 16, 2007, Trudeau was talking to 600 high school student at Leadership Windsor/Essex, a group that grooms youth to become leaders in their communities. Trudeau told the gathering of presumptive future leaders that time and space have become two big problems. "Time, because everything is accelerated." Trudeau, then 35, said, "The world is moving faster and faster and faster. The vast majority of you in 10 years will be working at jobs that don't even exist (today). We need to think differently about how we prepare for the future." The "space" problem he described was that people were "using up everything on the planet." He blamed the "capitalist machine" saying the free market system results in the exploitation of natural resources. "Our capitalist model has given us tremendous things," Trudeau explained. "But the time has come for us to look at it critically and try to improve on it, given the accelerated pace of change and the fact that we have limited space." He questioned whether free markets and the environment were compatible. As examples he complained that, "We consume more water per capita than anyone else on the planet," and, "We produce more solid waste than just about anyone else on the planet." That is because we are a wealthy country. Is he proposing a reduced standard of living? Who knows, he doesn't offer policy prescriptions to go along with the problems he identifies.

The platitudinous message resonated with the high school students. The *Windsor Star* reported that the teens "rushed toward the stage following Trudeau's hour-long talk" and they "swarmed Trudeau as though he were a rock star, flashing their camera-equipped cellphones." Jonna Reaume, 17, said to her "icon" that, "I can't wait to vote for you one day." On the day the Tories won their majority in 2011, Reaume took up tweeting and said it was time to "flee the country," but shortly thereafter the now 21-year-old announced she was going to travel around the country in a van. So maybe Trudeau just attracts a certain kind of fan.

There is a certain irony in the person collecting thousands of dollars for delivering speeches critiquing capitalism, but beyond the hypocrisy is the Trudeauvian inclination against free markets. Trudeau gives lip service to the role of private enterprise, but there is an underlying distrust that free markets produce optimal results and therefore the economy needs government intervention to make life fair. Questioning whether "free markets and the environment" are even compatible tells us much about his distrust of the private sector. Trudeau has never abandoned or clarified this skepticism of capitalism, so much of his economic policy should be seen in light of his critical view of free markets.

There are three key elements to every Dauphin utterance about economic issues. Trudeau's positions are usually solidly interventionist with an eye to more government combined with the need to help the middle class cope with their post-2008 financial crisis economic anxieties mixed with rhetoric about the need for fiscal responsibility. When he launched his leadership campaign in 2012, he wrote in the October 30 *Toronto Star* in a column titled, "Canadian Middle Class Left out of the Growth Equation."

"I have nothing against wealth; I believe that government has a role to play in creating it by supporting pro-growth policies. However, success comes with responsibility. Proportion matters, broadly felt economic security matters, and upward mobility matters. We are losing all of those. If we do not attend to this problem, we should not be surprised to see the middle class question the policies, and the very system, that values and encourages growth." As we've seen when Trudeau talked to students five years earlier, Trudeau himself will be among those questioning Canada's predominantly free market economic system.

It is clear that Trudeau thinks that government can solve the problems of the middle class. But knowing that Canadians tell pollsters they prefer balanced budgets to deficit spending, he is careful to insist that his economic plans –

vague as they are – are fiscally responsible. During the summer Liberal caucus meeting in Edmonton in 2014, the party leader was talking about "investing more [in] infrastructure" but stressed that while a Trudeau government would spend money on large projects, "the Liberal Party continues to be committed to fiscal responsibility."

He told *Maclean's* that infrastructure would grow the economy which "is a good way to help with a deficit," but that "fiscal discipline and responsible spending – and smart decisions," are what is necessary. That is not a commitment to balanced budgets or paying off debts. Fiscal discipline and fiscal responsibility are phrases Trudeau throws around without ever defining them.

On Balanced Budgets

Trudeau has spoken out of both sides of his mouth on balanced budgets. In his first year as a Liberal backbencher on the opposition side of the House, he supported deficit spending for stimulus purposes but said that the Conservative minority government in Ottawa, unlike "the budget my friend Dalton McGuinty presented" in Ontario, did not have the right "narrative behind" it. Both governments were ramping up spending to deal with the 2008 financial crisis, including handing out money to auto manufacturers, but what Trudeau meant was not obvious. One assumes that the Tories did not prioritize spending the same way the Ontario Liberals did –and the federal Liberals would have (although they abstained from voting on the budget) – or the Conservatives did not describe their spending as "investments" in human resources as Liberals do.

The next year, he told *Tandem,* the Toronto English-language weekly for the Italian community, "There's nothing wrong with running a deficit, but harm can come in how the money is spent. If it is invested in jobs, for research, schools, and so on, then there will be a beneficial return to the entire nation. But if money is just spent on building or repairing roads, then there's no return."

Yet Trudeau has backed infrastructure funding, endorsing the call by cities for more funding from Ottawa for building and repairing roads, as well as bridges and public transportation. This, however, is precisely what the Harper government did in the 2009 budget.

The infrastructure component of Canada's Economic Action Plan, announced in the 2009 budget, included $33 billion for 43,000 projects designed to stimulate the economy by creating construction jobs, enrich the lives of people within communities, and enhance the long-term economic value of infrastructure. Most of the spending through Building Canada involved joint projects with other levels of government to build and repair airports, bridges, highways, ports, public transit, recreational facilities, and roads. There were investments on First Nation reserves, including energy systems and transportation infrastructure. It also repaired and modernized facilities at federal government operations from national parks to border security.

In an interview with Peter Mansbridge on his first day in parliament after being elected Liberal leader in 2013, Trudeau said he "would much rather be part of a government that had a surplus than a deficit," but he also said that borrowing can be beneficial, implying that infrastructure spending can contribute to economic growth. "If you go and spend it on on a new flat-screen TV, that's different than if you go and invest it in your buddy's start-up company out of his garage and he goes on to succeed. One way you're going to have trouble paying back that debt, and the other way you're going to profit from it and it's keeping the economy rolling."

The implicit argument Trudeau was making is that the Harper government was not spending money on the right projects. But as usual, Trudeau did not point to specific infrastructure projects that shouldn't have been funded or even what kind of projects the government was supporting that did not contribute to economic growth.

At the same time, Trudeau told *La Presse*, "Of course I would eliminate the deficit, but it must be done in a way that reflects the reality for Canadians." There were no specifics, and no explanation for what reflecting the reality of Canadians meant? One reality that Trudeau did not mention is that government must pay for today's deficits with future taxes and higher interest payments.

Later in 2013, the Dauphin called balanced budget legislation, suggested by the Conservatives in the Throne Speech, a "reasonable proposal," but noted that the Tories had (at the time) five consecutive budgets with deficits. Saying it was "reasonable" implied it was supportable, but he never said whether he would vote for or enact balanced budget legislation. By not being opposed to the idea of a balanced budget law, it helped him look fiscally responsible. But by early 2014 Trudeau had a new line.

In an interview with CPAC after the 2014 federal budget was released, Justin Trudeau said the path to balanced budgets was a "commitment to grow the economy and the budget will balance itself." He implied the same thing a year earlier in his interview with Peter Mansbridge when he said, "The way to do that [balance the budget] is to grow the economy." In his August 2014 interview with *Maclean's*, Trudeau said, "One point of GDP growth is about $4.5 billion directly to government coffers, so that's the way you grow an economy and grow a capacity to invest in the kinds of things you need."

Trudeau was mocked by some on the right, including the governing party. Tory MPs took to political panel programs to deride Trudeau's comments. The Conservative Party launched an attack ad: "How can someone who thinks that budgets balance themselves be trusted with jobs and the economy" before the tagline, "He's in way over his head."

Mike Moffat, an assistant professor at the Richard Ivey School of Business and widely published economics commentator who was later appointed a member of Trudeau's Economic Council of Advisers, said that the idea is not necessarily ludicrous. Moffatt noted that both Ronald Reagan in his first term and Stephen Harper as economic policy adviser to the Reform Party before the 1993 election said that economic growth would increase profits and employment which in turn would lead to growing revenue (taxes) for government. There are two main paths to balanced budgets: to cut spending or increase revenues (or a combination of both). But if deficits are structural – if they would exist even if the economy was vibrant and performing at capacity with full employment because spending levels are higher than the levels of revenues government could reasonably expect to collect – it is impossible to grow the economy enough to eliminate budget surpluses.

Moffatt said that Canada did not appear to have a structural deficit and therefore unlike in the early 1980s America and early 1990s Canada, deep spending cuts were not necessary to balance the budget in the long-term. That assumes, however, there are no new large-scale government spending programs such as a national daycare or job-training scheme. Because Trudeau seems eager to fund education and research, on top of large-scale infrastructure projects, there is a danger that a Trudeau government could tip Canada into a structural deficit.

One reason Canada did not have a structural deficit in the early 2010s is because the Harper government did not enact extravagant new spending programs and (after the 2006 election) rescinded Ottawa's agreements with the provinces to fund universal childcare.

But Harper doesn't get all the credit. Liberal Prime Minister Jean Chrétien also prevented long-term structural deficits when his government made difficult choices about spending and made deep cuts in many departments to achieve balanced budgets by the late 1990s. Economic growth contributed, too, by increasing the government's revenue, a fact acknowledged by Trudeau when he praised Chrétien for reducing Canada's debt to GDP ratios in a YouTube video, "An economy that benefits us all." While a vibrant economy produces more income and profits to tax, it was program cuts (notably employment insurance reforms) that did most of the heavy lifting when it came to balancing the budget, a fact Trudeau did not acknowledge in his YouTube video.

Trudeau would back away from his "budgets will balance themselves" comments within a few months, telling *Maclean's*, "I think growing an economy is a good way to help with a deficit, but, ultimately, it's about fiscal discipline and responsible spending–and smart decisions." Of course, he never defines fiscal discipline and responsible spending and it might not mean spending restraint, but within seven months Trudeau went from an unequivocal "the budget will balance itself" because of economic growth to a growing economy "is a good way to help with the deficit." Perhaps his equivocation is a reflection that he knows he is not on solid ground when talking about economic principles.

The Dauphin desires to manage the economy. Trudeau told Mansbridge that "the economy needs to be managed right now." Trudeau's management of the economy would include, at the very least, "investing" in education and making "the right kind of infrastructure spending," although, once again, he doesn't offer specifics. This kind of spending, he claims, will "actually grow the economy." With his Keynesian belief that government spending creates jobs and enhances productivity, all of which has a multiplier effect that every dollar Ottawa spends trickles into other economic activity, spending can become its own justification. With such a view of economics, how long before Canada has a structural deficit?

Trudeau seems convinced that he will spend money on infrastructure that will grow the economy to the point that it will automatically balance the budget. If he truly believes that, there will be little of the fiscal discipline he used to mouth platitudes about, because there is no need to rein in spending; the economy, which will return to growth levels not seen in decades, will magically make the deficit disappear. Such a view is a recipe for fiscal disaster.

The Liberal leader seems a little confused about where he stands on balanced budgets, with an ever-evolving view on the matter. But perhaps that's because he does not consider fiscal responsibility a virtue in itself. In an interview on CBC Radio's "The House" on February 22, 2014, Trudeau said, "I would rather not" run a deficit, because "the idea of being fiscally responsible is something that goes to the core of what it is to be a Liberal, because we believe in government and therefore the best way to demonstrate that government can be good, unlike the Conservatives, is to demonstrate that government can be responsible fiscally, and that's where they have fallen flat because they want to prove that government is bad." To the extent that Trudeau's rambling sentence means anything, fiscal responsibility is a means to an end: increasing the stature of government as competent and beneficial. It does not mean providing value for what taxpayers hand over to Ottawa.

Whatever Trudeau's stated intentions are, Canadians might want to consider what other Liberals are saying. Huffington Post Canada talked to sitting and former Liberal MPs at the 2014 Liberal convention in Montreal and all four that are quoted suggest that deficits in the future are no big deal, as long as it is their party that is in charge. Former Liberal MP Omar Alghabra, who wants to run again in Mississauga, said, "Balanced budgets are important, but we just witnessed the necessity of running deficits at a time to help the economy ... I don't know what the budget situation in 2015 will be, but people need to know that taxpayers' money is spent wisely to help them. That's really what they care [about]." That sounds like laying the groundwork for defending budget deficits under a Liberal government. Alghabra said that "if you have a good platform that reassures [voters] that the government is spending their money wisely, I'm comfortable with that." Former Toronto Liberal MP Rob Oliphant said that any budget deficit would be temporary and eventually the Liberals would balance the books. "Liberals have proven, frankly, that we are the people who don't run deficits. We cut deficits." That was true under Jean Chrétien (after 1997) and Paul Martin, but Pierre Trudeau ran a deficit every budget year from 1971 through 1985.

Also in that Huffington Post piece from the Montreal convention, Scott Andrews, MP for the Newfoundland riding of Avalon, said the Liberals will have no difficulty getting elected with a platform of higher spending and a return to deficits. "I think people are looking at the big picture. It's not just taxes and deficits, it's social programs and the vision you have for the country and how you are going to stimulate the economy. It's a whole package."

It appears that the people who fill out his caucus (although Andrews was later suspended and ejected from caucus) have no concerns about deficit spending, as long as they are the ones doing the borrowing and spending.

Indeed, the Liberals at their 2014 convention supported numerous new programs and expenditures, substantially expanding the size and scope of government. The convention endorsed numerous expensive policies and programs: "national housing plan that would produce affordable, safe housing for Canadians at all income levels" including "the development of market rental housing" and ensuring "existing affordable housing and homelessness investments are permanent"; a "national strategy for a Universal Early Childhood Education and Care plan" that pegs federal funding of a provincial daycare programs to one percent of GDP while developing "national standards and monitoring mechanisms"; increase Canada Pension Plan payments to workers making $30,000-$80,000 and lowering the age of eligibility for Old Age Security Benefits from 67 to 65; reinstating the 2005 $5.085 billion, five-year Kelowna Accord with First Nation communities to fund education, housing, and health with "dutiful consideration of changes in costs and inflation"; investments "in research and development into ways to reduce costs of green energy technologies"; examining the feasibility of a basic income supplement (a guaranteed income for low-income Canadians) through pilot projects with municipalities or provinces. There are also unspecified commitments to so-called "green energy" schemes. The resolution on health care indicated support for a pricey national pharmacare system by lamenting that under the Harper government it (and other programs) were "unable to progress according to plan." Furthermore, the commitment to "a Transformative Canadian Infrastructure Investment plan" which would be funded at a level of one percent of GDP annually, but any debt (and debt charges) accrued for infrastructure would be disclosed separately from other accounts for the Government of Canada, suggesting a Liberal government would treat them as capital expenditures and not count them as general spending thus making it easier to claim the budget is not in deficit.

Another area in which the Liberals might increase spending is by increasing transfers to the provinces or funding partnerships on specific programs, like the Paul Martin government tried to do when it negotiated separate deals with the provinces on universal childcare. Campaigning with Rolf Dinsdale during a 2013 by-election the Grits thought they could win in Brandon-Souris (Manitoba), Trudeau told the *Brandon Sun* that the federal government should pay for affordable seniors' housing because provinces do not have the funds to do so: "The federal government is the only level of government with any money at all anymore. Provinces and municipalities are all extremely strained, and we have more and more seniors retiring into poverty, and not even just retiring with meagre pensions but retiring into debt as well." He said that the federal government needs to take "leadership" on a number of files, including seniors' housing. In a YouTube video released in early 2014, days before the Liberal convention, Trudeau said the same thing. He said that provinces, like the middle class, are "tapped out" and that only Ottawa has the fiscal room to invest; the federal government "needs to step up" with both financial commitments and leadership.

Trudeau has said that "much of the debate in politics" – that is the 2015 election – will be about how the "surplus is spent." He opposed the government's plan to return money back to the people through various (targeted) tax breaks such as income-splitting for couples where one spouse makes significantly more than the other.

That was in early 2014. Later that year and in early 2015, the price of oil declined precipitously. In mid-2014, the West Texas Intermediate price of a barrel of oil was north $90, but fell by more than 50 percent by early 2015. In January, the Conference Board of Canada estimated that the fall in oil prices would cost the federal government approximately $4.3 billion in revenue (and the provinces another $10 billion). While Trudeau has been quick to note that the

Harper government's various tax breaks are unaffordable with the loss of oil revenues, he has not stated how those losses will affect Liberal priorities, and the programs his party endorsed at its convention a year earlier. In early 2014 he said that while families and the provinces are "tapped out ... the federal government has room to invest." But the decline in oil prices means that Ottawa does not have the money Trudeau wants to spend, and yet the Liberal leader still touts the same old line about investing in infrastructure and the middle class.

Not that it really matters to the Dauphin. Trudeau said in his YouTube economics video that "real fiscal responsibility over the long-term" is achieved through "growth" with the federal government taking a "leadership" in "finding solutions." What is becoming clear is that when Trudeau talks about fiscal responsibility, he is not talking about the federal government living within its means with a balanced budget. He means something quite different – perhaps his father's Just Society – in which the state is directing the economy for some set of undefined optimal results.

Taxes

It is a mantra for Justin Trudeau that the middle class is being squeezed. To the degree that's true, a contributing factor – not that Trudeau admits it – is the high tax burden of Canadians. Not just income taxes, but sales taxes, payroll taxes, and property taxes. According to the Fraser Institute study, "Taxes versus the Necessities of Life: The Canadian Consumer Tax Index, 2014," the total tax bill for the average Canadian family rose 1,832 percent from 1961 to 2013, faster than shelter (1,375 percent), clothing (620 percent), and food (546 percent). The increase in the tax burden for families was almost three times higher than the increase in the Consumer Price Index (682 percent). As a consequence of the growing tax burden, income, sales, property and other taxes combine to be the largest budget item for the average family. In 1963, just a third of family income went to pay taxes (33.5 percent) but today the tax bill takes 41.5 percent of their income. If you included the cost of servicing debt – a form of deferred taxes – the increase would be greater.

But Trudeau doesn't usually mention taxes when he talks about the middle class. When he's pressed, he indicates that he will not raise taxes, but there is no talk of lowering the tax burden. Trudeau told the editorial board of *La Presse* in April 2013 that he would not raise the Goods and Services Tax, which was decreased by the Tories after they won in 2006, because although he understood the economic arguments in favour of consumption taxes over income taxes, he thought increasing the GST would hurt the middle class. The following year, talking about taxes in general, he said, "We need to ensure that governments keep costs as low as possible, especially for middle class households. The middle class is already having a hard time making ends meet and struggling with debt. Tax increases for them are not in the cards and not on the table." Not in the cards is language that suggests circumstances can change, like a new hand being dealt.

In late February 2014, Trudeau told the CBC's Evan Solomon that he wouldn't raise corporate, income, or payroll taxes, but by the next week, he once again amended his promise. "I did make a solid commitment to not raise taxes for the middle class. Anything else is simply not among my priorities." He is suggesting he will not raise taxes on higher incomes, but in fact he is not committing to anything. Either he is deliberately misleading the public about his intentions or he has not thought enough about the revenue he needs for his spending promises. Asked by journalists if he would raise taxes on higher income Canadians, he again evaded, saying, "I've been consistent that it is not my intention to raise any taxes and certainly will not be raising them on Canadians who are suffering under an overly heavy tax burden as it is." Asked again, he would not rule out a tax increase while insisting it was not a priority. But those are weasel words. Not his intention, not ruling out, not in the cards, and not being a priority, means Trudeau is almost certainly going to be raising some tax rates or creating new taxes, he just isn't indicating what taxes, for whom, and by how much.

Also, circumstances have changed but Trudeau has not clarified his stance. In February 2014 he told the CBC, "I don't think we need to raise any taxes," because "the government takes in plenty of money." In August, he told *Maclean's*, "I think we're taking in enough money as a government." But since then oil prices have tanked and Ottawa is collecting less revenue from the oil patch. With that money gone, at least for now, is Trudeau contemplating a tax increase to make up for the shortfall?

Stephen Harper is talking tax relief for Canadian families. In the fall of 2014, he indicated several new targeted tax breaks for families, including doubling the Child Fitness Tax Credit and the Family Tax Cut which allows parents in which one spouse earns more to split the income to possibly fall below the threshold of a lower tax bracket. The overall savings are modest, but for families struggling to get by as much as Justin Trudeau says they are, every penny counts.

At the end of his first year as leader, Trudeau described income splitting as "a decent idea, but it doesn't help the most vulnerable. "So there's advantages in some ways, but it's not exactly the panacea that they're pretending it is." He was expressing skepticism, without dismissing the policy entirely. But two months later, when then finance minister Jim Flaherty began expressing some

Pilgrimages to the Holy Door are encouraged throughout the Holy Year:

St. Peter's Cathedral Basilica, London welcomes pilgrims – individuals and groups – to the Cathedral, which is open Monday to Friday from 7 am – 4 pm. Individuals are welcome to visit the Holy Door throughout the day and also for daily Mass: Monday, Wednesday and Friday at 12:05 pm, and Tuesday and Thursday at 7:30 am.

Opportunities for group pilgrimages, including celebrating liturgy and a Cathedral tour, are possible throughout the week on Tuesdays and Thursdays as well as the afternoons on Monday, Wednesday, and Friday. Some evenings and weekends may be available upon request. To arrange a pilgrimage to the Holy Door in London, contact C.J. Nyssen at 519-432-3475 or by email at cjnyssen@dol.ca.

St. Patrick's Church and Shrine, Merlin is open 7 days a week, with confessions available during the day. Groups of 10 or more may request a special Mass time. To arrange a pilgrimage to the Holy Door in Merlin, call 519-689-7760 or email olrshrine@bell.net.

You are a part of our parish family. Most of us place a very high value on sharing the joy of our faith with future generations. Please prayerfully discern how you might repay the gift of faith you have received by sharing it with future generations. Consider our parish family in your planned giving. Thank you for your generosity.

Thank you for your support of the parish.
Do you have a question or need help with something? Please ask.
Is there anything you think is needed for the parish? Please let us know.
If you or a loved one are hospitalized please ensure they are registered as Catholic and receive pastoral care.
Are you new to the parish? Welcome! Please contact the parish office to register

Quote of the week... Three things that never return. The spent arrow, the spoken word, and the lost opportunity.

Ancient Persian proverb.

What is God telling me this week?
What is one thing from Mass today that will help me to become a better person this week?
How did I do last week?

Mexico Mission Trip Memories 2016 02 14-21
It was an experience of a life time to go on a Mission trip in the jungle and working along side the Mayan Indians. The Mayans are wonderful, friendly, loving Christian people. We were like a large family and formed a great friendship among all. We said Mass daily at church as well as prayers everyday. We slept in hammocks, had cold showers, ate outdoors, rode in open trucks to work, singing the Rosary and ate with the Mayans who made us delicious meals. There were many jobs to do. I was one of the painters. Last day with the Mayans we had a great meal, cake and pop and exchanged gifts. We swam in their Cenote, and zip lined over a beautiful lake. Fun day on our way home, visit the Lady of Fatima church, swam in a larger Cenote, and the ocean. We biked, climbed the Pyramid and ate in a restaurant. Thank you Father Steve for this memory, also for looking after us, our safety and own spiritual needs.

God Bless, Joan Molson.

doubt that the policy would be enacted with the first balanced budget expected in 2015, the Liberal leader made it clear where he stood: "We're quite pleased that they're thinking twice about it because it has been shown that it does not benefit close to 86 percent of Canadians."

When Prime Minister Stephen Harper and Finance Minister Joe Oliver announced details of broad family-friendly tax breaks in October 2014, including income-splitting for couples with children under 18, Trudeau became more explicit. "Income-splitting," he said, "disproportionately benefits the rich." It doesn't help the people who need it most and it costs Canadians an awful lot to do. It doesn't make sense," he told the CBC, saying that he would reverse the policy if the Liberals are elected.

He also wrote a column for the *Toronto Star*, "Income Splitting Not a Wise Investment for Canadians." In it he said that income splitting will "eat through virtually the entire federal surplus without providing any benefit to most Canadians, without creating a single job, and without helping one young person get some opportunity to get ahead." None of this is terribly relevant or on point as neither Prime Minister Stephen Harper nor Finance Minister Joe Oliver has ever linked income splitting with job creation. Furthermore, any tax relief would "eat" into the federal surplus because most tax cuts reduce revenues, but it puts more money into the pockets of average Canadians.

Trudeau also complained in his column that income splitting will "benefit the wealthiest Canadians most of all," with "nearly half the benefits [flowing] to those making over $100,000 a year." Trudeau paints income splitting as a scheme by the Prime Minister to reward the wealthy: "Mr. Harper appears to believe the Canadians who need the least should be given the most. That's not fair." While on the surface that sounds unfair, the reason those benefits accrue disproportionately to high income earners – many of whom describe themselves as middle class – is that they pay a larger portion of total income taxes. Nearly one-in-three adult, lower income Canadians do not pay any income tax at all, so no form of income tax break is going to benefit them.

When the 2015 budget was released, Trudeau said that it was an "electoral document" that "gave help to those who need it least," and had "nothing to the middle class." Indeed, Trudeau repeatedly invoked the middle class, but never defined it or said specifically what a Liberal government will do for it. He railed against policies that supposedly benefit the rich such as income splitting and nearly doubling the contribution Canadians can make to the Tax-Free Savings Account to $10,000. Trudeau said that increasing the cap for the tax-free investment account was part of the "measures that help the wealthiest Canadians." Yet 9.6 million Canadians have opened a

TFSA, which represents about one in three tax filers. Certainly not all of them are rich.

Trudeau also indicated opposition to the government's plan to lower the small-business tax from 11 percent to 9 percent because, he claims, it helps the wealthy. Trudeau said that some wealthy Canadians incorporate themselves to lower their tax burden. According to Industry Canada, there are more than one million small businesses (1-99 employees); Trudeau cannot seriously argue that most of these are nothing more than tax dodgers. Is he willing to prevent tax relief for small businesses just to carry out his class warfare against some so-called wealthy people who lower their tax burden for contract work or providing a service by incorporating themselves? Many of these so-called incorporated individuals are accountants, doctors, interior designers, and lawyers who provide services but do not necessarily make exorbitant incomes.

While Trudeau attacks the Harper government for policies that favour the rich, a parliamentary budget office analysis in 2014 found that the government's tax policies, including the Child Tax Credit and Working Income Tax Credit were "progressive overall and most greatly impact[ed] low- and middle-income earners." The PBO found that those making between $12,200 and $23,300 increased their after-tax income by about four percent under Conservative policies, as opposed to a 1.4 percent boost for those in the top ten percent earners. Kevin Milligan, a University of British Columbia economist who serves on the Liberal leader's economic advisory council, told *Maclean*'s, "A lot of the tax policy of this government hasn't been terribly pro-rich."

On May 4, the Liberals announced "two big parts of our plan to stand up for middle class Canadians," in a speech simply entitled "Fairness for the Middle Class" during a campaign-style event in Aylmer, Quebec. After attacking the government's budget as unfair for allegedly helping the wealthy more than the middle class, the Dauphin announced a 7 percent income tax cut for the second lowest tax bracket, those making between $44,701 and $89,401 – "for the people who need it most." While a 7 percent cut sounds great, it is in fact a 1.5 percentage point cut from 22 to 20.5. Every little bit helps, but an individual making $50,000 would save less than $90 in taxes, while someone making $60,000 would save about $225 and a $75,000 earner could keep an extra $450. This is hardly going to make a major dent in the bills of a middle class family.

Trudeau's economic advisers say that the cost to the federal government of his modest middle class tax cut is $3 billion. "We'll pay for it by asking wealthy Canadians to do a little more," said Trudeau. To pay for the middle class tax cut he would increase taxes on the top one percent of individuals who make at least $200,000 by creating a new tax bracket of 33, an increase of four percentage points from 29. Trudeau of course is not "asking" them to pay more, he would increase their taxes. Finn Poschmann, vice-president of policy analysis at the C.D. Howe Institute, told the *Ottawa Citizen*, "The separating line between Trudeau and Harper is on going after the top one percent. It's a little bit of class warfare here." It also illustrated how Trudeau operates. For two years he said that he did not "intend" and it wasn't a "priority" to raise taxes on higher income earners, but eventually the Dauphin had to admit that if he was going to help the middle class through tax cuts or spending programs, he needed to raises taxes on someone. But raising taxes on the highest earners might backfire. The *Globe and Mail* reported, "The Liberal proposal for a new tax bracket would push the top combined tax rate in most provinces to nearly 50 percent or more, a psychological threshold that economists have long warned will encourage tax avoidance and disappoint government expectations for extra cash." In other words, the plan is unlikely to be revenue neutral considering that combined with the highest tax rates at the provincial level, half of Canada's provinces – Manitoba, Ontario, Quebec, Prince Edward Island, and New Brunswick – would have top income tax rates above 50 percent. Furthermore, the *Globe and Mail* reported that many economists worry that higher tax rates on the wealthy could hurt Canada's competitiveness, therefore slowing economic growth and job creation. For all of Trudeau's talk of "fairness for the middle class," if he is successful in getting elected and implementing his economic agenda, he could tamp down employment and wages.

In the same speech Trudeau announced a major new program for families with children: "We'll give more to help middle class parents with the cost of raising their kids." Trudeau said that if the Liberals formed the next government, they would create a new Canada Child Benefit that would replace the Conservative government's (taxable) Universal Child Care Benefit of $160 a month for children up to five years old and $100 a month for all other kids six to 18, as well as two other means-tested programs, the Canada Child Tax Benefit and National Child Benefit Supplement. Trudeau calls it a "simple, meaningful, monthly, and tax-free" benefit for families with children under 18, but it is provided on a sliding scale. The Liberal's Canada Child Benefit starts at $6400 per year per child under the age of six and $5400 per child 6 to 17 years old, but the sliding scale quickly claws back the benefit. That means that most middle class families will not receive $6400 per young child each year or $5400 annualy for kids 6 to 17 years old. In his speech, Trudeau said, "A typical family of four, earning $90,000, will get a tax-free payment of $490 every month," or $5880 per year (for both children) – or about half of what the Liberals are trumpeting as their $6400 and $5400 child benefits. Families in households making $120,000 – probably about the upper end of middle class – would be receiving a benefit of under $1700 per child. The new CCB would cost a total of $22 billion, about $4 billion more than the existing programs. Trudeau said that the shortfall would be covered by cancelling income splitting and the 2015 budget provision increasing the limit that individuals can put into a Tax-Free Savings Account. Trudeau said that those tax expenditures benefit only the wealthy, although more than half of all TFSAs are used by middle class voters, and every household that pays income tax where one spouse makes more than the other will benefit from income splitting.

After two years of holding his policy cards close to his chest, Trudeau announced policy that still had a $2 billion gap between new program spending and tax expenditures and the increased taxes, cancelled tax cuts, and folded old programs. But after raising taxes on the wealthiest one percent and still producing a shortfall, Trudeau would need to go into deficit again to fulfill his promise to restore the $5 billion (plus inflation) Kelowna Accord for First Nations and any other spending like infrastructure, child care, or the environment, unless he planned to gut other spending or increase other taxes.

As for corporate taxes, it is once again difficult to pin down the Liberal leader. He conditionally supported lowering corporate taxes, but that was a long time ago in 2011, before he was the Liberal leader. During a campaign stop with Brampton Liberal MP Rudy Dhalla in 2011, he said that Liberals have been, and will in the future be, "committed to reducing corporate taxes," but only when the economy is strong and the budget is in surplus. He ran against tax breaks for "the largest" companies during the recession – companies that needed resources to hire more workers at the time – so the government could spend more money on education and pensions.

But during year-end interviews in 2013, as the economy was growing and the federal budget was on track to be balanced by 2015, he told the CBC, "I think we're pretty much where we need to be on corporate taxes ... where they are right now is something OK with me." He repeated his message on CTV's Question Period: "I think corporate tax rates are about where they should be," and implied that tax rates should be remain where they are – and not raised – because "being competitive on the world stage is very important for our businesses." But Trudeau added some Occupy Wall Street-type rhetoric: "Certainly if we get into a position of surplus or balanced books there is a tremendous opportunity to make sure that everyone gets to benefit, not just a few, and that will be very much our focus." That sounds like he could be planning to tax corporations to spread the wealth. But in the very next sentence he added: "Being competitive on the world stage is very important for our businesses." That would imply lower taxes. Either Trudeau's mouth gets ahead of him and he offers gibberish, or he deliberately muddies the waters by suggesting support for very different policies. Or he has no idea what he's talking about.

Trudeau gives lip service to the idea that lower taxes for companies are beneficial, but when the opportunities to lower them arise by meeting his previously stated criteria, he backs away from his earlier position. No doubt the Dauphin needs the government to raise the revenue necessary for the massive spending increases he has planned: infrastructure, pharmacare, daycare, First Nations. Still, one wonders why he does not entertain the possibility that the middle class is being squeezed because companies are paying higher taxes rather than higher wages. It is standard economic theory that companies "pay" for taxes by passing the costs onto others through higher prices, lower wages, or hiring fewer employees. None of those are good for the middle class Canadians Trudeau purports to champion.

Free Trade

As an MP, Trudeau has supported free trade, at least in principle. In 2009, he voted for the Bill C-24, *An Act to implement the Free Trade Agreement between Canada and the Republic of Peru*. In 2010, he gave a speech in the House of Commons about the free trade agreement between Canada and Colombia where he talked about the need to balance the economic issues and moral issues regarding the human rights situation in Colombia. He defended the need for free trade to remain engaged with Colombia to "make positive change," saying, "We must get involved" and jeopardizing the then $1.3 billion trade exchanged between the two countries would only harm Canada's leverage in dealing with the South American country. He championed the agreement's encouragement of "long-term investments that will benefit the Colombian people" and increased trade, especially in agriculture. The Liberals took credit for a human rights monitoring mechanism in the free trade agreement which was vital for the party's support. Still, Trudeau prioritized the economic benefits over the human rights concerns in his speech.

As Liberal leader, Trudeau supported the Foreign Investment Promotion and Protection Agreement with China (FIPA) and free trade with Europe, Panama, Honduras, South Korea, and Japan. In a June 6, 2014 speech to the Regina and District Chamber of Commerce, he said Liberals "are passionate supporters of free trade" and "that's why we chose not to play politics with the recently announced free trade agreement with the Republic of Korea, as well as the agreement in principle with the European Union. We are broadly supportive of those agreements." Fair enough. That might be part of Trudeau's engagement with the world. Liberals from Alexander Mackenzie and Wilfrid Laurier through to William Lyon Mackenzie King and C.D. Howe supported free trade; it wasn't until the Pearson-Trudeau era that Liberals began to oppose free trade on nationalist grounds, culminating in John Turner's opposition to the Canada-U.S. Free Trade Agreement in 1988.

As leader he responded lukewarmly to the news that the government had ne-gotiated the Comprehensive Economic Trade Agreement (CETA) between Canada and the European Union. On the October 18, 2013 announcement that Ottawa had agreed in principle to the CETA, Trudeau reiterated that the Liberals support free trade "as this is how we open markets to Canadian goods and services, grow export-oriented businesses, create jobs and provide choice and lower prices to Canadian consumers." But he provided wiggle room to change his mind. "We are broadly supportive of CETA, though we have yet to see its details, as this is only an agreement in principle," he stated in a press release. He said that the increased trade with the EU would "increase opportu-nity for the middle class." He congratulated the "Canadians from all political parties, all orders of government and the public service who have played major roles" in negotiating CETA and welcomed a public debate on free trade with Europe. He also hinted that Harper would demonize opponents when he said, "The prime minister has a responsibility to lead the discussion in a positive and generous manner."

That statement had a little of everything. It provided support for free trade which is generally popular, left room for the Liberals to eventually oppose it if the political winds shifted, pandered to the middle class by invoking un-named benefits for workers and consumers, diminished the role the Conserva-tive government played in securing the CETA deal, and chastised Harper for something he hadn't yet done, namely go on the attack against opponents of the deal.

Earlier in 2013 Trudeau indicated support for the principle of freer trade say-ing that it was one of the few positives in the Canadian economy and that fu-ture economic growth would come with increased trade with Asia. He finally put actions behind his rhetoric.

The Canada-China Foreign Investment Promotion and Protection Agree-ment has been in negotiations on-and-off since Jean Chrétien's first term, but ramped up during Paul Martin's government. Ottawa has dozens of FIPA agreements that spell out the legal rights of corporations to ease investor-state disputes. The Department of Foreign Affairs, Trade and Development Canada describes the "main purpose" of any FIPA: "To ensure greater protection to foreign investors against discriminatory and wholly arbitrary practices, to provide adequate and prompt compensation in the event of an expropriation and to enhance predictability of the policy framework affecting foreign in-vestors and their investments." The idea is that foreign companies want to be treated fairly when they invest and do not want to be subject to discriminatory laws. Most of these FIPAs are with smaller countries (other than Russia, the next largest countries are Argentina, Philippines, and Poland), so an agree-ment with Beijing caused an unusual amount of consternation.

Many on the political Left had hoped Trudeau would join the NDP in opposing FIPA. Instead, the Liberals joined the Conservatives to vote against an NDP motion in April 2013 that would inform Beijing that parliament would not ratify the Canada-China Foreign Investment Promotion and Protection Agreement. Trudeau's trade critic, Joyce Murray, explained that the motion, which was non-binding on the government, was opposed by the Liberal Party of Canada because it was an "outright rejection" of FIPA, which would benefit Canada by encouraging investment, creating jobs, and promoting trade between the two countries.

Typically Liberal statements endorse trade agreements when they are announced by saying, "We are broadly supportive" of CETA or free trade with South Korea, but that they want to "see its details," while calling on Harper to be more transparent on negotiating these deals. This is all fair enough. Since Trudeau has become leader, the Liberals have voted with the government on all its free trade agreements and they have appeared pro-free trade, with Trudeau saying, "We need trade with the world," to boost jobs and improve the standard of living for Canadians. Perhaps the Dauphin realizes if he is going to grow the economy so that the deficit will take care of itself, then he needs astronomical trade-led economic growth.

Employment

In 2012 the Harper government implemented new Employment Insurance rules. They required repeat claimants to look for, and take jobs, that paid at least 70 percent of the wages or salary of their former job and were located within 100 kilometers of their homes to qualify for EI payments. The goal was to expand the definition of a "reasonable job search" and "suitable employment" to get seasonal workers to find more regular work and not rely on a government cheque as a matter of habit between fishing or farming seasons.

When Employment Insurance reforms were implemented in 2013, Trudeau took issue with changes to rules on seasonal workers that he said would disproportionately affect Atlantic Canada and Quebec. He complained, "The government does not understand the issues of the regions. The Conservatives are still talking about seasonal workers when in fact it is necessary to work seasonal work." He said, "The reality is that we have four seasons, we have cyclical industries," and that expecting people to relocate or travel far each day to where work might actually exist would be unfair to these workers. Trudeau condemned the government for its talking points: "I don't talk about seasonal workers. It's not about seasonal workers, it's about seasonal work."

He said if elected, he would scrap the government's reforms. The Dauphin said he understood regional economic realities better than the Harper government. The Conservatives did not do their homework to "understand what their changes meant for people on the ground." Saying that the changes were "cooked up in backrooms" in Ottawa and Toronto, Trudeau charged the government with being obsessed with "quotas and targets for reduction" of the number of people receiving EI. He also said the only motivation the Tories had was mistaken belief that "Canadians are defrauding the system."

In defending seasonal work, Trudeau never explained what to do with workers between fishing or harvest season. He told a media scrum that EI "needs improvement" but did not say how. He only said that the reforms would be "rejected wholesale and we'll start again from scratch" if the Liberals were returned to power. He later said that the Liberal goal was to have people "move out of the cycle of dependency" so they would not be "stuck with seasonal work." What Trudeau failed to recognize in his rush to condemn the government was that their EI changes were also designed to move people out of the cycle of dependency as workers bounced back and forth between a paycheck and government check after each fishing or growing season. He could not comprehend that the Conservative government wanted to encourage people to be self-sufficient rather than rely on government handouts or that it wanted to protect the interests of taxpayers.

Employment Insurance, formerly Unemployment Insurance, was originally meant to help workers who were down on their luck, and facing unexpected times without paychecks due to broader problems in the economy. Trudeau views EI as an entitlement for workers who can expect annual bouts of joblessness because of their chosen careers. But the Liberal leader also sees such workers as passive victims, when he describes seasonal workers as people who "fall into the situations where they need" government help.

Trudeau said in January and May of 2012, that seasonal work was a reality in many regions of the country, but offered no specific ideas on what he would replace the government's bill with. By August, during the Liberal caucus meeting at the Rodd Brudenell River Resort in Prince Edward Island, he was talking up job training and skills development to move workers to new industries, but admitted he "isn't entirely clear" how he would fix EI. He said that his government would consult workers in different regions across the country before introducing their own reform bill.

Jobs

Like any good politician, Justin Trudeau talks a lot about jobs, specifically about creating them. Yet he seems blithely unconcerned about the jobs that people have and may lose, or have recently lost.

During the Liberal national caucus meeting in London, Ont., in January 2015, he told the *London Free Press* that southwestern Ontario, which has seen numerous factories close in recent years – Ford in St. Thomas, Caterpillar and Kellogg's in London, Heinz in Chatham, Volvo Construction Equipment in Goderich, Smucker's in Dunnville and Delhi, to name a few – that the region was "transitioning away from manufacturing-based employment as a driver in the economy to much more innovation and high-tech and a more knowledge economy." This came off as a snide remark that people have to get used to the fact that the automotive and food processing industries were moving production to the southern United States and Mexico. Well-paying jobs in which a breadwinner could support his or her family were disappearing and the Dauphin appeared to be callously shrugging his shoulders. Trudeau said that the jobs of the future in the area would be in health science and research, ignoring that many erstwhile factory workers did not have the education or training to transition to these new jobs. Trumpeting "the jobs of the future" does little to help the unemployed of today. Since 2000, Canada has lost 501,500 manufacturing jobs, including 10,300 in London alone. Many of those people found other jobs, but not always salaries close to what they were paid, and many have retired early or dropped out of the labour market completely.

Asked by the *Free Press*' Norman DeBono about the possibility of a national automotive policy Trudeau merely replied, "The short answer is we are building a platform that will be responsible." DeBono followed up: "Will there be more money for automotive industry incentives?" Trudeau said that it depended "whether there will be a surplus, what type of fiscal framework the government has." That wasn't ruling out an automotive strategy, but neither was it an endorsement of a comprehensive policy to shore up the slumping manufacturing industry in southwestern Ontario, an area in which the Liberals have only one seat (Guelph).

Asked by the *Windsor Star* about creating an automotive strategy, Trudeau offered bafflegab: "One of the things we need to look at is a plan for growth and prosperity that is based on diversifying our economy but also understanding our pillars and our strength." Again he has no plan. He did not explain his understanding of the pillars and strengths of the Canadian or southwestern economy. He did not answer the question of whether he favoured an automotive strategy. He did say that Ottawa has "a role to play" in building infrastructure and (perhaps) training or retraining workers for business. Trudeau uses buzzwords like "innovate and invest in 21st Century prosperity" to cover up his lack policies.

Trudeau told a rally in London following the caucus meeting that "what we need is a plan" although he notably failed to offer not only details of his plan to create jobs, but to even suggest what the plan might broadly address. Pressed on the lack of a plan, Trudeau reiterated, as he often does, that he will release a platform closer to the October 2015 federal election.

There are plenty of questions for the platform to answer. Trudeau said at the biennial convention in Montreal in February 2014 that, "We want to make sure the economy is diversified and resilient." And, "What we're after is an economy that provides well paying, good jobs for as many Canadians as possible." Do not these goals of a diversified and resilient economy that provide quality jobs include creating the conditions for manufacturing to flourish? Or does he think the "jobs of the future" – great employment opportunities that are both rewarding and pay well but which seem to occur more in political rhetoric than reality – will entirely replace factory jobs?

Trudeau talks a lot about the jobs of the future, or, sometimes, the jobs of tomorrow. Again, these jobs are never described or defined. Presumably they will be good, even better than what we have now. He sometimes suggests that they will be attainable through more education. He also suggests they will be in the fields of health, research, green energy, and the environment. These jobs sound great, but they are part of the planner's fantasy world and they are not materializing.

Conclusion

While occasionally security or health care pop up as top concerns among voters, polls consistently show that economic issues are among the most important to Canadians. Whether it is the overly broad category of "the economy" or broken down to its constituent parts such as "jobs" and "taxes" people are concerned about bread and butter issues that directly affect the affordability of everyday life.

Alongside national security, the most important responsibility of any government is to manage the economy competently. Justin Trudeau has no training in economics, no experience in business, and shows no indication that he has studied political economy or the details of economic policy in a serious way. When he talks about fiscal responsibility, he links it to the need to "demonstrate that government can be good." In other words, the Dauphin wants to appear responsible in fiscal matters so that the public will trust government to do more. The irony is that over time, the more government does, the more it risks a structural deficit of programs that cost taxpayers more and more.

Trudeau's rhetoric provides little insight into the specifics of an economic policy Canadians might expect if the Liberals were elected to government; Trudeau says wait until the election and the Liberals will release a more detailed platform. Perhaps, but more likely it will highlight the broad principles of Liberal planning (infrastructure, helping the middle class) and reiterate opposition to specific Conservative policies such as income-splitting. Certainly, with falling oil prices at the end of 2014 and early 2015 threatening Ottawa's ability to balance the budget, the leader who suggested that budgets can balance themselves cannot be trusted to set the sorts of priorities that will be truly fiscally responsible.

But even if the Liberals were to release a detailed policy of their economic agenda, Trudeau must know that, as Kim Campbell famously said, campaigns are not the time to discuss policy. The pros and cons of the Liberal economic plan would likely dominate the media coverage for a day or so, be targeted by their political opponents in attack ads and during the leaders' debate, but otherwise become ignored and forgotten. Releasing a platform during a campaign ensures lots of heat but little light, and voters would not likely be able to give it the careful consideration such important matters require. Even if the platform was released in the months before the writ is dropped, few people will take out of their summer schedules to study the details of policies being proposed by a political party. This assumes, of course, that Trudeau has a detailed and costed economic plan. Trudeau and the Liberals will call their platform detailed, but saying it is detailed does not make it so.

According to an Abacus Data survey in January 2015, more Canadians thought Stephen Harper better suited to be CEO of a large company (47 percent compared to 23 percent), to give advice on how to invest your money (46 percent vs. 24 percent) or provide advice about a career (41 percent compared to 24 percent) compared to Justin Trudeau. In each case, NDP leader Thomas Mulcair also finished ahead of Trudeau. On economic matters, Canadians trusted Harper more than the Dauphin.

Abacus also asked fun questions to determine the so-called likability of the prime ministerial contenders. Trudeau did much better on these measures. He was the first choice for voters to take a vacation with (55 percent), choose a good movie to watch (53), sing your favourite song (47), babysit your kids (44), to have over for dinner (43), cook the best meal (42), and look after your pet (40). In most cases, Harper finished behind Trudeau and Mulcair.

The takeaway from all this is that Canadians want Harper handling economic matters but if you need someone to watch your dog, Justin Trudeau is your guy.

Canada faces serious economic questions including ones about the degree that government revenues "depend" on oil and what to do when manufacturing is no longer producing the sorts of jobs that could provide a stable income for a family. The trust-fund kid who can't explain what he means by middle class and who simply tells southwestern Ontario workers that they need to prepare for an information economy because car and other factories are leaving for good, cannot be counted on to understand the daily struggles of millions of Canadians. Making ends meet is not a debating society talking point for economically anxious families, but a reality of their lives.

A Conservative talking point against Trudeau is that he isn't qualified to be prime minister because he was a substitute teacher and ski instructor. That's not entirely fair because he has also been an MP for seven years and has other life experiences, although nothing like what most Canadians go through making ends meet. But it is telling that in the Dauphin's memoir/political manifesto *Common Ground*, Trudeau spends more time on his personal ski stories than his economic views of the country.

Chapter 11: Justin Trudeau on Pipelines

Justin Trudeau's position on pipelines is either nuanced or all over the place because Trudeau's position on pipelines depends on the pipeline in question. He supports Keystone XL and has said so in both Calgary and Washington D.C. He opposed the Northern Gateway and in a rare case of specificity on policy has said he would do whatever he could to stop it if he were prime minister. As for the Kinder Morgan pipeline, he supports it if the project is done right. On the Energy East Pipeline, Trudeau's position depends.

All these positions are fair. Some projects might pass economic benefits tests or environmental standards or risk evaluations that others do not. The problem, as it usually is with Justin Trudeau, is that he is good at bashing the government for not doing what he thinks they should be doing without articulating specifically it is he wants the Conservatives to do.

Currently, oil from Alberta is moved by TransCanada Corporation's Keystone pipeline that travels east through Saskatchewan and Manitoba, and south through Nebraska before going to refineries in either Wood River, Illinois, or Cushing, Oklahoma, or the Patoka Oil Terminal Hub tank farm in Illinois. The Calgary-based TransCanada wants a direct 3,456-kilometre pipeline from Hardisty, Alberta through the southwest corner of Saskatchewan on its way through Montana, North Dakota, and finally Steele City, Nebraska. In another phase, it would extend by nearly 900 kilometres the southern portion from Oklahoma to refineries in Houston and Port Arthur, Texas, a move that would increase capacity to 1.3 million barrels of Alberta crude a day, up from 590,000 barrels currently, and allow Alberta crude to be sold on the world market rather than the American one. There has been American political opposition to the proposal due to concerns about the environment, with both climate change and construction through the Ogallala Aquifer in the Sand Hills region of Nebraska, raising the ire of environmentalists and their political allies.

111

The Enbridge Northern Gateway project would entail the construction of a 1,177-kilometre twin pipeline from Brudderheim, Alberta to Kitimat, British Columbia. The pipeline would move 525,000 barrels of oil daily to the Pacific coast and up to 193,000 barrels of imported condensate, a petroleum product used in the oil sands fields. Oil carriers would then ship the crude from Kitimat to refineries in Asia. Environmentalists worry about the forests and waterways the oil would travel through, and various native groups are unhappy at the company's proposed intrusion on aboriginal lands or what they see as insufficient economic benefits for their people.

Kinder Morgan, one of the largest energy companies in North America, already operates the Trans Mountain oil pipeline between Edmonton and Vancouver, and in 2013 it applied to the National Energy Board seeking permission to triple capacity by building a parallel line. It, too, faced opposition from environmental and native groups.

The impetus for all three projects is to get higher prices on the global market for oil from Alberta as American capacity is maxed out. Oil companies claim that they are stuck being paid lower West Texas Intermediate prices instead of the global Brent Crude Index price, which has cost them billions of dollars annually. Keystone would address both the U.S. oversupply (by eliminating the Oklahoma bottleneck) and access to global markets (with the Texas coast refineries). Both Northern Gateway and the Kinder Morgan expansion would bring more Alberta oil to the Asian market.

Keystone and Northern Gateway were both publicly proposed in 2010 and as of early 2015, neither had received the go-ahead to begin construction.

TransCanada announced in 2013 that with Keystone XL being delayed by American politics, it wanted to convert its natural gas pipeline from southern Alberta to eastern Ontario to transport oil in order to move crude from western Canada to refineries and ports in Quebec and New Brunswick along its Energy East pipeline; it would also require extending the existing line from eastern Ontario to the Atlantic coast. Environmental groups oppose Energy East, too, although the main objection of organizations like Environmental Defense Canada is that it will allow oil companies to make money from what it calls the "tar sands" projects.

The Conservative government has supported the building of pipelines, welcoming the economic benefits in terms of job creation that construction and higher oil prices would finance in oil sands development. Yet for the better part of a half-decade, an alliance of environmental and First Nations groups have blocked all efforts to expand pipeline capacity and few politicians are eager to cross them.

Trudeau's position is different. He supports some but not others, defending his position with only a modicum of argument or rationale, if that.

During the Liberal leadership race, Trudeau addressed about 250 students at Trent University in Peterborough, Ont., and he was asked about climate change. While he said that something had to be done about climate change, he did not offer any specific plan. Then he pivoted to use the opportunity to talk about Keystone XL and bash the Harper government. "Because this government has dragged its heels ... our largest trading partner is saying, 'No, we can't take your oil'," Trudeau inveighed. Yet it was dithering by the White House and American political considerations that were delaying the Keystone project. Trudeau blamed Harper and his cabinet for not "reassuring Canadians and our trading partners that we are managing environmental sustainability."

It is easier to attack one's political opponents than develop defensible policy during a leadership campaign. He also took aim at the "political games" being played by the NDP opposing Keystone. Just before the leadership convention, Trudeau said, "I'm very hopeful" that despite the NDP opposition, "we will see the Keystone pipeline approved soon." He told *Canadian Business* that Keystone is an "extremely important initiative" to get "our raw materials to market" and highlighted increased employment as one benefit.

While still on the leadership campaign trail, he went to Edmonton where he praised Alberta Premier Alison Redford's "balanced position" between economic development and environmental protection, without stating what, precisely, was balancing these concerns. Although he said in the scrum that getting Alberta oil to Asian markets was important, he did not comment on the Northern Gateway pipeline.

He seemed to be open to other pipelines when he said that the U.S. administration's approval of Keystone is not the "be all and end all" of getting Canadian oil to market. "There's been a lot of great proposals about how to get our resources to market but we have to do it in a way that is both economically responsible and environmentally sustainable." Unfortunately, he never states what he means by economic responsibility and environmental sustainability, or by what parameters these standards will be determined.

After winning the Liberal leadership, he was no longer evading questions about the Northern Gateway. During a stop in Vancouver in July 2013, he said that he was "absolutely opposed" to the pipeline because there was not enough information about its safety. At the same time he reiterated support for Keystone XL and said that he was open to the Kinder Morgan project as long as environmental and community-support requirements were met. It is odd that he opposed Northern Gateway because he didn't have the necessary information to come to a conclusion; why not take the same position on Kinder Morgan and support it as long as it complied with similar agreements?

If there is a constant in Trudeau's pipeline position it is that Prime Minister Stephen Harper never did enough to address environmental concerns.

Trudeau spoke to the left-wing Centre for American Progress in October 2013 in Washington D.C.; despite his extensive traveling to more than 80 countries, it was his first ever visit to the U.S. capital. He told the predominantly anti-pipeline crowd that he was in favour of Keystone XL: "I'm actually supportive of the Keystone pipeline because it's an extremely important energy infrastructure piece for both of our countries." He said the project had to not harm the environment and blamed Harper for not demonstrating its safety. He also said "in the long run" both Canada and the U.S. had to make "gains towards sustainable energy sources." In 2011, the Centre for American Progress, a Washington-based think tank ran by partisan Democrats, came out against Keystone, saying, "At a time when the United States should be doing everything in its power to reduce carbon dioxide pollution and speed the transition to cleaner fuels, the Keystone XL pipeline would be a step backward. Getting oil from Canada's tarsands is a dirty business." It is not surprising that with the White House's favourite policy shop opposed to Keystone, the Obama administration would delay its decision, precariously balancing the need to not offend business interests while not rocking the boat full of its supporters.

It was surprising to see Trudeau make the case for Keystone in front of an audience friendly to him but opposed to his policy, during a panel on "progressive politics." It ultimately didn't hurt his image with the audience, with Matt Browne, a senior fellow at CAP, saying many in attendance found his position "compelling" and "balanced."

Trudeau defended his decision to talk favourably about Keystone in front of its critics in Washington: "There were some people who raised an eyebrow ... a strong young progressive with an environmental background talking positively about the project, perhaps it got some people thinking about the fact that perhaps it's not as bad as it has been caricatured." He told Canadian reporters in the U.S. capital that his support for Keystone was "steadfast."

At the same time he reiterated there was no contradiction in supporting Keystone but not Northern Gateway. "I'm open to pipelines but done in the right way and in the right place."

"Done the right way" became his Northern Gateway mantra. Without specifying Trudeau said there were "extreme ecological sensitivities" that made the Northern Gateway pipeline unacceptable. But he didn't tell reporters or citizens what the right way was.

"They are very, very different proposals," Trudeau told reporters in Washington. He said that Keystone had already been approved by the National Energy Board, whereas Northern Gateway could harm those who rely on British Columbia's waterways for their livelihood if there was ever a spill. He did signal some hint of how he thinks about the issue: "It's important that we get our resources to market, but it's also important that we understand that it's not just up to governments to grant permits anymore. We have to get communities to grant permission and that's something that we need to spend more time focusing on." He would give local communities, especially native communities, an effective veto power over projects of national, even international importance.

In January 2014, he told the Calgary *Metro* that "pipeline policy in general is one of the most important responsibilities of a Canadian prime minister and of a Canadian government – to make sure we can get our resources to market. We are a natural resource economy and we need to do that." But, he added, "We need to do that in the right way." He offered boilerplate about "long-term strategy" to ensure "not just a sustainable environment but a sustainable economy." He said that local communities must support the projects. This would be repeated, like a broken record, whenever he was asked about Northern Gateway.

He went so far as to say in his *Metro* interview, "the only thing" preventing the United States from approving Keystone is that the Harper government "hasn't done a good job of demonstrating a level of commitment to doing it right and upholding environmental protections and regulations." A few months earlier, he gave a speech to the Calgary Petroleum Club on October 30 in which he said the same thing: "If we had a stronger environmental policy in this country – stronger oversight, tougher penalties, and yes, some sort of means to price carbon pollution – then I believe the Keystone XL pipeline would have been approved already." With the exception of a Terrence Corcoran column in the *Financial Post*, the comment about pricing carbon seemed to fly under the radar as the media mostly focused on Trudeau using American political wrangling as an excuse to bash Harper. When, in early 2014, the U.S. State Department decided not to approve the Keystone pipeline despite not finding serious environmental problems with the project, Trudeau said it was "Harper's political failure" rather than a "scientific or substance failure" that the U.S. did not okay the project.

At the same time he said that he was open to support the Kinder Morgan project if the federal government improved the approval process, without hinting what improvements he wanted. He said that Prime Minister Stephen Harper has not sold Canadians on the economic benefits of trade, choosing instead to vilify environmentalists and others opposed to pipelines. "Mr. Harper has demonstrated that he is not very good at working with anyone who doesn't share his ideology," he said in February 2014. Such partisanship, Trudeau charged, was "limiting the kind of growth that Canadians can have."

Over the next few months he would repeat his pro-Keystone, anti-Harper message. During a campaign swing through Fort McMurray in support of the Liberal candidate, Kyle Harrietha, in a by-election, Trudeau included the oil industry in his complaint: "The fact is that the oil sands have somehow become a poster child for climate change. That is a failing of both government and industry for allowing that to happen because they weren't doing enough to reassure people that the environment is a priority." He then tip-toed toward a policy: collaborating with the provinces a Liberal government would adopt a national climate policy aimed at reducing greenhouse gases. What such a policy would entail would not be articulated; nor did he mention pricing carbon as he had six months earlier in Calgary.

He also campaigned with Liberal by-election candidate Dustin Fuller in Okotoks, Alberta in the spring of 2014, and complained, in the heart of oil country, that Ottawa's heel-dragging on stricter environmental regulations was harming the oil and gas industry by making it harder to get the resources to the American market. Repeating his well-used line he said, "The oilsands have become, in the eyes of many, the poster child for climate change." As usual, he didn't offer suggestions on how to change the oil patch's unearned reputation as an environmental disaster. Perhaps he doesn't think the reputation can be fixed.

Trudeau has an appreciation for Canada's economic history. He told a reporter for *Your McMurray Magazine*, that from furs and forests to fossil fuels, Canada has always been a country that was dependent on its resources. "So I am supportive of pipelines that are done right and done in the right place," if they are supported by local communities and local First Nations. If these were well-worn phrases by now, at least he finally, in May 2014, stated his reasons for opposing Northern Gateway: "I don't feel that a pipeline through the Great Bear rainforest, putting large tankers passage to Kitimat has been properly thought through." Trudeau also questioned whether there was a "social license" for the project. He said while "a government grants permits ... only communities can grant permission." Presumably that means the public needs to support projects to lend them credibility. Trudeau has repeatedly referenced the "social license" for pipeline projects without stating what he means by that highfalutin phrase, but it seems to give local communities, especially natives, a veto over projects of national importance.

In the same interview, he said he wanted to get the "landlocked oil resources to market" and thus supported Keystone and was "very much in favour of the West/East Pipeline."

Except he wasn't.

In May 2013, Trudeau expressed concern about the West/East pipeline – later rebranded Energy East – telling CBC's Information Morning Fredericton he had questions about toxins in the bitumen being transported. "I think it is a proposal that is extremely interesting. We are waiting to look at how they are going to deal with both the community, local, aboriginal concerns and the environmental concerns," Trudeau said. That was a definite maybe. But, if there was a chance "it will cost on pollution," the project would be a no-go. Then federal Natural Resources Minister Joe Oliver said Trudeau was trying to have it both ways, appearing both cautiously protective of the environment while seeming to endorse the pipeline under the right conditions. Oliver said, "I just don't think we need the naysayers using cute wording to get on both sides of the issue." Trudeau's statement put New Brunswick's Liberal leader in a bind, because Brian Gallant supported the job-creating pipeline, praising both the anticipated growth in employment to build the pipeline, work the refinery, and ship the oil out of ports. "It is something we support whole-heartedly," Gallant said.

Nearly two years later, Gallant, by now the Premier of New Brunswick, was still trying to assuage concerns about Trudeau's position on the Energy East pipeline. The federal Liberal leader told *La Presse* that concerns about the environment and community support for the Energy East project had not been addressed by the TransCanada Corporation. Gallant said his federal counterpart still supported Energy East because, Gallant believed, those concerns would eventually be answered. "I think he's just commenting on something that we all know, that you need to ensure that communities have the chance to be heard, and that communities are as supportive of projects as much as possible." That is a charitable spin on the mostly negative comments about the pipeline Trudeau made to his predominantly French audience in Quebec, where polls showed Energy East was unpopular.

After the Tories gave provisional support to Gateway North – support that came four years after the company sought to build the pipeline and that comes only with meeting 209 conditions, including obtaining community support and certain safety standards – Trudeau complained that Ottawa was giving the pipeline "rubber stamp" approval. He was asked by reporters if he still supported Kinder Morgan and he wavered. CTV reported, "He would not say whether he would let the project go ahead if he were prime minister." Trudeau was now only promising to create "a level playing field" although it is unclear what that meant for the building of pipelines.

Even his tepid support for Kinder Morgan's Trans Mountain pipeline seemed to fade.

In the course of five months, Trudeau went from being "very interested in the Kinder Morgan pipeline" saying, "I certainly hope that we're going to get that pipeline approved" when he was talking to the Calgary *Metro* in February 2014, to being non-committal when talking about the same pipeline to the media in June. To be fair, Trudeau's office contacted the *Vancouver Observer* in February to clarify that he did not "unconditionally support" Kinder Morgan's Trans Mountain pipeline, but they did not disavow his words about hoping it was approved.

What is Trudeau trying to do? The most charitable view is that Trudeau is considering evidence about each pipeline and altering his position as he processes each new set of data. That is unlikely. The second most charitable view might be he is making a political calculation, attempting to position himself between the knee-jerk say-no environmentalism of the NDP Official Opposition and what he labels the oil industry cheerleaders in the Conservative government. By saying yes to one project, no to another, and seemingly evolving his views on the other two, Trudeau appears middle-of-the-road and open-minded. He is not saying no to an important industry and a major driver of economic growth in western Canada, but he is not turning his back on his environmental credentials, either. He almost admitted he is deliberately positioning himself when he told reporters at the Calgary Stampede in 2014, "So the fact that the Conservatives are attacking me out here for not being pro-pipeline enough and the NDP are attacking me in Toronto for being too pro-pipeline sort of reassures me that I've found a balanced place that I think most Canadians are going to appreciate."

The least charitable explanation is that Trudeau has no idea what he's doing or making it up as he goes along, or, worse, he does know what he's doing and some of his previous positions on various pipeline projects were disingenuous.

His different take on each pipeline and his shifting positions on some of those pipelines, might confuse voters, who deserve to know precisely Justin Trudeau's position on what he himself says is one of the most important jobs of a prime minister: getting natural resources to the global market. It would seem Trudeau has a precise policy, but his evolving position and his trumpeting of the social license veto for communities raises enough doubts about the Dauphin's commitment to getting Canada's natural resources to the global market.

Chapter 12: Justin Trudeau on the Environment

Justin Trudeau identifies himself as an environmentalist, and took to environmental activism at a young age. In his memoirs, Trudeau writes fondly of his time with family, canoeing, hiking, and camping. When he was 20 years old he rafted with his father in the Yukon and northern British Columbia to – in his words – "raise awareness of the potential environmental dangers to the region posed by a copper mind," although that might simply be a high-sounding justification for what was really just a family outing. He later worked with the Canadian Parks and Wilderness Society in their campaign to protect the Nahanni National Park Reserve in the Northwest Territories. He clearly loves nature.

In *Common Ground*, Trudeau admitted that while he was speaking regularly on youth and environmental issues, he had no formal expertise in the latter. He considered that teaching and his involvement with the federally funded youth volunteer group Katimavik were qualifications to talk about youth issues, but, "I recognized I needed a deeper understanding of environmental issues." So he enrolled as a Masters student of Environmental Geography at McGill in 2005 but dropped out the next year when he became a full-time speaker; he only needed to write his thesis, which he said he would return to if his career in politics didn't work out, but evidently one year at school qualified him as an expert on environmental issues so he could start charging thousands of dollars to clients to share his wisdom.

The folks at Sun News mocked the Liberal Leader in September 2014 when he told a group of University of Western Ontario students: "We have to realize that the way of thinking that got us to this place no longer holds. We have to rethink elements as basic as space and time, to go all science fiction on you in this sense." In many ways it sounds bizarre, Trudeau questioning the settled science of space and time.

In fact, this is a standard bit of rhetoric from Trudeau. When he was on the professional speaking circuit before becoming an MP, Trudeau would tell high school students with "the environmental crisis that is upon us," society needed to rethink not just capitalism – which he railed against as inevitably leading to the destruction of the natural environment – but to rethink the concepts of time and space: "Time, because everything is accelerated ... the world is moving faster and faster and faster ... we need to think differently about how we prepare for the future." The "space" problem related to the fact that "we are using up everything on the planet." This stuff might impress high school students, but what does it all mean? And, more importantly, what would Trudeau have society and government do about it? He gave that speech in 2007 in Windsor, when he was thirty-five. Then, he did not like the "capitalist machine" because it exploited natural resources. Speaking in Whitehorse in September 2005, he said that trade and investment could be good for Canada but added, "My concern is that we make sure that the wealth coming in, we don't spend it on buying more cars and more trucks and bigger houses." He said that part of the solution to greenhouse gas emissions was a ban on gas-guzzling SUVs, but he admitted that any politician who advocated such a policy "wouldn't last two weeks in office."

Justin Trudeau has dropped the Marxist rhetoric since being elected MP and Leader, but has he changed his thinking? Thirty-five is hardly a youthful flirtation with discredited ideology. And he recognized at a young age that politicians who advocated the policies he once thought were necessary to protect the environment would have short political careers.

As Liberal Leader the Dauphin talks about the topic of the environment incessantly, but hardly ever offers solutions to the problem that he described as a professional speaker as society's "path towards collapse." If civilization itself is at risk of collapsing, you would think that Justin Trudeau would do more than exhort the Harper government to act more environmentally responsibly – like when he called then Environment Minister Peter Kent "a piece of shit" during Question Period because Canada had officially withdrawn from the Kyoto Protocol – and perhaps outline precisely what the Canadian government needed to do to avert the impending disaster.

Trudeau blamed Harper's lack of action on climate change for the Obama administration's obstinate refusal to okay the Keystone XL pipeline. But the Liberal Leader never offered any hint of what the Prime Minister could have done, other than impose a price on carbon. As *Alberta Oil Magazine* said, "He's been even vaguer on green issues than on energy policies, repeatedly stressing the importance of environmental regulation but rarely how that regulation would look."

Trudeau sometimes still calls himself an environmentalist. After speaking in favour of the Keystone XL pipeline to a liberal audience in Washington, D.C., in October 2013, he said he raised eyebrows because here he was, "a strong young progressive with an environmental background talking positively about the project." And yet he never describes himself as such in his memoirs. The environment barely comes up as often as the economy, with both receiving about a half-dozen mentions each in the 343-page book.

But Trudeau's allies in the radical environmental movement still consider him one their own. "Environmental professional" Dan Beare wrote in the online *Alternatives Journal*, which describes itself as "Canada's environmental voice," that like Barack Obama, who has done little in the way of pushing the environmental agenda in the United States, Justin Trudeau has a personal "support base which believes strongly in government regulation to protect the environment."

As an MP in 2009, Trudeau told an Alberta audience that native peoples are not being sufficiently consulted although he did not address specific concerns that aboriginals had with the development of oilsands. Trudeau gave lip service to the benefits of extracting more from the oil patch, including touting the jobs and tax revenues it would create, but said it needed to be done properly. "We don't want to mortgage our future," he insisted, without stating what sorts of limits he had in mind. The following year he said that the oilsands are "a necessary part of the economy in Canada right now," although he wanted "alternatives" to be found. Of course, he did not talk about what kind of alternatives, none of which create many jobs or are as efficient as fossil fuels.

Trudeau supports Keystone XL to move oil to the American south, but opposes most other pipeline projects. Yet environmentalists have not screeched their opposition to Trudeau's Keystone XL position or questioned his acknowledgement of the importance of the oilsands industry to both the Albertan and Canadian economy? Why the silence? Do they understand that the Dauphin is merely mouthing support for an industry to appear moderate but know that he would institute severe restrictions that would cripple the oilsands industry if he ever became prime minister? Perhaps they paid attention to what he said in October 2012 that "there is no sense in being in an incredible rush" to get oil out of the ground if five or ten years from now it harmed "ourselves ... in either monetary terms or in ecosystem terms." That indicates a desire to regulate oilsands developments that would appease environmentalists but might leave a lot of the economic advantages of the natural resource on the table – or under the ground, as it were. He has also often said by way of explaining opposition to Keystone XL that "the oilsands have become, in the eyes of many, the poster child for climate change." This signals to radical environmentalists that he shares, or at least appreciates, their concerns. Trudeau is an expert at indicating his support for a project or policy while recognizing opposition to it. This tact makes it appear that Trudeau could be on either side, a not always disadvantageous positon for a politician to be in. It is possible for voters to only see what they want to in a candidate. It also makes him appear reasonable and open-minded. But it might be a pose, deliberate positioning to deflect criticism that he is a radical environmentalist or knee-jerk liberal.

He did it again during an August 2014 swing through Atlantic Canada, when he told reporters in Nova Scotia that "Canada obviously needs to develop its natural resources but we need to do it in a responsible and sustainable way." This appears moderate, balancing ecological and economic issues. So is asserting that "we're demonstrating that we're not risking the future of our children either in an economic or environmental way." But the Liberal Leader has never indicated how he would balance these two opposite sides of the scale.

Before he became an elected official, Trudeau did not sound so moderate. He said if the oil sands were going to be exploited, then money made from the projects should be invested in building technology that does not require gas and oil. But in 2005 he also used inflammatory rhetoric that exposed his contempt for the oil industry; he wanted to create "a world that won't need to be exploited by leaching cyanide into the river systems and ruining a caribou herd and habitat." Then he was playing for cheers from youthful or zealous audiences, not seeking the votes of millions of Canadians.

For two years as Leader, Trudeau talked about a national climate policy, which he said would limit greenhouse gases. He did not elaborate how this would be done, but said it would target both consumers and the energy industry. He said his government would act unilaterally to implement such a program, and claimed it would enhance oil sands profits. He was treading on ground that has already proven disastrous for Liberals.

In June 2008, four months before the anticipated fall election, then Liberal Leader Stephane Dion unveiled his Green Shift that would have pegged the price of emitting fossil fuels such as oil, gas, and coal, at $10 per tonne initially but which would rise to $40 a tonne within four years. Ostensibly businesses would pay these carbon taxes but they would pass the cost along to consumers, which Dion estimated would take $225-$250 out of the average household budget. He also proposed reducing income taxes so that the new Green Shift levy would be revenue neutral for the government. The Harper government called the Green Shift a "tax on everything" because it would have affected transportation and thus the costs of moving goods around the country.

Dion never recovered from proposing his environmental tax and announced he was leaving as party leader after what up to that point, had been the Liberals' worst electoral showing in Canadian history.

Trudeau talked about carbon pricing – a euphemism for a carbon tax or government regulations that increase the price of carbon-producing fuels – but again he lacked specifics about how he would go about doing that. Asked by the *Edmonton Journal*'s Mariam Ibrahim in an August 2014 interview how he would "enhance Canada's environmental reputation," when he becomes prime minister, Trudeau answered that Canada would have to "be serious about putting a price on carbon pollution," after consulting with scientists and the provinces. "What we need is a responsible debate and discussion around it, and unfortunately what we're getting right now is fearmongering and attack ads." Yet again, Trudeau avoided stating his position, passing the buck to scientists and the provinces.

The Liberal website, over top of its leader's picture, says a Trudeau government will meet the provincial leaders and "work with them to set national targets on carbon emissions and pricing."

In a speech to the Calgary Petroleum Club, on October 30, 2013, Trudeau brought up carbon pricing. He called for a national energy strategy with "a national approach to pipelines and development, within an overall framework that includes a policy that puts a price on carbon pollution." Such a strategy had to be "based on science and evidence." Perhaps Trudeau is unaware of this, but science cannot set prices. Markets – that is people and government – do.

In an interview with Bloomberg News during the June 2014 by-elections, Trudeau said, "The Liberal Party is somewhat agnostic" about what form a carbon tax should take in Canada. He suggested that the issue was fraught with electoral pitfalls: "We recognize the fact that the discussion around carbon pricing has been incredibly polarized politically."

On February 6, 2015, Trudeau was back at the Calgary Petroleum Club. He said, "Many in this room believe that a price on carbon is good for the environment, for the economy, and for Alberta's oil and gas sector …You know Canada needs to have a price on carbon. The good news is that we're already on our way." Trudeau said, "British Columbia, Alberta, Quebec – and soon, Ontario – have all committed, in various forms, to a price on carbon. Combined, those jurisdictions represent over 85 percent of the Canadian economy." In his clearest statement on carbon prices he said, "Our children's future requires us to reduce carbon emissions; and carbon pricing is an effective way to get us there."

The Dauphin has long charged Harper with failing to have Ottawa lead on the issue. He told Calgary's oilmen, "The problem is that the provincial approaches are uncoordinated, and limited by a lack of federal leadership." Not all provinces were participating in a carbon pricing scheme.

Different provinces take different approaches. Alberta taxes carbon above a certain level of production, although that might change with the NDP government elected in May 2015. British Columbia implemented a carbon tax in 2008, which is imposed on consumers in order to encourage conservation and the use of alternative fuels, although many environmentalists claim it is set too low to actually change consumer behaviour. Quebec and Ontario have a cap-and-trade system which limits the amount of carbon a company can produce, after which it must buy credits from companies that have come under their allotted carbon production (as set by the government). It is effectively a tax on carbon because it sets a price on producing greenhouse emissions after a certain level.

Trudeau told Bloomberg back in 2014 that the business community needed clarity because companies "want to know where the benchmarks will be, what the expectations will be, for the next 10 years, for the next 25 years." He said it helps them create a business model for dealing with greenhouse gases, but he attacked the Harper government for failing to provide that clarity.

So what does Trudeau support? In his 2015 speech to the Calgary Petroleum Club he said the individual provincial programs "make sense for their own economic contexts and priorities." He also condemned the NDP's "one size fits all solution from Ottawa." These comments indicate he has moved away from the idea that Ottawa needs to provide leadership. Trudeau said he intended "to build on these provincial initiatives," but did not say how.

Just a few weeks earlier, Trudeau told AM980's Andrew Lawton that it "should be up to various provinces because they've already taken the lead on that, and what the federal government needs to do is co-ordinate that and oversee the implementation." As Andrew Coyne observed in the *National Post*, after two years of chastising Prime Minister Stephen Harper for abrogating his responsibility to lead on enacting a price on carbon, Justin Trudeau was likewise abrogating federal leadership on the question of carbon pricing. "He might not have been clear on which sort of carbon 'price' he preferred, but he was clear that he would be the one to impose it." Then, all of a sudden, ten months before the federal election, Trudeau passed the buck to the provinces.

Justin Trudeau learned the lesson of Stephane Dion: do not talk about carbon taxes. So he called them carbon pricing, which was the central plank of his environmental agenda. But as the election neared, Trudeau abandoned it.

Five months before the October 19, 2015 federal election, the Liberal Party website had a total of 72 words on environmental issues. A Liberal government would meet with the provinces to "set national targets on carbon emissions and pricing" and they would "support clean energy and energy-efficiency projects to help reduce climate change causing gases." On the one hand, that's thin gruel for a party led by a committed environmentalist. On the other, it commits the federal government to push the provinces to implement carbon taxes that will increase the price of everything, from the gas that goes into the family vehicle to the family groceries.

Chapter 13: Justin Trudeau on Cities and Infrastructure

Even before he became Liberal leader, Justin Trudeau was talking about the need for more federal support of cities, in particular funding infrastructure projects. Since becoming leader, he has linked infrastructure to his middle class narrative, to improve the well-being and economic security of that group of voters. Trudeau says that if Ottawa were to invest in the right projects, middle class life would be more affordable, more convenient.

Trudeau has complained that cities receive just eight cents of every tax dollar collected in Canada, compared to the federal government which takes half, while the provinces take 42 cents. Trudeau said that in an increasingly urban country, with large cities facing numerous social problems, municipalities need more revenue to tackle issues. "How do we ensure all levels of government have the revenue, and the revenue sources we need, to fulfil our responsibilities to Canadians?" he wondered in a June 2013 campaign-style swing through British Columbia. He returned to this theme in Edmonton the next January. "The vast majority of services to citizens are delivered by municipalities, but only a minute fraction of the ability to raise money and spend the public purse is available to municipalities," he told the Edmonton *Metro*.

He has returned to this theme repeatedly.

He told Vancouver's News 1130 in August 2014, that, "We have a government that is no longer working as a partner with other municipalities or provinces, and at a time when we need to increase productivity and make sure that people aren't wasting their time on commutes as they are." This issue offers much in one punch for Trudeau: he is attacking the governing Conservatives, he is implying he will play nice with various levels of government, and tackles issues such as economic growth and transit – macro and micro economics – all at once. Hitting the productivity notes allows listeners to insert their aspirations about jobs and shorter commute times which means financial stability and more time with the family.

Trudeau told the Federation of Canadian Municipalities at their annual conference in Niagara Falls in May 2014 that "Canadians, for the most part, are not all that interested in the finer details of inter-governmental funding," because voters and taxpayers "just want to be able to get to work, to get their products to customers, on roads that are in good repair, on bridges that aren't crumbling and with a rail system they can rely on."

The Dauphin attacked government cuts to infrastructure spending, without noting that the program to support such projects was coming to an end (and would be replaced by a new program the following year). Trudeau said, "Infrastructure funding needs to be substantial, predictable and sustainable." That has become a mantra when he talks about infrastructure. He also said that if the federal government increased the amount of funding for infrastructure, then local governments could borrow against that revenue stream.

He told the Edmonton *Metro*, "Ultimately when different levels of government focus on the different levels and the jurisdictions that they have, they tend to forget that the fact is we all serve the same citizens." Indeed, that's true and there is only one taxpayer, but such thinking can also be used to justify ignoring separation of powers and blur constitutional and legal distinctions that provide the necessary division of responsibility and thus accountability. It sounds pragmatic, but when a project does not work out, who is going to take the blame? No one.

Despite Trudeau offering to partner with cities by providing more money for them, he hasn't been forthcoming as to what precisely that means. The Huffington Post's Althia Raj was in Edmonton for the August 2014 Liberal caucus meetings in the Alberta capital, where Brock Carlton, the CEO of the Federation of Canadian Municipalities, brought Regina Mayor Michael Fougere and Edmonton Mayor Don Iveson along to hear details of what a Liberal government would do for cities. She reported that they didn't get any.

While Trudeau told reporters at the caucus meeting that there are "very, very real needs" across the country, he said that the Liberals would increase infrastructure funding by up to one percent of GDP, but "it won't happen in the first year," as "it will be something that the Liberal party has to work seriously on getting." The party endorsed the idea of increasing infrastructure investment by one percent of Gross Domestic Product at its 2014 Montreal convention, but party delegates routinely use a percentage of GDP as an expression of financial commitment without putting flesh on those bones, or stating where the money comes from. Sometimes, it seems, that people who invoke spending a particular percentage of GDP on some worthy project, think the money can be grabbed out of an account labelled Gross Domestic Product when in fact GDP is a statistic that merely reflects all economic activity.

Trudeau usually – but not always – qualifies his support for handing money over to cities for infrastructure with the line that the "Liberal Party continues to be committed to fiscal responsibility." Still, despite his claim that, "The Liberal party has been very clear over the past months that we believe that infrastructure spending is necessary on a significant and serious scale to be able to grow our economy in the right way," he hasn't provided any specific projects he would fund or describe what he means by the "right way" to grow the economy. His proviso that these be both economically beneficial and environmentally sustainable sounds like an important qualification, but it, too, is vague: economically beneficial for whom and what trade-offs are acceptable?

Michael Fougere, the Mayor of Regina, said that he asked the Liberal caucus what exactly they meant when the party pledged to spend one percent of GDP on infrastructure. "Is it conditional? Is it attached to provincial growth? Is it done by per capita [on] how you distribute it? Or is it done provincially or by cities?" He added, "Because if it is one percent of GDP, it could actually be a reduction of transfers versus an increase," if the economy shrank, but many economists favour pumping-priming the economy with infrastructure spending when the economy contracts. Fougere stressed that he wasn't criticizing Trudeau or the Liberals, but rather that their promises did not provide the answers municipal leaders were looking for.

The Federation of Canadian Municipalities' Carlton had no problem with the lack of specific Liberal program, saying he felt "a genuine interest" among the Liberal caucus to help municipalities address issues. He said the Liberals "are thinking that through" and "we are offering some ideas."

In 2013 and 2014, Justin Trudeau repeatedly said that the federal government needed to fund cities and provinces to "invest now" in transit, housing, and education. He did not press the Harper government for any specific funding, and despite the call for investment "now" he said that he would release his spending wish-list during the 2015 election campaign. "The more specific debates," he said, were going to be what the 2015 election was about.

That promise to the 2000 mayors and city councillors at the 2014 FCM annual meeting in Niagara Falls of more federal money if the Liberals were elected the government could be viewed as a bribe to local politicians, and their community networks, in the lead-up to the next federal election. It's no secret that many big city mayors are not fans of the Harper government and Trudeau is solidifying a potential beneficial electoral relationship with political machines that are in place across the country. But the tact also displays a mindset. The federal government is the sugar daddy for lower levels of government.

An important insight into Trudeau's thinking is his line that "the federal government should be helping out." During an interview with *Metro* Calgary following a fundraising event in the city, Trudeau explained that the Harper government "doesn't do a very good job of working with other levels of government." He said that the prime minister should be meeting with provincial and municipal leaders more often. But it is more than personal engagement, Trudeau said, Ottawa must be willing to share its wealth with the lower levels of government. He praised past Liberal governments for the New Deal for Cities, Paul Martin's 2005 plan to fund infrastructure, and the Martin government's Gas Tax Transfer.

He told the Edmonton *Metro* that "federal leadership" was needed, by which he meant money. He said in early 2014 that a national strategy that recognizes each city has its own goals but needs federal funding to achieve them would be a centerpiece of his government, although precisely how he would create a program that had such flexibility was not spelled out. "I think there is a great opportunity to be a flexible, but as a present partner with strong stable funding that understands that investment in transit is an investment and not just an expense."

A few months later he gave an interview to the downtown Toronto urban weekly *The Grid*, which is owned by the *Toronto Star*. He was about to recruit Adam Vaughan, a member of the left-wing faction at Toronto's city council, to run for the federal Liberals in a by-election to replace Olivia Chow, who resigned her downtown seat to run for mayor. Vaughan could have just as easily run for the NDP, but he was recruited by the Liberal leader when Trudeau was in town for the funeral of former finance minister Jim Flaherty. According to *The Grid*'s Courtney Shea, Vaughan agreed to run for the Liberals only if Trudeau promised a national urban agenda, presumably one in which the erstwhile city councilor would have a say. Asked about it by Shea, the Dauphin said that Vaughan would provide invaluable input on what cities need, whether it's housing or transit. Trudeau said that he was open to "an actual national transit strategy" so "public transit is seamless and properly used and reliable" and then "people will get out of their cars" and there will be less traffic. To make it work, Trudeau said, the strategy must look beyond the next election and have a 10-year or 20-year vision.

But helping cities with infrastructure does not take just vision, but money. The family benefits Trudeau offered in May 2015 envision spending the budget surplus and then some, while raising taxes on the wealthiest Canadians. The large-scale infrastructure spending the Liberals under Trudeau are talking about will require more tax hikes or gutting existing spending. The question for Trudeau is that if there is only one taxpaying citizen, as the Dauphin has noted, why not allow taxpayers to pay for their local transit and road improvements themselves?

Tellingly, Trudeau has not said what he would do differently than the Harper government. When one considers how much the Liberal leader has said about investing in infrastructure, it would be easy to conclude that the federal government has not been spending money on infrastructure during the nine years the Conservatives have been in power. Trudeau has called for more funding from Ottawa for building and repairing roads, as well as bridges and public transportation. This, however, is precisely what the Harper government was doing.

The infrastructure component of Canada's Economic Action Plan, announced in the 2009 budget, included $33 billion for 43,000 projects designed to stimulate the economy by creating construction jobs, enrich the lives of people within communities, and enhance the long-term economic value of infrastructure. Most of the spending through Building Canada involved joint projects with other levels of government to build and repair airports, bridges, highways, ports, public transit, recreational facilities, and roads. There were investments on First Nation reserves, including energy systems and transportation infrastructure. It also repaired and modernized facilities at federal government operations from national parks to border security, many of which were long overdue.

If Harper is not doing the right kind of projects, which, if any, would Trudeau stop funding? During his speech at the 2014 biennial convention, Trudeau said, "As a progressive party, as a Liberal Party, we need to ask ourselves, what is the right role for government in creating that economy? Too much government is an enemy of freedom and opportunity, but so too is too little." There was no sense, however, of what the balance would be.

Chapter 14: Justin Trudeau on International Issues

Growing up at 24 Sussex Drive, Justin Trudeau has a better idea than most of what is involved in being prime minister, and perhaps that is most true when it comes to foreign affairs. In *Common Ground* he says, "Sometimes I had a front-row seat at events of major importance," as he travelled with his father meeting foreign dignitaries. Perhaps the best known of these front-row seats was attending the funeral of Soviet dictator Leonid Brezhnev in 1982 when the Dauphin was just ten years old. The lesson he learned as he met world leaders such as U.S. President Ronald Reagan, British Prime Minister Margaret Thatcher, and German Chancellor Helmut Schmidt, was that "in foreign relations, [personal] relationships are vitally important." As a young lad, Trudeau admits, he had neither the interest nor the intellect to understand arms control and trade agreements. But as a young child he noticed that Pierre Trudeau's briefings after these meetings focused on the personalities involved much more than the issues discussed.

Trudeau touts his travel – both as the son who tagged along with his father on international jaunts and as a jet-setter son of privilege after graduating from high school – as a qualification for prime minister. He told the weekly Farsi paper *Salam* in Toronto in April 2014, "All my life I've been an international traveller; I've spent years travelling around the world seeing all sorts of different countries." He boasted of visiting 90 countries. And he criticized Stephen Harper because he hadn't travelled. "Stephen Harper didn't do much travelling, if any, before he became prime minister, and the lens through which he looks at foreign affairs is always, 'Is this going to help my electoral prospects back home'," said Trudeau.

As sure as Trudeau is in his ability to conduct foreign policy, one can't help look at Trudeau's statements on international issues and wonder if he's ready to be prime minister. Trudeau seldom talks about international affairs, and when he does, he demonstrates insensitivity and poor judgement. His off-the-cuff commentary on international issues shows a lack of seriousness about some of the world's most serious issues and hot spots.

Over the course of 12 months Trudeau committed three serious missteps when talking about global affairs. Alone, any one of them could be dismissed as an ill-advised joke, but taken together they betray a troubling lack of maturity for someone seeking the country's highest elected office. None of them were about policy, and all of them were impromptu remarks.

On November 6, 2013, the aspiring prime minister held a "Ladies' Night with Liberal Leader Justin Trudeau," which had attracted controversy even before the event was held. The marketing material was amateurish and treated women as if they were vapid. The electronic invite suggested the ladies could ask questions such as, "Who are you real-life heroes?" and, "What's your favourite virtue?" While these can certainly be revealing questions, providing real insight into the mind of a political leader, the implication was that women voters cared more about personal feelings than policy. Still, about 100 women paid $250 to attend Trudeau's Ladies' Night.

That didn't mean, however, that it would be an easy evening for him. One of the ladies in attendance asked Trudeau which country's government he most admired: "Which nation, besides Canada, which nation's administration do you most admire, and why?"

Trudeau considered the question for an extended length of time, during which event host Amanda Alvaro gave him some time to think by saying, "Not the fluffy questions some were expecting." It was not the type of question that should have stumped him, although it provided more opportunity for reflection that the typical softball he was presented with throughout the night.

He finally answered after thinking about it for a while. "You know, there is a level of admiration I actually have for China because their basic dictatorship is allowing them to actually turn their economy around on a dime and say 'we need to go green fastest ... we need to start investing in solar.' I mean there is a flexibility that I know Stephen Harper must dream about of having a dictatorship that he can do everything he wanted that I find quite interesting."

There is a lot to that statement.

The Chinese regime is one of the most brutal in the world, and any admiration for a country that routinely intimidates, arrests, imprisons, and tortures political opponents is misplaced. They are among the worst human rights abusers in the world according to Amnesty International, Human Rights Watch, and the U.S. State Department.

Trudeau said that he liked the Chinese system because of its ability to deal with pollution. The problem is that pollution in China is rampant. The Chinese economy depends on coal. It is used in making steel, cement, and electricity. China is the biggest consumer of coal in the world, burning 3.8 billion tonnes in 2012, and while other countries are decreasing their coal consumption, China's use is growing. Some analysts, such as Wood Mackenzie, estimate coal use in China will double by 2030. Beijing's air quality index regularly exceeds 300 – the World Health Organization says anything above 25 is dangerous (Mexico City averages 52 and Los Angeles 25). Talking about China as an environmental beacon due to their one-party government betrayed a shocking lack of knowledge about the country's environmental problems.

This was not some esoteric detail of China's pollution problem. In the weeks before Trudeau proclaimed his appreciation of Beijing's ability to produce environmentally friendly policy, there were reports in Canadian newspapers of Chinese schools and airports closing due to smog, and a women's golf tournament in Beijing witnessed participants playing with masks on to protect themselves from the noxious pollution. The city of Harbin, the *Globe and Mail* reported, had a "1,000 on an air quality index that puts an upper limit on safe air at 25."

Justifying his admiration for the Chinese dictatorship for environmental reasons does not make any sense considering the country's terrible environmental record. Ignoring the human rights record of one of the world's worst regimes is inexcusable.

Ironically, he says that Stephen Harper can only "dream" about having the power of the Chinese dictatorship, yet it was Trudeau who was professing admiration for the communist government in Beijing. Trudeau criticizing Harper for being a dictator or dictator-wannabe while admitting his "level of admiration" for China's "basic dictatorship" is rich. Meanwhile NDP leader Tom Mulcair chastised Trudeau: "I'm not a big fan of dictatorships. I rather prefer democracies. I don't understand how someone can say that their favourite government was a dictatorship, frankly." It is also notable that it was his father, some three decades earlier, who said something very similar, praising Fidel Castro's ability to get things done without worrying about democratic niceties during a prime ministerial visit to Havana. Respect for dictatorships runs in the family.

To be fair to Trudeau, he redirected himself and provided a second answer: "But if I were to reach out and say which kind of administration I most admire, I think there's something to be said right here in Canada for the way our territories are run. Nunavut, Northwest Territories, and the Yukon are done without political parties around consensus. And are much more like a municipal government. And I think there's a lot to be said for people pulling together to try and solve issues rather than to score points off of each other. And I think we need a little more of that."

There are two problems with that answer. The question was about what "nation's" administration and the three northern territories are not nations. Furthermore, Yukon does have political parties. Indeed, at the time of Trudeau's comments, the Yukon Liberal Party featured their interim leader, 38-year-old Sandy Silver, meeting Justin Trudeau, on its website.

Trudeau concluded his remarks about China (and the territories) with a joke: "Sun News can now report that I prefer China." The Sun News team went on the attack. Over the next few days, no fewer than four Sun News personalities chastised Trudeau for his comments about the Chinese dictatorship he admired: David Akins, Adrienne Batra, Ezra Levant, and Brian Lilley. Either Trudeau was callous in his disregard for China's brutality, uninformed about its environmental problems, or he genuinely admired a dictatorship, none of which reflects well on the man who wants to lead Canada's government.

But it wasn't just Sun News that took Trudeau to task for his China remark. The CBC's Rex Murphy said that Trudeau's admission that he admired China's murderous regime "wasn't just dumb … it was almost weird, it was certainly immensely careless, and, no, it wasn't a joke."

The problem with Trudeau is that when it comes to foreign policy, he cracks inappropriate jokes. It is kind of his thing, perhaps covering up his ineptitude on substantive matters of international affairs.

During the 2014 Winter Olympics in Sochi, Justin Trudeau joked about Putin invading Ukraine days before Russia invaded Ukraine.

Appearing on Radio Canada's *"Tout le Monde en Parle,"* which takes a humorous approach to current affairs, Trudeau was asked about violence occurring in Ukraine. Admitting it was "very disconcerting" he proceeded to his punchline, "Especially since Russia lost in hockey, they will be in a bad mood, we are afraid of a Russian intervention in Ukraine."

He made the joke on an episode taped on February 20. On February 26, Russia annexed Crimea, a region of Ukraine with a large Russian population. But the criticism was immediate on the panel as the joke illustrated bad judgement. *"Tout le Monde en Parle"* host Guy Lepage asked incredulously, "Just because of hockey?" Fellow guest Dan Bigras, a singer and actor, reminded the Liberal leader that there were massacres going on in the former Soviet republic; according to the Ukrainian ambassador to Canada, up to that point 82 people had already been killed in riots and conflict between government loyalists and

Russian sympathizers. Trudeau tried to explain himself: "No. That's trying to bring a light view in a situation that's extremely serious."

Opposition MPs condemned Trudeau's remarks.

Three of Harper's cabinet ministers, Employment Minister Jason Kenney, Citizenship Minister Chris Alexander, and Industry Minister James Moore all condemned Trudeau. In a scrum outside the House of Commons, Kenney said Trudeau's invasion joke showed poor judgement "to make light of the deadly crisis in Ukraine." Kenney also tweeted: "So Justin Trudeau, whose favourite regime is 'the basic dictatorship of China,' thinks the deadly crisis in Ukraine is a laughing matter." Talking to reporters, Alexander said, "Trudeau apparently thinks the situation is Ukraine is something to joke about. We don't and we are concerned that there is not just one statement of this quality, there's a pattern here of support for communist dictatorship, of belief in ... budgets balancing themselves and now of whimsical comments, offensive comments about Ukraine's future based on the result of a hockey game in Sochi." In a tweet, Moore simply called Trudeau's words "Unreal."

NDP leader Thomas Mulcair also called out Trudeau for joking about a serious topic. "I fail to see the levity when you've got dozens of people being shot dead in the street of their own capital, so you don't make jokes about that," he told reporters. "If he's making jokes, I think that he'd better start explaining himself, if and when he ever accepts to take questions from journalists."

Vadym Prystaiko, the Ukrainian ambassador to Canada, demanded an apology from the Liberal leader.

The Liberal Party's foreign affairs critic Marc Garneau – who had himself challenged Trudeau on international affairs when he ran against him for the Liberal leadership a year earlier, complained that the Tories and NDP were scoring "cheap partisan" points against Trudeau and said his leader had nothing for which he needed to apologize because of the light-hearted nature of the popular French-language program on which Trudeau appeared. Still, Trudeau was forced to apologize, days after the program taped and a full day after it aired he waded into a pool of reporters to apologize: "I regret my comments about Russia which made light of some very real fears that Ukrainians have." He said he waited a full day to express his regret because, "I wanted to make sure that I had the chance to express directly to leaders within the Ukrainian community how seriously the Liberal Party takes the situation in the Ukraine."

Between the taping of the show, which occurred on a Thursday, and its airing, on Sunday night, the Liberal Party convention, which was being held in Montreal that weekend, voted for a resolution supporting the transition to democracy in Ukraine and calling on Prime Minister Stephen Harper to prevent any foreign countries from interfering in Ukrainian affairs.

CTV's Tom Clark reported that Liberals admit off-the-record that they are concerned about statements like Trudeau's joke about Russia because it gives credence to partisan attacks that he is not up to the job. These criticisms were unlikely to hurt Trudeau in the immediate polls – they did not – but they could feed into the Conservative attack that Canada needs Harper's disciplined and experienced leadership and that in a time of geopolitical uncertainty, being flippant is hardly an asset.

Twice in several months Trudeau showed himself to be utterly unserious about Russia and China, two of the most important and challenging countries in the world.

It wouldn't be long until another inappropriate joke escaped the Liberal leader's lips. In September and October 2014, the government prepared the Canadian response to the growing threat of the Islamic State in Iraq, Syria, and elsewhere in the Middle East. Active under various names since 1999, the Islamic State (Islamic State in Syria and Islamic State in Levant, ISIS and ISIL respectively), became more active in the summer of 2014, carrying out a terror campaign that included beheadings and mass murder. Several victims were western civilians. As a self-declared caliphate, it claims authority over all Muslims worldwide and is trying to establish an Islamic state beachhead in Syria and Iraq. In July they claimed more than 6300 fighters, while other estimates had their numbers at 10,000. In August, they threatened genocide against Yazidis and Christians in Iraq. In both Canada and the United States, there were greater calls for action, and in August, the United States began aerial bombing as part of a humanitarian mission to protect vulnerable communities.

In October, the Conservative government said that it was preparing plans to become involved although no specifics were released as neither the government nor the military had finalized the details of what was necessary.

On October 2, 2014, Trudeau attacked the Harper government, saying it was playing political games with the lives of Canadian soldiers as it prepared to send them to battle in Iraq. The Dauphin chastised Harper for failing to win an all-party consensus on military engagement with the Islamic extremists. Speaking at a conference sponsored by Canada 2020, a progressive think tank linked to the Liberal Party, he said, "Unlike prime ministers for decades before him, Mr. Harper has made no effort to build a non-partisan case for war ... instead, he dares us to oppose his war, staking out not moral territory but political territory." Trudeau said that he wanted to see Canada limit itself to a non-combat role in the fight against the Islamic State.

Then Trudeau went personal and juvenile. "Why aren't we talking more about the kind of humanitarian aid that Canada can and must be engaged in, rather than trying to whip out our CF-18s and show them how big they are? It just doesn't work like that in Canada." He said a humanitarian response – "strategic airlift, training, medical support and humanitarian aid for the thousands of displaced Iraqis" – rather than deploying "a handful of aging war planes" would be a more substantial Canadian contribution to the war against the Islamic State.

Former U.S. secretary of state Hillary Clinton, who was also speaking at the Canada 2020 conference, said that non-military action was needed including an "information war" and increased humanitarian aid but she also said that military action was "essential" and "critical" to prevent the Islamic State's "further advance."

But whatever Trudeau was trying to say about military and foreign policy was lost in his phallic reference. Yes, Justin Trudeau dropped a dick joke in the middle of a serious policy debate on how to end what the United Nations Human Rights Council would eventually suggest was genocide that included systemic rape and mass murder.

The Conservatives struck back at Trudeau's schoolyard-style comments. "Mr. Trudeau's comments are disrespectful of the Canadian Armed Forces and make light of a serious issue," said Jason MacDonald, the prime minister's spokesman. "Our involvement in the fight against ISIL is, and has been, motivated by a desire to do our part in fighting a group that has made direct terrorist threats against Canada and Canadians, in addition to carrying out atrocities against children, women, and men in the region. As the prime minister has said, we take that seriously and will do our part." Trudeau preferred to eschew the reason for deployment – the atrocities committed by the Islamic State – in favour of personal insults. Defense Minister Rob Nicholson said Trudeau's "whip out our CF-18" comments showed "poor judgment ... regarding a global terror threat" and were "disrespectful words regarding the work of our Canadian Forces." Employment Minister Jason Kenney said that making a "juvenile high school joke" about the campaign against a "genocidal terrorist organization" raised questions about Trudeau's judgment. On Twitter, Kenney unleashed a torrent of criticism: "Remarkable that Justin Trudeau uses juvenile humour ("whip it out") to describe use of force in combatting genocide" and he wondered, "Is this how Prime Minister Justin Trudeau would conduct himself in discussing use of air power at a NATO Summit?" Kenney then tweeted links to past controversies such as when the Liberal leader "joked about Russia's aggression in Ukraine while protestors were being shot" and the "same J. Trudeau whose 'most admired country' is the 'basic dictatorship of

China'." Immigration Minister Chris Alexander tweeted that Trudeau's comment was "shameful" and "another bozo eruption" insulting the work of Canadian Armed Forces.

It was not only Tories who found Trudeau's comments offensive. NDP Leader Tom Mulcair, who agreed with Trudeau in opposing Canada joining the international combat mission, had no patience for Trudeau's "childish jokes."

Despite Trudeau's attack on Harper's supposedly macho response, the Liberal leader was not ruling out endorsing the government's action, whatever it would have ended up being. Trudeau said Harper needs to make the case "openly and transparently, based on clear and reliable, dispassionately presented facts." Trudeau also charged, "Mr. Harper is intent on taking Canada to war in Iraq. He needs to justify that. He has not made the case for it. He hasn't even tried." He said that the prime minister was repeating the mistake Harper made as leader of the opposition by endorsing the 2003 American invasion of Iraq, a policy opposed by then-prime minister Jean Chrétien.

The day after Trudeau's ill-advised joke, Harper announced that Canada was deploying CF-18 fighter jets as well as surveillance and refueling planes, that would join the U.S.-led action against the Islamic State in Iraq, but not because of some macho need to prove his manhood, as Trudeau implied. Harper told the House of Commons that Canada had to join the fight because "free riders" are not "taken seriously" in the international community, and the atrocities committed by the jihadists demanded a response. The prime minister said that allies do not stand on the sidelines when an enemy is recognized and responded to, especially one with the capability of harming Canadians. Harper argued that the threat to Canada was real as ISIS could "launch a terrorist jihad" on a global scale if it established a regional beachhead in the Middle East, and the Islamic State had "specifically targeted Canada and Canadians. ISIL's words are matched by its actions." Harper limited Canada's military role to training local police and troops to respond militarily to the jihadist assault and also announced a humanitarian plan to aid refugees.

The government does need legislative approval to send military troops into action, but by tradition governments consult parliament. The Harper government made parliamentary approval a prerequisite for becoming involved, which was more a formality considering the party controlled both the House of Commons and the Senate. He proposed a limited six-month mission involving fewer than a dozen planes and about 600 personnel.

Trudeau came out against the Conservative plan to join the airstrikes and all but one MP voted along with the leader. Irwin Cotler, an internationally recognized human rights expert, abstained from the vote after publicly stating his disagreement with his party leader, who said that Canada should not take part in hostilities but rather limit its participation to delivering humanitarian aid.

Cotler, a proponent of the liberal idea that governments have the Responsibility to Protect vulnerable populations, released a statement explaining what he called a "principled abstention," from the government's motion. He explained, "I have been advocating for some time" the sort of combat mission the government was proposing in order to uphold the "the Responsibility to Protect (R2P) doctrine, which states, simply put, that where there are war crimes, crimes against humanity, ethnic cleansing, or genocide, and the government of the region in question is unable or unwilling to take action – or worse, is the author of the criminality – the international community has a responsibility to intervene to protect targeted innocent civilians." Cotler also supported the sort of non-military options Trudeau was calling for, such as humanitarian aid for refugees in Syria and Iraq. Yet Cotler maintained that inaction three years earlier in the Syria civil war was a reason for the heightened conflict in 2014 and the urgent need for a more vigorous response. Cotler expressed concern over the government's lack of details about how the military was going to be deployed, but unlike Trudeau, not the principle of becoming militarily involved.

Incredulously Trudeau claimed the statement as a vindication of his policy: "Mr. Cotler, who is a friend and valued member of the Liberal team, is in the position where for three years he has been calling for airstrikes in Syria. At the same time, his statement was unequivocal: he cannot support this government's approach on this."

Jason Kenney read it a different way. "This is an ignoble day for the proud Liberal Party of Canada, underscored by Irwin Cotler's absence tonight," he said after the vote on the motion. He went on to say, "Tonight we're talking about sending six fighter [jets] to defend innocent civilians from a maniacal, genocidal death cult. As far as I'm concerned, this was the easiest call that a government or parliament has faced in the deployment of force in decades."

Cotler was not alone among Liberals, however, in criticizing Trudeau's position.

Former MPs such as Rudy Dhalla, Michelle Simson, and Bryon Wilfert all endorsed the government's actions. Dhalla and Simson invoked the Responsiblity to Protect, and Wilfert said, the "case has been made" for military action.

Bob Rae, the former Liberal interim leader and an acknowledged international affairs expert within the party, took to the pages of the *Globe and Mail* to express support for the air mission. He wrote: "It is now apparent that the forces of radical violence have metastasized, and that Islamic State represents a clear and present danger to the people over whom it rules, to any minorities around the area, to the region and potentially to the world." Ujjal Dosanjh, who served as Paul Martin's health minister, was an opposition MP from 2006 through 2011 and during that time was critic of National Defence, Public Safety, and Foreign Affairs. He also sat (at various times) on the Standing Committee on National Defence, the Committee on Public Safety and National Security, the Committee on Foreign Affairs and International Development, the Committee on the Canadian Mission in Afghanistan, and the Committee on Justice and Human Rights. He brought that expertise when he expressed support for the government's "robust" mission. Dosanjh said that the military action should be "beyond partisan politics." Former Liberal foreign affairs minister Lloyd Axworthy told CTV that Islamic State "have to be whacked, and whacked good" because "if you really want to stop them, you're going to have to give a full-court press." Former senator Romeo Dallaire went further than the government, saying that ground troops were also necessary.

Even Quebec's Liberal Premier Philippe Couillard supported the mission, saying that Canada "cannot escape its obligations." He called the Islamic State "a significant threat" to Canada and Quebec: "Let us not be so naive that we think because Quebecers have been fortunate enough to live in peace for centuries that we're immune to this risk. The risks also exist for us. These murderous movements are mobile, they are imaginative in the worst sense and they won't hesitate to attack those they consider enemies, which are democratic societies." Couillard's son serves in the Canadian Armed Forces.

The only prominent non-sitting Liberal to come to Trudeau's defence was former prime minister Jean Chrétien. He wrote a column in the *Globe and Mail* saying that Canada should provide a "massive" humanitarian response while admitting that "Islamic State's atrocities must be stopped," without offering a plan on how to do so from the sidelines. Chrétien wrote, "Western countries must be cognizant of the region's history in deciding how to act." He also condemned Harper's rush to war, reminding readers that 11 years earlier he had been Chrétien's loudest critic in not joining the U.S. war in Iraq.

Despite Chrétien's support for Trudeau's position, even most Liberal voters were inclined to support the mission against the Islamic State. According to the generally Liberal-friendly Ekos Research, a poll taken October 10-15, a week after the controversy, 53 percent of Liberal supporters backed the mission while 45 percent were opposed. Trudeau was on the wrong side of Liberal voters.

The government motion passed 157-134 on a party-line vote. Joining the Tories were independent MP Brent Rathgeber, a former Tory, and Bruce Heyer, an NDP-turned-Green MP. Cotler did not vote. The motion endorsed the government's plan to have six CF-18 fighters, two CP-140 surveillance planes, one aerial tanker aircraft, and 600 personnel join the international airstrike mission. Harper released a statement after getting parliamentary approval for the plan saying, "We do not take this step lightly." He explained, "If left unchecked, this terrorist organization will grow and grow quickly. They have already voiced their local and international terrorist intentions and identified Canada as a potential target." The comment about not taking action lightly was clearly a response to Trudeau's joke about whipping out Canada's CF-18s.

The funny thing about that vote was that Trudeau was not there for it. Despite calling for a full debate on Canada's military response to ISIS in the House of Commons, Trudeau was not present in parliament for the vote. He explained during a media scrum, "First of all, I have tremendous confidence in the Liberal team," whom he trusted "to put forward and explain the Liberals' position." But that does not explain why he missed the debate and vote that he himself had called for. On an issue as important as sending Armed Forces abroad the Liberal leader didn't show up. He didn't take part in the formal debate. He didn't stand up with his fellow Liberals in parliament opposing the government's mission.

Sun News contributor Lorne Gunter surmised that Trudeau called for a parliamentary debate because he thought he could win Canadians over to his position, but the Liberal's pacifist position was politically unpopular, and the Grit polling numbers declined steadily for the next five months.

At the same time as the brouhaha over his juvenile joke, Trudeau was asked about Article 5 of the NATO Treaty. Asked during a scrum whether Article 5 kicks in if the Islamic State, which was already fighting Kurds on the Iraq-Turkey border, attacked Turkey, a NATO member, Trudeau looked perturbed at the question. He inquired, "What's Article 5." Once the unidentified journalist described it, Trudeau said, "Ah, the NATO trigger" and hemmed and hawed a bit before saying, "We will all have more discussions about what Canada will need to do." Monte Solberg, a former Conservative MP turned Sun News commentator, said, "Justin initially didn't know what it was and then seemed to think if the Turks were attacked our response would be a discussion."

In some ways it might not be fair to criticize the 42-year-old leader of the third place Liberals for not knowing the details of specific treaty articles, even one as important as the NATO agreement to come to the defense of our alliance partners. But Trudeau has told us how smart he is and how prepared for the job he is that holding him to a higher standard of knowledge is fair game. More importantly, however, Trudeau seldom shows much intellectual depth, preferring platitudes to policy specifics. Having criticized military options, it is incumbent upon journalists to ask him about treaty commitments that obligate

Canada to military action, especially when a current conflict is at the border of the one of the alliance members. The would-be prime minister needed to have a better idea of how to respond to what might have been an imminent attack on a vulnerable ally in the volatile region.

More than four months after the mission was approved, the Dauphin was asked about Canada's role in Iraq during his interview with Andrew Lawton on AM 980, in London, Ont. He said that he was "unequivocal" in his support of Canada being involved but still questioned what the country's specific role should be. He said that Canada should be "robustly engaged against ISIS" but wanted to focus on humanitarian and medical assistance. Asked by Lawton about if there were any circumstances where military involvement would be justifiable, Trudeau replied it would be "warranted if there is a reasonable chance of success," and claimed that Harper misled Canadians about the extent of military involvement; earlier that month it had been reported that Canadian soldiers killed enemy combatants and the opposition parties criticized the government for crossing the line between training and involvement in the theatre of war.

Trudeau clarified and limited the role he envisioned for Canada's military: "If there is a way that Canada can offer expertise that other parts of the world is unable to provide," then the Canadian Armed Forces could be called into action. Trudeau said that Canada should be limited to do what other countries can't, implying that NATO allies and other countries cannot deliver humanitarian aid.

Asked several times by Lawton to clarify his position, Trudeau repeated that Canada should only do what other countries' militaries cannot and he made it clear that he does not think there is a military solution to conflicts in the Middle East. Lawton pressed. "Is there any scenario you can give where Canadian military involvement is justified?" Trudeau couldn't provide any scenario and returned to his theme that Harper "misled" Canadians on whether troops would be involved in ground combat.

The national media picked up the story the following day and Lawton revisited the interview on his show. He said that Trudeau had "danced around the question, finger pointed at the prime minister," and left the impression that the conflict with jihadists as limited to the Middle East. Lawton concluded that the Dauphin "might be a pacifist but won't admit it."

A few weeks later, he was on *Winnipeg's Morning Show* on 680 CJOB. Host Kathy Kennedy asked Justin Trudeau what he thought about U.S. President Barack Obama announcing he would ask Congress to okay military intervention against ISIS. Trudeau said that Harper should bring the issue before parliament – which the prime minister did five months earlier, a debate Trudeau called for but for which he didn't show. Did he forget that the Canadian parliament had already debated and voted on the issue? Was he unaware that the Harper government was committed to another round of debate and a vote as the original six-month deadline for involvement was ticking closer?

Aside from Trudeau's flip remarks and the earnest belief that backpacking in Greenland and travelling with students in the Caribbean qualify as important foreign affairs credentials – recall that a repeated Dauphin criticism of Harper is that the Tory leader had not travelled abroad before becoming prime minister – what else does Trudeau offer Canadian voters when it comes to international issues?

In August 2014, Trudeau was asked by a reporter from the Sun News Network what the greatest threat to global security was. The Dauphin replied: "The biggest threat to global security is the kind of violence and misunderstandings and wars that come out of resource depletion, economic uncertainty, concerns of lack of hope for generations growing up in a world that is getting smaller and seemingly less and less fair." Perhaps, but he gave this answer at a time of instability in the Middle East and north Africa, a resurgent Islamic terror threat, Iran flaunting anti-proliferation rules, and conflict between Russia and Ukraine. Perhaps his root causes argument had merit, but despite the sociology textbook answer, Trudeau doesn't have any answers to these problems. Nor did he seem all that committed to tackling them as a serious threat. A few months later in an interview with Indigo CEO Heather Reisman in which he was asked the same question, he said it was Ebola and other pandemics although he couldn't name another disease.

Whenever there is a crisis, Trudeau returns to the mantra of humanitarian assistance, approaching the problem essentially as a social issue. He eschewed military solutions even before he was an MP. In 2007, Trudeau joined the children of famous 20th century leaders and activists at the Gen II Global Peace Initiative in Britain, joining famous names – and darlings of the Left – such as Kennedy, King, Mandela, Rabin, and Tutu in an effort to promote nonviolence. Martin Luther King III, son the slain American civil rights activist, said, "It is incumbent upon us, the second generation of peace keepers, to continue to carry on our parents' dreams and visions to make our world what my father called the Beloved Community." King's group, Realizing the Dream, Inc., founded Gen II. During the initiatives proceedings, Trudeau said that he hoped the group would shift global policy from defence to development. "The balance, I think everyone would agree, is heavily weighted to defence, not enough on development and diplomacy," said the second generation Trudeau.

The Gen II initiative issued a press release after meeting at the luxurious Savoy Hotel in London, England – the five-star hotel where federal cabinet minister Bev Oda infamously expensed her $16 glass of orange juice – with a declaration of its goals to "peacefully resolve current conflicts; extend respect for basic human rights in situations where it is absent; and foster harmony." They vowed to develop plans for crises in Darfur, North Korea, and elsewhere, met two years later in Toronto, and weren't heard from again.

Also in 2007, Trudeau called on Canada to increase its foreign aid commitment and UN peacekeeping contributions. He said that Canada was "a tremendously wealthy, lucky country" and it should share its wealth because "with that good fortune comes responsibility" that the government was not living up to. While the Conservatives were just arriving to power during his criticism, Canada has long failed to live up to the 0.7 percent of gross national product that Lester Pearson identified 50 years earlier as the benchmark for help that developed countries should devote to foreign aid. That said, according to the Center for Global Development's Commitment to Development Index, Canada ranks ninth in the world in giving foreign aid.

Trudeau also complained that "our longstanding reputation as impartial referees on the global stage" had "dwindled" because the number of Canadian personnel taking part in United Nations peacekeeping missions "could fit into two school buses." Again, Canadian contributions to peacekeeping were already on a long-term trend downward. The highwater mark for Canadian peacekeeping in terms of personnel was 1993 when there were 3,336 soldiers taking part in various missions around the globe, but by 1998 that number fell to under 500, and in most years since then only 200-300 soldiers were abroad as part of United Nations peacekeeping efforts. Trudeau was essentially holding up the 1960s Liberal model of foreign involvement, which has been popular in the political rhetoric of the country but has not reflected the reality of Canada's conduct in foreign affairs for some time. For someone who prides himself on his forward-thinking and willingness to question the status quo, he is stuck in the past when it comes to how Canada should be a player on the international stage.

The fact is that opposition leaders don't give much thought to foreign policy. It isn't usually an election issue. Typically they take positions merely to oppose whatever the government of the day is doing. Justin Trudeau, who touts himself as a new kind of politician, falls into these same old traps: chastising the Harper government without offering constructive criticism such as viable alternatives.

When Trudeau isn't proclaiming his love for China's brutal government, he condemns the Conservatives for not doing enough to engage with the communist regime. In an interview with *Canadian Business* during his

146

leadership bid, Trudeau remarked on Harper's shift in China policy which began by shunning the most populous country and second largest economy over its dismal human rights record to becoming "Mr. Panda Man" who engages Beijing and wins the right for Canada to borrow a pair of pandas to rotate among several Canadian zoos over the next decade or so. The problem for Trudeau, apparently, is that Harper has shifted his position. The Liberal, however, isn't giving any indicaiton as to which of the two positions he approves. The point isn't that Harper's policy was necessarily wrong, but that he flip-flopped. Trudeau is trying to score political points over an apparent inconsistency on the part of the government.

Trudeau told James Cowan of *Canadian Business*: "Thanks to the history of Sino-Canadian friendship … there's an opportunity for us historically, there's an opportunity for us geographically, there's an opportunity for us geologically, because we have so many resources China needs right now … For me, it's either we set the terms now and take the lead role, or 20 years down the line, we're the poor cousins who accept any deal thrown our way." That's a lot of words, but there is no policy there. While Trudeau is implying that Canada should engage China, it isn't clear how Canada should engage except vaguely as a trade partner, albeit an important trade partner.

It is also silly to suggest that Canada can set the terms of any agreement now, but won't be able to 20 years from now. According to the International Monetary Fund, the Chinese economy is about ten times larger than Canada's today – $17.6 trillion compared to $1.5 trillion – and while Beijing wants access to Canadian resources, but in no way is it dependent on Canada.

Prior to becoming leader, Trudeau said that Iran's nuclear ambitions presented "a credible and real threat that I am extremely worried about." In early November 2012 he acknowledged Iran was "a threat not just to the security of Israel but to the stability of an entire region that is volatile and, to a certain extent, the stability and prosperity and security of the entire world." But earlier that year, he told *Salam Toronto*, a Farsi-language paper, "I'm of the school of international relations that says it's important to talk to each other and it's especially important to talk to regimes that you disagree with and that disagree with you, and make sure that there is means of communication." He specifically condemned the Harper government's decision to sever diplomatic relations with the Islamic Republic, expelling Iranian diplomats from Ottawa and shutting down the Canadian embassy in Tehran. While acknowledging in the *Salam Toronto* interview that "there are very, very real concerns about the government in Iran that need to be addressed," Trudeau added "but one has to make sure that you think about the citizens of Iran and the Iranian government differently." This closing of diplomatic relations, Trudeau suggested, represented, a "weakening of Canada's fairness and openness to the world." He also told the Jewish National Fund's annual Negev Dinner in 2013 that while he understood the Israeli government's concerns over an international agreement being negotiated between Iran and the United States, "I choose to be optimistic."

Trudeau counts himself as a "strong supporter" of Israel but dismisses Harper's support of Israel as a political ploy. He condemns the Harper Tories for courting Jewish votes through their close relationship with Israel. Before becoming leader, Trudeau said, "My concern is that [Harper] continues to make support for Israel a domestic, political, strategic issue," a criticism he has repeated often since winning the party's leadership. Trudeau has affirmed that "Israel has the right to defend itself and its people. Hamas is a terrorist organization and must cease its rocket attacks immediately." It is unclear why when Harper says the same thing it is political, but for Trudeau it is a sincere declaration of strong support for an ally. To his credit, the Dauphin has publicly disagreed with his filmmaker brother Alexandre's anti-Israeli views – Alexandre Trudeau made an anti-Israel documentary called *The Fence* that skewed heavily in favour of Palestinians in their conflict with the Jewish state.

Despite the generally positive tone toward Israel, including praise for being the only democracy in the region, Trudeau told a Radio Canada panel in February 2014 that the "friendship" does not preclude being "critical regarding the colonizations and other issues." The term colonization, which is never explained, is problematic, raising questions about how hard a Trudeau government would press the Israelis over the West Bank and Gaza Strip. Trudeau also says he supports a two-state solution with a democratic Israel and Palestine. Yet, he told an audience of 200 at the Beth Emeth Bais Yehuda Synagogue upon receiving (*in abstentia*) an award from the Canadian Friends of the Meir Medical Center, that "the Liberal Party of Canada will have Israel's back." That came a mere week after telling a Farsi-language paper that the Tories support Israel only to court the domestic Jewish vote; Harper, he told *Salam Toronto*, is "very, very much focused on what is going to play well at the ballot box,"

Few opposition leaders want to get into the nitty-gritty of foreign affairs, partly because not many voters cast ballots on international issues, but also because criticizing the government over international issues can appear unpatriotic. Trudeau's favoured paths are attacking the prime minister for politicizing foreign issues for electoral gain and making entirely inappropriate jokes about grave matters in international affairs. Stephen Harper admitted after becoming prime minister that international issues take up an unexpectedly disproportionate amount of his attention. In other words, it is important part of the job of prime minister. When the Liberal leader ventures into talking substantively about foreign affairs he appears completely out of his depth.

Chapter 15: Justin Trudeau on Terrorism

On April 15, 2013, two bombs exploded near the finish line of the Boston Marathon, killing three and injuring more than 260 others. It was a few days before any information about who might have carried out the deadly attacks became available. Trudeau was interviewed by Peter Mansbridge on the CBC the next day during which he offered boilerplate condolences for the victims and their families, and support for the first responders. He wondered what, if anything, Canada could do to help. But then the real insight into Trudeau's thinking about such violent terrorist attacks kicked in: "And then at the same time, you know, over the coming days, we have to look at the root causes. Now we don't know now whether it was, you know, terrorism or a single crazy or, you know, a domestic issue or a foreign issue, I mean, all of those questions. But there is no question that this happened because there is someone who feels completely excluded, completely at war with innocents, at war with a society. And our approach has to be, okay, where do those tensions come from?" Trudeau continued: "We need to make sure that we're promoting security and we're, you know, keeping our borders safe and, you know, monitoring the kinds of, you know, violent subgroups that happen around." But he also urged "people to not point fingers at each other and lay blame for personal ills or societal ills on a specific group, whether it be the West or the government or Bostonians or whatever it is, because it's that idea of dividing humans against ourselves, of pointing out that they're not like us and, you know, in order to achieve our political goals we can kill innocents here. That's something that no society in the world that is healthy, regardless of ideology, will accept ... Of course, I'd be worried about what specific targets there are. But there will always be more targets, more shopping centres, more public events, you know, more gatherings than we can evacuate or than we can deal with. I mean, there's... yes, there is a need for security and response and being proactive and making sure that we have information, but we also need to make sure that as we go forward we don't emphasize a culture of fear and mistrust, because that ends up marginalizing even further people who are already, you know, feeling like they are enemies of society rather than people who have hope for the future and faith that we can work together and succeed."

There's a lot to unpack there.

The most basic is Trudeau's inability to label the attack terrorism. Most people would call an attack near the crowded finish line at the Boston Marathon that killed three and injured more than 260 others an act of terror. Trudeau seems to suggest that individuals are not capable of carrying out such acts: "We don't know now whether it was, you know, terrorism or a single crazy." There is the disturbing suspicion that while correctly warning that there should not be a rush to judgement about who might have carried out the barbaric attack, Trudeau was overly concerned about not offending would-be terrorists. He did not want fingers pointed "at each other" or to "lay blame on each other for personal ills or societal ills."

Aside from not casting blame on any particular group, presumably Muslims, Trudeau goes out of his way to find excuses for why anyone or any group of people would attempt to murder and maim hundreds of innocent people. The Dauphin said that "we have to look at root causes" and indicated he knew the root cause of the Boston Marathon massacre: someone or some people felt excluded. Even before the public knew any details about any of the individuals involved in the attack, Trudeau knew their motivation: "There is no question that this happened because there is someone who feels completely excluded." Prime Minister Stephen Harper chastised Trudeau for his root causes statement, saying, "When you see this type of violent act, you do not sit around trying to rationalize it or make excuses for it or figure out its root causes." The following year, the Conservatives briefly released an online attack ad that showed a part of Trudeau's interview with Mansbridge that concluded with a voice-over: "How can you make excuses for terrorists and keep Canadians safe? Justin Trudeau. He's in way over his head."

The suggestion that social exclusion leads some individuals to terrorism puts at least some of the blame for terrorist attacks on the broader society: government, schools, neighbourhoods, the economy. There is a fundamental difference between liberal and conservative responses to the problem of terrorism. Conservatives generally want to take the fight to terrorists, to have intelligence on those who want to harm the West, and take precautions to prevent those who kill innocents to advance a religious or political agenda from carrying out their violent plans. Liberals love looking for root causes. It is about avoiding being judgemental and not assigning blame, but it also feeds into the welfare state they want to build. Government programs, whether through welfare spending or education, it is thought, show enough goodwill to buy the loyalty of citizens, including those at risk of being radicalized.

Lorrie Goldstein, a columnist at the *Toronto Sun*, summarized the Dauphin's view on combatting terrorism: "Trudeau believes we must perpetually walk on eggshells, so as not to risk offending potential terrorists, lest we make them feel excluded from society."

Two Chechen brothers, Dzhokhar and Tamerlan Tsarnaev, were suspected of carrying out the terrorist attacks in Boston. Tamerlan was killed during pursuit by police when brother Dzhokhar ran over him following a firefight with police. After Dzhokhar Tsarnaev was apprehended by the police, he said during interrogation that he and his brother were jihadists influenced by Muslim radicals, opposed to the wars in Iraq and Afghanistan, and learned how to build the pressure-cooker bombs through al-Qaeda websites. On April 15, 2015, Dzhokhar Tsarnaev was found guilty of murder and conspiracy to commit terrorism. Trudeau may or may not be correct about these brothers feeling socially excluded. Yet it is not clear what can be done to make the supposedly vulnerable to feel included, and other than not criticizing terrorists, Trudeau has not offered any policy to reduce the sort of exclusion that allegedly leads some people to commit terrorist acts. Both the RCMP and FBI have issued reports that say while some terrorist suspects come from poor families and lack education, many come from well-to-do homes and have had access to excellent schools. According to the security experts, marginalization is a popular explanation for susceptibility to radicalism, but there is, at best, mixed evidence about the connection and even less agreement on how to address the problem.

On October 22, 2014, terrorism hit closer to home for Canadians and parliamentarians. Corporal Nathan Cirillo was shot and killed during sentry duty at the Canadian National War Memorial by Michael Zehaf-Bibeau, who proceeded to enter the parliament buildings. He was killed by Commons Sergeant-at-Arms, Kevin Vickers, in a shootout with security and police in the halls of parliament. The building went into lockdown as there were rumours of more than one attacker. Many parliamentarians, staffers, and journalists were stuck inside for most of the day before the building was deemed secure and it was safe for everyone to come out. When Trudeau emerged, he spoke, delivering a carefully prepared speech. He said he was "deeply saddened by today's horrific events here in Ottawa and unreservedly condemn these brutal and heartless acts of violence. This attack is unforgivable." He said Cirillo's murder was a "cowardly act" and that if there were any other perpetrators, they had to be caught and punished. But he never called the attack terrorism. Instead, he focused on remaining calm: "We cannot let this get the better of us. Losing ourselves to fear and speculation is the intention of those who commit these heinous acts." He warned against blaming Islam, saying "Canadians know acts such as these committed in the name of Islam are an aberration of your faith."

That same evening, after being whisked away safely and briefed on security measures, Prime Minister Stephen Harper went on television to address the nation. He called Zehaf-Bibeau's attack "a terrorist act" and said, "Together we will remain vigilant against those at home or abroad who wish to harm us." He vowed the government would respond to a terrorist threat whether it came from home or abroad and that there would be no safe haven for terrorists.

The RCMP said the attack was by definition a terrorist act under the Criminal Code. In the days after the attack, NDP leader Tom Mulcair was adamant that the incident was not a terrorist attack even though the government and RCMP labelled it as such. Trudeau, who initially refused to call it a terrorist attack, relented and deferred to the experts: "The RCMP was clear, these were acts of terrorism, [so] these were acts of terrorism."

But was Trudeau merely acknowledging the expertise of the RCMP or was he playing politics? John Robson, a columnist for the Sun newspaper chain, wrote that he feared, "Justin Trudeau's flip-flop on saying 'terrorism' was driven by politics rather than any serious effort to think through the matter." Canada is not a hawkish country, but fierce patriotism and willingness to defend the symbols of Canadian democracy were worth defending. Trudeau may not have understood, as Robson said, that terrorism is "a particular kind of evil, with particular methods and goals ... Violence intended to change public policy by spreading fear among civilians." But Canadians understood it, and Trudeau needs to not look weird or out-of-touch to them. The RCMP calling Zehaf-Bibeau's murder of Cirillo and breaching of parliament's doors with a gun in his hand a terrorist act – they said they had evidence of Zehaf-Bibeau's jihadi motivation for the attack – gave Trudeau cover for his flip-flop, deferring to experts rather than looking like he was blowing in the winds of public opinion. Yet Robson said, "Surely a man who would be prime minister should agree with them because he agrees with their reasoning not because the cops said so."

In some ways, it was impressive that he could eventually use the word terrorism. Trudeau has been noticeably reluctant to utter the word. Just weeks before the terrorist incident in the nation's capital, Trudeau was in downtown Toronto, promoting his new book *Common Ground*. He was interviewed by Indigo CEO Heather Reisman who asked him what he considered the greatest global threat facing Canada. He said Ebola. As journalists noted at the time, even though the disease that broke out in West Africa was making headlines, no Canadian had become ill with the disease. Presumably not satisfied with that answer Reisman asked for the next greatest threat. "More pandemics," replied the Dauphin. Ezra Levant called the answer "childish and uninformed" as the Liberal leader could not name another disease. "He didn't even believe his own answer enough to come up with the name of this supposed national threat," Levant observed.

Even if Trudeau could not take the threat of terrorism seriously, the Conservatives did. In February 2015, Steven Blaney, Minister of Public Safety Canada, introduced C-15, the *Anti-terrorism Act, 2015*. It's full name is *"The Anti-terrorism Act, 2015: An Act to enact the Security of Canada Information Sharing Act and the Secure Air Travel Act, to amend the Criminal Code, the Canadian Security Intelligence Service Act and the Immigration and Refugee Protection Act and to make related and consequential amendments to other Acts."* The first major amendment to anti-terror laws since the aftermath of September 11, 2001, it was introduced four months after the attack on Parliament Hill. The *Anti-Terrorism Act, 2015* amended about a dozen laws to permit government agencies to more easily share information about Canadians, criminalized speech that advocates or promotes terrorism, gave the Canadian Security Intelligence Service new powers to disrupt activities that threaten Canadian security, expanded the definition of national security, and lowered the threshold for holding suspects in preventative custody. Both the NDP and Liberals were worried that CSIS had new powers but lacked sufficient oversight by parliament, and civil libertarians joined the opposition parties in raising concerns about privacy through government monitoring. Both the NDP and Liberals have also raised the possibility that the government could use the cover of combating terrorism to criminalize the work of groups like environmental organizations or First Nations that oppose government policy. Prime Minister Harper dismissed those last concerns as conspiracy theories.

The NDP opposed C-51 and many pundits thought the Liberals would, too. How the tiny Liberal caucus of 36 MPs voted was irrelevant to whether C-51 would pass, considering the government's majority. Even before the *Anti-Terror Act, 2015* was tabled in the House of Commons, Trudeau expressed serious concerns about the bill but said his party would still support C-51. While hammering the Tories for introducing the bill as nothing more than a political ploy to stir fear in order to win votes, he vowed to amend the law if the Liberals were elected to government. While appearing to take a stand on principles of defending some civil liberties, Trudeau treated his problems with C-51 as mild qualms to be tinkered with when the Liberals won power.

Trudeau said when the bill was unveiled that he shared the concerns of critics about "overbroad" language in C-51, but insisted the law would "significantly increase the safety and security of Canadians." He cited coordination between agencies, a strengthening of the no-fly list, and greater preventative arrest tools for police as measures vital to protecting Canada against terrorism.

Three specific changes the Liberals wanted to see included greater MP oversight of intelligence agencies, reducing the "disruption" mandate of CSIS that allowed the intelligence agency to commit a wide range of crimes with a warrant in order to apprehend terrorists, and a mandatory three-year review of the legislation. Yet support for the bill was not contingent on amendments to these effects being passed.

There was broad opposition to the bill, some of it close to home for the Liberals. Chantal Hebert of the *Toronto Star* reported that even as former leader Stephane Dion, Liberal critic for Canadian Heritage, Official Languages, and Intergovernmental Affairs, was publicly defending his party's position on C-51, his wife, Janice Krieber, an expert on security issues, was on Radio-Canada "echoing most of the NDP's concerns" about civil liberties and privacy about the proposed legislation.

Critics of C-51 included Amnesty International, four former Prime Ministers – Joe Clark, John Turner, Jean Chrétien, and Paul Martin – who co-wrote an open letter concerned about the potential for "human rights abuses," and Daniel Therrien, the federal Privacy Commissioner, who worried that various agencies had been granted too much power to investigate individuals without sufficient evidence. A long list of academics co-signed a statement against the bill as over-reaching.

During a visit to his alma mater, the University of British Columbia, on March 5, 2015, Trudeau faced criticism from students opposed to the bill, with the issue dominating the one-hour question-and-answer with youth. Trudeau was repeatedly asked questions about why he was supporting a bill he claimed to oppose even if the amendments the Liberals were proposing were rejected. He was asked why he was not standing up for the privacy of Canadians. Trudeau offered babblegab, not really answering the question: "I appreciate that. Yes, I appreciate that. Yeah. Thank you for expressing your concern and I've heard this. We've heard this from Canadians and I share those concerns about this bill." But, he said, the Liberals were powerless to defeat a bill proposed by the government who had a majority in the House of Commons, and put the onus for reversing the troublesome provisions on the students and others opposed to C-51. "That's why," Trudeau explained, "the pressure that you and everyone else are putting on this government is getting them to understand that if they don't bring in oversight, they're going to have a very difficult time in the next election campaign." The UBC pushback on C-51 was a rare case of Trudeau being forcefully challenged on anything in any university setting.

Most baffling, however, was the admission that the Liberal vote for C-51, despite grave misgivings, was pure political calculation.

The Liberal leader condemned the government's anti-terrorism bill as part of the Conservatives' plot to ride a wave of fear about terror to re-election in 2015. Trudeau complained that C-51, a bill which he partially supported, "fits into their fear narrative" and "their desire to bash people." That implied the law was unnecessary, but the Liberals were still voting for it. The obvious question, though, is why Trudeau would lend the Conservative fear narrative any credence by backing C-51. Trudeau admitted the Liberals were voting for C-51 for fear of being labelled soft on terror by Stephen Harper and the Conservatives. "I do not want this government making political hay out of an issue … or trying to, out of an issue as important as security for Canadians," Trudeau explained. "This conversation might be different if we weren't months from an election campaign, but we are." That is a stunning admission of cowardice on the part of a political leader. While almost everything in politics can been viewed through the prism of electoral politics, it is rare for a party leader to admit to either the political calculation or of being scared of one's political opponents.

To add to the confusion, on March 14, Adam Vaughan, a downtown Toronto Liberal MP, was seen among the protesters at the #StopC51 rally outside Toronto's Nathan Philips Square just days after voting for it in the House of Commons. On Twitter Vaughan claimed to be merely listening "to all sides of the debate" and he told Desmond Cole of Newstalk 1010, a local radio station, he was "in complete lock-step with my leader" on C-51.

The *Toronto Star*'s Thomas Walkom condemned Trudeau for supporting the bill: "That the Liberals are faint-hearted when it comes to supporting civil rights is not surprising." Walkom cited Jean Chrétien's "sweeping anti-terror laws" from 2001, but he was also hinting at Pierre Trudeau's invocation of the *War Measures Act* during the FLQ Crisis. The Liberals know, he wrote, "from their own experience, that draconian security laws can make governing easier."

It is easy to understand Trudeau's support for C-51. The political aftermath of the October terrorist attacks at home, an Angus Reid poll in February showing 82 percent support for the government's anti-terror bill (with majority support in every province, including Quebec), and fear about being labelled soft on terrorism, especially after the political fallout over his comments and vote on Canadian military engagement with ISIS, could all contribute to a politician being cowed to do something he or she does not want. But Trudeau is not just any politician. He offers himself not only for the job of prime minister, but as a beacon of hope that does politics differently. In his admission that he took a position on C-51 because of its proximity to a federal election and fear of being attacked, Trudeau admitted to putting his own well-being and the well-being of his Liberal Party, ahead of the principles of liberty and privacy about which Trudeau and his party supposedly care so deeply.

While the economy will probably be the most important issue in the 2015 federal election, security will still be near the top of the minds of many voters as Canada approaches the one-year anniversary of the terrorist attack on Parliament Hill. Canadians are going to want a prime minister that takes the security of the country seriously. Justin Trudeau seems to fear a Stephen Harper attack ad more than he does murder and mayhem at the hands of terrorists. The Dauphin wants to look at root causes but we know little about how he would tackle terrorism. In his memoirs Trudeau recalls talking to his students in British Columbia on the morning of 9/11, hours after passenger planes became weapons of mass destruction on the American east coast. He told his young charges, "Never to forget where they were when they heard the grim news on September 11, 2001," saying it was necessary in order "that we remain vigilant in the fight against terror." That is the only mention of terrorism in his 343-page memoir-cum-manifesto and it seems as if he has himself forgotten to remain vigilant. When terror strikes at the heart of our democracy, as it did on October 22, 2014, the prime minister should be able to recognize the attack for what it is and offer a coherent response. Justin Trudeau is not that person.

Chapter 16: Justin Trudeau on Immigration and Multiculturalism

Justin Trudeau has fully if inchoately embraced immigration and multiculturalism as the defining ideals of Canada. In a well-worn line that sounds good but means nothing, Justin Trudeau often says that Canada might be "the only country in the history of the world that is strong because of its diversity, not in spite of it." A variation of the line shows up multiple times in his memoir *Common Ground* and again in his famous "Canadian Liberty and the Politics of Fear," in March 2015. He uses it whenever he talks about multiculturalism and immigration, or addresses ethnic audiences, such as the Reviving the Islamic Spirit Convention in December 2012. He is obviously very fond of the formulation.

The line that this country is strong because of its diversity and not in spite of it sounds great, but Trudeau only provides the most superficial examples of the benefits of multiculturalism: "a blossoming of ethnic restaurants, festivals, and community centres." Diverse communities such as his riding of Papineau have "elevated ... overall liveliness." Seldom does Trudeau acknowledge the challenges of multiculturalism, other than to note they exist. Trudeau laments "identity politics," apparently unaware that it might be connected to the official policy of multiculturalism his father implemented four decades ago that encourages new Canadians and their descendants to maintain their homeland's culture.

Trudeau believes that regardless of "where the people came from, what language they spoke, or how they prayed," they "shared certain values" once they moved to Canada, and it is those values, he explains in his memoir, that connects all Canadians. What values are those? Other than to cite his father's Charter of Rights and Freedoms, he does not say.

In February 2015, Prime Minister Stephen Harper defended his government's decision to appeal a Federal Court ruling permitting a Muslim woman to keep her face covered with a niqab while taking the oath of citizenship. Harper said: "We don't allow people to cover their faces during citizenship ceremonies. And why would Canadians, contrary to our own values, embrace a practice at that time that is not transparent, that is not open and, frankly, is rooted in a culture that is anti-women." During his March 9, 2015 speech, "Canadian Liberty and the Politics of Fear," Trudeau told an audience at the McGill Institute for the Study of Canada in Toronto that "Canadian liberty is all about inclusion." He condemned Harper's criticism of wearing a niqab as the politics of fear and division. He defended the right of Muslim women to cover their faces in public, including during citizenship ceremonies (and court proceedings), as an important part of their identities and expression of their religious beliefs. Harper, Trudeau complained, found the facial covering offensive "and was convinced that most Canadians did too."

Trudeau suggested that Harper might be wrong about the unpopularity of the niqab. Trudeau appeared certain he was taking a popular stand, standing up for the rights of a minority, Muslim women. His political instincts did not serve him well as polls would indicate exceptionally strong support for Harper's position. A Leger Marketing poll found that seventy percent of Canadians agreed with Harper that the niqab should not be worn during the citizenship ceremony. Furthermore, sixty percent said it should be "banned in public spaces" such as government offices and courts. Nearly six in ten (fifty-eight percent) said, "The niqab is imposed on women by their families and communities" while fewer than one in five disagreed with the statement. According to an Ipsos Reid poll, nearly nine in ten Canadians (eighty-eight percent) supported the requirement that people show their face during a Canadian citizenship ceremony, with nearly two-thirds of respondents strongly supporting the position; also, seventy-two percent agreed with the prime minister that Muslim facial coverings are symbols of oppression and an anti-women culture. Conservative pundit Gerry Nicholls tweeted: "Poll shows only Canadians who oppose PM Harper's niqab policy are Justin Trudeau & the Parliamentary Press Gallery." The public was on the government's side.

This might be all part of what Ezra Levant has called Trudeau's courting of the Muslim vote, a pursuit for the Liberal leader that included visiting the radical Assuna Annabawiyah mosque in Montreal in 2011. Several Sun News Network hosts attacked Trudeau for visiting a mosque that had links to terrorists, including al-Qaeda, according to U.S. intelligence sources. At the very least the mosque promoted radical views, including positions that relegated women to second-class citizens, with features on their website advising men to avoid shaking hands with women and that women stay in their homes except in "urgent cases." Richard Klagsburn said on his blog, Eye on a Crazy Planet, "But its history and the values the Assuna Annabawiyah mosque espouses are hardly of the sort that a responsible political leader should give implicit approbation with a high-profile visit." That is, unless Trudeau can explain how keeping women indoors is consistent with the Charter of Rights and Freedoms. When in August 2014 Trudeau was asked by Paul Wells of *Maclean's* about attending an event at the Assuna Annabawiyah mosque, Trudeau said, "You can disagree with them and you can be worried about what some people might be preaching, but, for me, it's more important that my message of respect and inclusion ... is an approach I will consistently take." Trudeau is willing to overlook a mosque's possible connection to terrorism as part of his efforts to promote respect and inclusion.

The Dauphin seems to define multiculturalism as celebrating foreign cuisine and clothing, while ignoring difficult questions about cultural practices that might be problematically imported to Canada. He is fine with other cultures when they are reduced to their most superficial aspects like food and garb, but he does not pay much heed to the core values that are inherited by a culture's tradition and religious heritage. Indeed, he told immigrants in *Common Ground* that they must shuck their social conservatism to be good Canadians, and that they had to accept same-sex marriage and equality between the sexes.

Trudeau gives lip service to the notion that all cultural expressions respect Canadian values and law in return for Canadian society accommodating as much of immigrant culture as possible, but he does so without acknowledging a multitude of examples when cultural expression might bump up against the precious Charter rights Trudeau celebrates. How, for example, do honour killings, genital mutilation, and treating women as second-class citizens fit into Canada's multicultural mosaic?

It is not that Trudeau accepts these relics of backwards foreign cultures, it is just that he will not be willing to challenge them. Yet, if the Conservative government ostracizes such cultural practices, Trudeau will condemn the government for the politics of division and fear. Before becoming leader, in March 2011, Trudeau condemned the new *Discover Canada* study guide for immigrants seeking to become Canadian citizens. In it, the federal government advised those preparing to become citizens: "Canada's openness and generosity do not extend to barbaric cultural practices that tolerate spousal abuse, 'honour killings,' female genital mutilation, forced marriage or other gender-based violence." Trudeau had no time for this two-year-old addition to the guide: "There's nothing that the word 'barbaric' achieves that the words 'absolutely unacceptable' would not have achieved." He added: "We accept that these acts are absolutely unacceptable. That's not the debate. In casual conversation, I'd even use the word barbaric to describe female circumcision, for example, but in an official Government of Canada publication, there needs to be a little bit of an attempt at responsible neutrality." In other words, the government should be neutral about honour killings or sensitive to those who embrace female genital mutilation. Immigration Minister Jason Kenney accused Trudeau and the Liberals of choosing political correctness over women's rights.

It is telling that the Dauphin reserved his scorn not for the practices of honour killings and forced marriage, but a two-year-old government citizenship document condemning those practices. For Trudeau, scoring political points on the supposed intolerance of Conservatives is more important than naming and shaming foreign practices that might run afoul of the Charter, the law, and Canadian values.

Trudeau, like most federal politicians, embraces immigration as a net positive for Canada, but he goes further than that. Immigration helps define Canada. The waves of new immigrants "joined in this great project over the years" are what make Canada the country it is today. As he said in announcing his bid for Liberal leader in October 2012, Canada "was founded on a bold new premise: that people of different beliefs and backgrounds, from all corners of the world, could come together to build a better life for themselves and for their children than they ever could alone." Diversity, he insists, is strength and "the heart and soul of the Canadian success story."

Immigration and multiculturalism are central to Trudeau's conception of Canada. It is therefore unsurprising that Trudeau wants more immigration, and more multiculturalism. As immigration critic in 2010, Trudeau said that Canada should expand immigration: "I think we can look at getting over the 250,000 mark up to approaching one percent of our population, if not going beyond that."

Despite his pro-immigration views, Trudeau would later defend environmentalist David Suzuki's anti-immigrant comments to the French-language *L'Express* newspaper in July 2013. Suzuki said "Canada is full" and that continuing to bring large numbers of immigrants into Canada "to support economic growth" was "crazy" because "our useful area has been reduced." Trudeau said of the environmentalist's statement, "There is a way to reconcile concern, legitimate concerns about environmental sustainability, and Canada's continued openness and strength around immigration." But he would not condemn Suzuki's statement. Several Conservative cabinet ministers slammed Suzuki, including then Natural Resources Minister Joe Oliver who called the comments not only economically mistaken but "morally shocking." Trudeau, who couldn't bring himself to criticize Suzuki, did however take on his critics: "I think this is a great example of how this government is choosing to pick fights whenever it possibly can." One might wonder how a federal political leader who celebrates immigration and calls for more, ignores calls to stop mass immigration from a noted public figure, and goes so far as to legitimate the concerns, yet turns around and attacks the government for daring to defend immigration. It is crass political opportunism.

The odd thing is that Trudeau takes a noticeably different tact in his memoirs, disagreeing with the gist of Suzuki's argument. Trudeau says that he understands "that immigration is essentially an economic policy," but more importantly that "immigration's most critical role for Canada" is as "a nation-building tool." Immigrants, Trudeau says, "come from abroad to find a new life, not just a better job." All this, Trudeau suggests, makes Canada a better country.

Justin Trudeau likes the idea of multiculturalism and immigration. But his praise for these policies seldom goes beyond platitudes and he does not demonstrate much serious thought about the contradictions and challenges that massive immigration, especially from some cultures, poses. Trudeau is breezily indifferent to the ways in which some imported cultures might challenge or change what makes Canada great, including the values of tolerance and equality that the Dauphin himself often espouses. None of this is to say that immigration is good or bad, but that it raises complex issues that the Liberal leader does not seem to care about or even comprehend.

Chapter 17: Justin Trudeau on Crime

The familiar Justin Trudeau patterns of opposing whatever the Conserva-tives are doing, relying on what science and experts say, and looking for root causes, all come into play on the issue of crime. But that is not to say that Trudeau does not believe what he says about crime and the justice system. In-deed, there are subtle hints of his true ideological colours in approach to crime and punishment.

Trudeau says locking up criminals is taking "the easy way out." He complains that the Harper government and his backbenchers (through various private member's bills) are cynically exploiting a get-tough-on-crime agenda for po-litical gain. As a candidate running to become an MP in 2008 Trudeau criti-cized the Tories "tough on crime" agenda that cynically won votes but did not cut crime. "It's not about building more prisons," he said, "it's about building more community centres." The remark suggests that the best way to reduce crime is to give youth alternatives to life on the streets. It was very reminis-cent of President Bill Clinton's first term in the White House when he pushed midnight basketball and ballroom dancing as a way to get vulnerable teens off the streets.

In his first term as MP he railed against Harper for his "build more prisons and lock 'em up" approach. He dismissed as simplistic the Conservative view that criminals are "just bad people anyway." He said that "real leadership" does not mean "doing the thing that 80 percent of the people say they want, it's about doing what you believe is right, no matter what." Trudeau said govern-ment should "find ways to help prevent them" – presumably criminals – "from becoming bad in the first place." This is a classic root causes argument.

When first elected MP, he told the *Hill Times* that Canada has a lot to learn from Quebec, including how to approach crime. In his attempt to pander to Quebeckers' vanity, Trudeau claimed, "Our crime rates are lower than anywhere else around the country." According to Statistics Canada that's not true, regardless of the metric used to measure crime. Although is below the national average in every major measure, they are not at bottom for any of them: for assault, Ontario and Prince Edward Island had significantly lower rates in 2008; for robberies all of Atlantic Canada had much lower rates; both New Brunswick and Newfoundland and Labrador had lower homicide rates; Ontario, New Brunswick, PEI, and Newfoundland and Labrador all scored better on the Crime Severity Index of major crimes. To score points and flatter Quebec voters, Trudeau casually made a claim that was not only untrue but easily disproven.

Trudeau's larger point, however, was that Quebec could "share more of the solution with Canada," on a number of issues including law and order. He said, Quebec's "criminal justice is a lot more focused on socialization, rehabilitation rather than incarceration. And it is effective here." As the 2008 crime numbers from Statistics Canada shows, Quebec's policies do not seem to make much of a beneficial difference among provinces in Central and Eastern Canada.

The Conservatives have pushed mandatory minimum sentences as a key feature in fighting crime and improving public security. The idea is that minimum sentences might deter crime but more importantly signal society's strong disapproval of particular crimes and punish criminals for their actions. The social science is mixed on whether tougher sentences deter crime, but the signalling and punishing aspects of punishment are values-based considerations.

The Dauphin mostly disagrees with mandatory minimum sentences.

On November 10, 2013, Trudeau took to Twitter for a Sunday afternoon answering questions from his (then) 270,000 followers. After taking such important matters such as his favourite movie ("probably *The Shawshank Redemption*") and last iTunes purchase (an album from the independent band Fun), he replied to policy questions. Asked, "Would a Trudeau-led federal government reconsider the slew of new mandatory minimum sentences recently rolled out by the (Conservatives)?" the Dauphin replied: "I (and the Liberal party) trust the judiciary to do their jobs well, so yes." That was it. A general principle was articulated – "trust the judiciary" – but not specific mandatory minimums with which the leader or party disagreed. The Sun Network's David Akin asked Trudeau's office for some elaboration; which particular provisions he might rescind. Trudeau's spokesperson did not reply.

It was possible that Trudeau believed all mandatory minimum sentences should be rescinded.

Later that week he told reporters, "We need to reduce crime, we need to reduce victims of crime. In order to do that we have to be smart about our approach."

He once again attacked, "the Conservative approach" of "imposing mandatory minimums on anything and hoping that that will solve the problem [which] hasn't solved the problem nearly enough."

Sun News Network's Marissa Semkiw tracked down Trudeau when he was in the city campaigning for Chrystia Freeland in the Toronto Centre by-election and asked him if he would rule out lifting mandatory minimum sentences for individuals who committed sexual offenses against children. He replied that he would "trust the judiciary ... and make sure there is less crime." Semkiw asked which mandatory minimums he would get rid of. He replied "all of them." Semkiw asked again about whether his opposition to mandatory minimums included such sentences for convicted child-sex offenders. "No, I wouldn't rule out repealing mandatory minimums for anyone. I'm looking at opening, listening to evidence, listening to experts, trusting the judiciary."

Among the mandatory minimum sentences the Conservative government had passed were five years for incest with a minor (under 16), and one year for sexual exploitation of a minor, acts of bestiality in the presence of children, making child pornography, and distributing child porn.

Liberal justice critic Sean Casey would parrot Trudeau's position that they would scrap all minimum sentences before back-tracking a little; he said they would eliminate all mandatory minimum sentences except for murder. Trudeau himself had not offered that clarification.

A question for the Dauphin is whether he dislikes Harper's mandatory minimum sentences or minimum sentences in general. He seems to ignore the fact that that minimum sentences were part of the criminal justice system prior to Stephen Harper becoming prime minister in 2007. According to the Canadian Bar Association, in the first seven-plus years of the Harper government, parliament passed laws doubling the number of mandatory minimum sentences from 29 to 57. The Jean Chrétien Ministry was responsible for almost as many, 21, most of them for gun-related offense. In fact, in 1977, Pierre Trudeau's government implemented mandatory minimum sentences for gun crimes involving automatic weapons.

Trudeau also supports getting rid of the mandatory victims' surcharge. The Harper government has enacted a minimum $100 surcharge on all criminal convictions with proceeds going to a fund that helps agencies that work with victims of crime. Asked by CTV's Robert Fife in early 2014 about the policy, Trudeau non-responded: "I think my, my base position is we need to make sure that we're creating less crime in this country and that comes a lot of different ways, but we need to base ourselves on the facts and we need to base ourselves on what works." He added, "I tend to defer to our, our justices, our legal system, our judges, who tend to know very well how to engage with this and we need to base ourselves on fact and not trying to play politics with advantageous, you know, policies that are all about getting votes and not actually about reducing crime levels, which are already on the way down, but need to continue, because any crime is too much." There is plenty of bafflegab but no answer. The boilerplate answer he gives to all crime-related questions does not once address whether those convicted of crimes should also pay the minimum $100 surcharge that funds victims' services. It is almost as if Trudeau had no idea about what he was talking and hearing the word "minimum" thought he was answering a question about mandatory minimum sentences.

Trudeau and the Liberals complain that the get-tough-on-crime approach does not work; it does not deter crime, it does not rehabilitate criminals. Prime Minister Stephen Harper has explained the Conservative position on punishing crime: "It's time that the Liberal Party learns that our justice system is based on accountability." That's another way of saying that most Conservatives believe in the just desserts theory of punishment that is often colloquially put as "can't do the time, don't do the crime." It is based on the view that when people break the law, part of the purpose of punishment is to express society's outrage at the violation and serve as retribution for the transgression.

Trudeau has also stated that the tough-on-crime approach – which he juxtaposes with his vague smart-on-crime approach – is unnecessary because crime rates are declining. But again, if punishment is meant to signal that a criminal act is taken seriously and to provide retribution to the criminal, crime rate is irrelevant to what is an appropriate punishment.

Justin Trudeau maintains that he favours policies that are based on evidence, but he ignores the fact that that much of policy is still based on values. Deterring crime is a value, and policies to that effect might be measurable (although the causes of crime are in dispute and so multivariable that it could be impossible to know if a certain set of policies "work" or not). Trudeau and his party do not buy into the idea that first and foremost criminals should be punished for their wrong-doings, because they believe the focus of the criminal justice system should be on rehabilitation. But that is also a value-judgement.

This is a standard ideological debate between the Left and the Right: is punishment primarily about retribution or rehabilitation? It should come as no surprise that Trudeau does not view retribution as the primary purpose of punishment, preferring to rehabilitate those who break the law. During the Pierre Trudeau government, Canada formally abolished capital punishment and life sentences.

It is telling that in early 2015, the Liberal Party website had more information about the leader's position on legalizing marijuana – a statement with statistics along with a YouTube video – than it did on punishing convicted criminals. The Liberal website states: "We believe in strong penalties for serious crimes, but we do not believe that 'after the gavel' justice – sentencing alone – is sufficient to keep our communities safe." Neither Trudeau nor other Liberals have indicated what they consider "strong penalties" but Canadians can be sure they do not include minimum sentences. There is also the suggestion that more efforts be made to rehabilitate criminals, but again there is no indication of what that entails. The website continues: "There is a critical role for judges in determining sentences, and mandatory minimum sentences should be restricted to serious and violent offences only." Other than Sean Casey's statement that the Liberals support minimum sentences for convicted murderers, there has been no effort to make clear what offenses would qualify for minimum sentences and how long those sentences would be.

There is also a statement on the party website that "smart and sustainable investment in law enforcement resources is essential." That is a statement with which few Canadians would disagree. Even putting aside the fact that policing is mostly a municipal and provincial responsibility, there is no indication if such a comment even commits a Trudeau government to increasing law enforcement budgets. When Trudeau welcomed former Toronto police chief Bill Blair as a candidate for the Liberals in Scarborough Southwest, he announced that a Liberal government would create a federal fund to pay benefits to up to $300,000 to the families of police officers, firefighters, or paramedics killed or permanently injured in the line of duty. But there was still nothing about improving front-line emergency services.

There are serious discussions to be had over the most effective way to combat crime in terms of policing, and separate discussion about the role of punishment when criminals are convicted. Justin Trudeau does not seem interested in engaging either of those issues. He prefers to use the issue in the same cynical way he accuses Stephen Harper of doing, ignoring that politicians, like the Canadians they represent, have many different priorities when it comes to the problem of crime.

Chapter 18: Justin Trudeau on Guns

Justin Trudeau voted for scrapping the gun registry and later said he wouldn't bring it back. That isn't necessarily an inherent contradiction. Politicians can change their minds, and sometimes do so because they are actually convinced that their new position is the correct one, rather than merely convenient. As for the gun registry, it could make sense for a supporter to not want to waste the resources bringing back a highly controversial and expensive program, wasting political capital and, worse, handing a great issue to one's opponents for fundraising and vote-winning purposes.

Still, Trudeau's flip-flop on the gun-registry reeks of crass political opportunism.

The gun registry was created by the Jean Chrétien government Bill C-68, *An Act Respecting Firearms and Other Weapons*, which was passed into law in 1995. It was to be fully implemented by 2003 at an estimated annual cost of $2 million. In fact, it cost more than $2 billion to create and no one knew either the compliance rate for registration or its effectiveness as a crime prevention tool.

Popular in urban centers and among editorialists for the big city papers, the gun registry was despised by rural voters and in the West. The Conservatives made scrapping the registry a centerpiece of their 2011 campaign after flirting with the idea in previous elections. With its majority, C-19, *The Ending the Long-Run Registry Act*, was passed on February 15, 2012, by a vote of 159 to 130. Trudeau, who had not yet publicly declared his intention to run for the Liberal leadership, opposed the bill just as every other member of his caucus did, but unlike many of his colleagues he did not participate in the debate in the House of Commons, with his only comment limited to interrupting Conservative Larry Miller's speech with an, "Oh, come on," as the Bruce-Grey-Owen Sound MP spoke in favour of the bill.

But nearly ten months later, in the early stages of the Liberal leadership race, Trudeau attempted to clarify his position with a seemingly contradictory statement on the legacy of the gun registry: "The registry saves lives," but it was a "failed public policy." To add confusion to his position, Trudeau then seemed to flip-flop on the issue. He said he still supported the registry, at least in principle, but that it was too divisive to bring back. "I voted to keep the firearms registry a few months ago and if we had a vote tomorrow I would vote once again to keep the long-gun registry," he said. But, he admitted, "It was so deeply divisive for far too many people, it no longer exists," and said he would not bring it back if the Liberals formed government. "I'm not going to resuscitate that," he said. This position acknowledging the deep political divisions over the registry does not jive with his stance on the Conservative government's tough-on-crime approach; Trudeau said several times that political leadership means sometimes doing what is right not popular. But when it comes to the gun registry, Trudeau admits to a political consideration: it is just too divisive to bring back.

It was surely no coincidence that Trudeau made his comments about not re-opening the gun registry debate in Hawkesbury, Ont., in the rural, eastern Ontario riding of Glengarry–Prescott–Russell. In a campaign stop during his leadership bid, he said, "There are better ways of keeping us safe than that registry which has been removed."

So according to Trudeau, the long-gun registry saved lives, was failed public policy, and there are better ways to reduce crime. That's a little bit of everything for everyone: if one likes the gun registry there is some hope he will bring it back, but if one is skeptical one might convince oneself that the Liberals under the Dauphin won't resurrect the program. Trudeau must have known he needed to connect with rural voters because he stressed his own pro-gun bona fides: "I grew up with long guns, rifles and shotguns," noting that he was surrounded by RCMP guards growing up and, "I got to play with [their guns] every now and then." He said he hiked across Greenland as a teacher and had a gun "slung over my shoulders" to protect him and his charges from polar bears.

Trudeau also explained, ""I was raised with an appreciation and an understanding of how important in rural areas and right across the country gun ownership is as a part of the culture of Canada." He said there was no contradiction "between keeping our cities safe from gun violence and gangs, and allowing this important facet of Canadian identity which is having a gun," although that seemed a comment to reassure the locals rather than explicate an anti-crime policy, because none was forthcoming.

Then Trudeau did what he often does and blamed his opponents for playing politics, for highlighting certain issues for political gain. "We have a government, or successive governments, that have managed to polarize the conversations around gun ownership to create games in electoral ways – when you don't have to have a conflict." Yet even as he tried to assure the crowd that he would not bring back the gun registry, he called for a balance in which "law-abiding hunters and farmers" had nothing to fear while developing some sort of policy for keeping cities safe. "I don't see that that's an unsolvable solution," he said, without offering a solution.

Still, Trudeau supported the notion that the gun registry be resurrected by the Quebec government, where gun control is much more popular. Trudeau said he favoured letting provinces "find different solutions" to gun violence, and if Quebec wanted to maintain the registry, including the information the federal government had already collected, that was fine. At the time, the Parti Quebecois government was suing Ottawa so it couldn't destroy the files, a legal challenge they ultimately lost. "What's important is protecting Quebecers from gun violence," Trudeau maintained, in yet another rhetorical nod to la belle province at the expense of the rest of the country.

The would-be Liberal leader certainly calculated that he isn't going to lose many votes of gun control supporters because they are generally liberal and find the sort of "common ground" that he counts on when he abandons small-l liberal principles. Assuming he has such voters in his back pocket, the Dauphin attempts to appear balanced and non-ideological in an effort to win over voters who might not be totally comfortable with the billion-dollar gun registry failure. Trudeau might criticize the Harper Conservatives for acting too political and unprincipled, but when it comes to the gun registry, Trudeau is cynically betraying his own stated preference for the gun registry while admitting he is doing so for political reasons.

The Canadian Press reported that Heidi Rathjen, a survivor of the mass shooting at the Montreal polytechnique in 1989, condemned Trudeau's duplicitous position: "It's just political garbage," she said. Rathjen explained: "He's basically saying that the registry is a good thing only where it's popular, but that's not what a political leader does, that's not how you lead – by implementing a public safety measure only where there's no controversy."

But just because Trudeau opposes the gun registry, it does not mean he and the Liberals oppose greater gun control measures. During the debate over C-42, the *Common Sense Firearms Licensing Act*, in late 2014, the Liberal Party of Canada issued a statement that said the bill should be split into two to allow quick passage of the sections they supported but permit more debate on the measures of which they disapproved.

If passed, C-42 would strengthen some provisions to keep guns out the hands of people deemed unfit, including prohibiting individuals convicted of spousal abuse from owning weapons, and streamline licensing while strengthening training requirements, but also make it easier to transport weapons that are legally owned and change the way firearms are classified for regulatory purposes. The Liberals said the bill as it stood "will put Canadians' safety at risk." Trudeau reiterated in the statement, "We will not bring back a gun registry," but added that Canada needs "smart and well-crafted gun control legislation."

By his own admission, Trudeau supports gun control, but will not admit what his favoured gun control policy looks like.

Chapter 19: Justin Trudeau on Drugs

Usually a politician trying to reach out to middle class voters would stay away from contentious issues. The middle class is generally considered cautious, if not outright conservative. Many middle class parents worry about their children's future and safety. Loosening Canada's drug laws would seem to be a risky debate for a national leader to wade into.

Pinning down Justin Trudeau's exact position on marijuana is tricky. He was against decriminalization before he was for it and then suddenly for legalizing pot. It's a journey that has taken twists and turns, but due to the media's fascination with the young Liberal leader and the multi-million dollar campaign by the Conservatives condemning the Dauphin's position on pot, there are few Canadians who do not know that Justin Trudeau wants to change the legal status of marijuana to be more permissible.

Under Michael Ignatieff, the Liberal Party officially favoured decriminalizing possession of small amounts of marijuana (giving fines instead of jail sentences for marijuana possession), a policy pushed by the party's youth wing for decades. And yet the party was not united in supporting liberalization of the drug and one of the critics of liberalizing pot laws was one of the most youthful voices within the party.

As a rookie opposition MP in 2009, Trudeau voted with his colleagues in favour of C-15, *An Act to amend the Controlled Drugs and Substances Act and to make related and consequential amendments to other acts*, which included a provision raising mandatory minimum prison sentences for drug offenders. That same year, he also questioned a Liberal youth motion calling on the party to support decriminalizing marijuana. He said it sent a mixed signal: the state was trying to get teens not to drink alcohol or smoke cigarettes, but then the government was turning a blind eye to smoking pot. He said that legalizing any drug would be a "step backward." The optics, he admitted, didn't seem quite right.

Following the annual pot protest on Parliament Hill in 2010, Trudeau told *Maclean*'s he was not in favour of decriminalizing pot. He said he witnessed the problems with marijuana with his own eyes: "I lived in Whistler for years and have seen the effects. We need all our brain cells to deal with our problems." He said, "It's not your mother's pot," explaining that marijuana today is stronger than it was in the 1960s.

Speaking of mothers, Trudeau's reticence to embrace full-fledged legalization could be related to the problems his mother, Margaret, had with the drug. The *Vancouver Province* reported in 2007 that Margaret Trudeau told a press conference promoting the Canadian Mental Health Association's Bottom Line Conference that as a hippy in the 1960s "I loved marijuana" but that later mental health problems that sometimes required hospitalization were connected to her use of pot: the first time when her middle son Michel was born, the third time following the deaths of Michel and her former husband Pierre. Margaret Trudeau admitted, "Marijuana can trigger psychosis. Every time I was hospitalized it was preceded by heavy use of marijuana."

Despite his mother's negative experience with marijuana, Trudeau would eventually come to endorse easy access to pot.

As recently as early 2012, he was still expressing concerns about liberalization. He told *The Hill Times* that decriminalizing marijuana sent the wrong signals and may contradict the interests of the government in promoting healthy lifestyles among young people. "My own issue is that we're trying to encourage people to drink less and smoke less tobacco. To legalize something else that we know is perhaps not as harmful but not necessarily healthy could be a step in the wrong direction." He also raised concerns that a permissive drug policy could lead to problems at the Canada-U.S. border when it comes to trade. These were pragmatic arguments against liberalization and yet he muddied the waters by adding, "But I do believe in free choice."

He took a strong stand in an interview with Red Dot Project at the January 2012 Liberal convention. Trudeau again stated his opposition to liberalizing drug policy, saying that using pot is unhealthy and that it "disconnects" an individual from the world. He said that decriminalizing marijuana might not be "entirely consistent with the society we're trying to build." At the same time he said he was "excited" that the party was debating the topic of liberalizing pot.

And yet at the same Liberal policy convention which considered a youth motion calling on the party to endorse decriminalizing marijuana, Justin Trudeau tweeted, "Liberals across Canada came together to support legalizing marijuana in 2012 because the status quo is unsafe and costly. #cdnpoli."

You could call that mixed signals or trying to have it both ways. But whatever it was, it marked the beginning of his public evolution on the issue of marijuana.

At a rally in Kelowna on July 26, 2013, three months after becoming the Liberal leader, Trudeau ignited the political debate about liberalizing Canada's marijuana laws. Greeting enthusiastic supporters in the British Columbia city, and saying he would answer their questions, the Liberal leader kicked it off. Trudeau pointed to a young man holding a sign about decriminalizing pot. Trudeau said, "I see my friend waving a sign about cannabis, I'll take that as a question." He continued: "I'm actually not in favour of decriminalizing, I'm in favour of legalizing it." He explained the "current model is not working, we have to use evidence and science to make sure we are moving forward on that."

What is notable about his policy-on-the-fly announcement on pot in Kelowna, was that he brought it up himself. He was not asked about it by a journalist or a citizen, although he pretended it was a query. Standing surrounded by circle of supporters he pointed to one person and used the opportunity to speak about the issue. He voluntarily addressed the issue.

Trudeau said he favoured full legalization of cannabis. "I'm actually in favour of legalizing it; tax and regulate it," Trudeau said to cheers from the crowd. "It's one of the only ways to keep it out of the hands of our kids."

The media jumped on the comments, featuring it on their front pages and top of their broadcasts. Gerald Butts, Trudeau's closest adviser, tweeted that it wasn't really news. Earlier that year, in February, Trudeau told students at the University of Western Ontario in London, Ont., that he had decided decriminalizing didn't go far enough, so he now supported legalization of marijuana after talking to experts and reading the most recent research. During his campaign for leader in London at UWO, Trudeau was asked a direct question about pot, and he told the UWO audience that he would go beyond decriminalizing marijuana and supported legalizing pot. He said users would have to show identification so it could be kept out of the hands of young people, but said he would not liberalize other drugs. Heroin users, he joked, would be "S.O.L."

Butts said the media focusing on the re-announcement in Kelowna indicated it was a "slow news day."

Trudeau reiterated his pro-legalization position shortly after becoming leader. Talking to the Dartmouth High School in Dartmouth, N.S., on May 24, 2013 – two months before everyone noticed Trudeau's position enunciated during his Kelowna appearance – the new Liberal Leader told teens that legalizing pot would "keep it out of the hands" of younger teenagers "and when you turned 18, well, you make your own decisions."

Three months before telling university students in London that he favoured legalization, Trudeau indicated his openness to such a policy to teenagers in Atlantic Canada, but was still favouring decriminalizing marijuana over legalization.

Speaking to high school students at Colonel Gray High School students in Charlottetown, P.E.I. in November 2012, he said the "war on drugs ... doesn't work." Saying it unnecessarily put people behind bars while profiting organized crime, Trudeau said, "I am a huge supporter of decriminalization." He added that he would consider legalization to help keep pot out of the hands of kids. He said he was worried that the drug negatively affected the brain development of adolescents and that it could send the wrong message to people about healthy lifestyles.

In the course of about one year – the Liberal policy convention in early 2012, through the fall, to just before his coronation as leader – Trudeau went from opposing liberalizing marijuana laws to decriminalization to legalization of pot.

Indeed, Butts was correct in wondering about the newsworthiness of the Trudeau comments in Kelowna, as it had already been getting national and regional media play for some eight months.

In November 2012, *Maclean's* reported that Trudeau, still then a leadership candidate, had views that were evolving on the issue. "I've certainly evolved from conversations with supporters and Liberals. I am fully a supporter of decriminalization. I think the time has come for that. I am actually very open to legalization and specifically tax and regulation the way they are calling it in the States." He called for "a lot of serious discussion about" it.

A few weeks later, the CBC quoted Trudeau saying, "I'm very much in favour of decriminalizing" and that legalization is "an automatic next step to look at taxing and regulation" of marijuana.

At about the same time, the *Vancouver Sun* quoted Trudeau's comments at length: "I think we should seriously look at legalization or taxing and regulation ... I think it's the way to keep it out of the hands of our kids. I think it's a way of keeping the profits out of the criminal gang industry and I think it's an idea whose time has come. It just makes no sense to criminalize a segment of society for smoking pot anymore. I think we need to send clear messages that it's not good for you, but I think we should be mature enough as a society to allow people to make their own choices around marijuana and focus our efforts on other and more pressing issues." Trudeau claims that legalization will make it harder for youth to acquire pot and it would mean the government could tax it, therefore putting more money in the federal and provincial coffers. Furthermore, the government would save the estimated half-billion dollars it spends enforcing the law and incarcerating those convicted of what he considers minor drug charges. He called the 475,000 people convicted of drug-related crimes in the first six years of the Harper government "lives ruined" although he did not seem to acknowledge that those nearly half-million people might have had something to do with that themselves. The Sun News Network reported that 475,000 people were not convicted of marijuana possession since 2006 as Trudeau claimed, but that number actually represented all police-reported drug incidents.

The Tories had not remarked on Trudeau's position on marijuana when he was a leadership contender, but after the Kelowna speech, the Conservative government's position was noted in press release; it had "no interest in seeing marijuana legalized or made more easily available to youth."

Not surprisingly, he has attracted enthusiasts for the cause of drug liberalization.

Marc Emery is known as the Prince of Pot. He once owned a used bookstore in London, Ont., that sold banned books and music (such as the misogynistic rappers Two Live Crew) and he promoted the idea of liberty without limits. He later moved to British Columbia where he focused on promoting marijuana decriminalization, but also went so far as to sell marijuana seeds through the internet. His activism and commercial activity earned him not only the nickname the Prince of Pot, but also a jail term in the United States. Marc Emery claimed to have smoked weed with the Dauphin "four or five times" back in 2003 when Trudeau lived in British Columbia, but later clarified that he meant "I have only smoked pot one occasion with Justin Trudeau. The '4 or 5 times' is four or five times that evening," he said once a video of an Emery speech was noticed on the internet.

While Emery served time in an American prison, his wife, Jodie, remained in Canada to continue her husband's pro-pot crusade. In the summer of 2014, Jodie Emery, nicknamed the Cannabis Queen, said that not only was she seeking the Liberal nomination in Vancouver East, but suggested that the Liberal Party and perhaps Trudeau's own operatives had approached her to do so. Trudeau denied the claim and initially did not prevent the notable pot decriminalization activist from running. He said Jodie Emery would be treated like every other candidate seeking a Liberal nomination. He told *Maclean's*, "She's got a process to go through. There'll be a green-light process to look into her and, ultimately, it will be Liberals in the riding who will decide whether they want her as a candidate. That's the way things are set up. There are a lot of people who are passionate about one issue or another who feel they want to move forward by stepping toward politics. In general, that's a good thing." Of course, people who are passionate about the issue of abortion need not apply for the Liberal nomination, but making pot legal was not initially a disqualifying issue for Trudeau.

In January 2015, the Green Light Committee red-lighted her nomination, preventing Jodie Emery from running for the Liberal nomination.

For the past two decades, it is has been commonplace for journalists to ask politicians for high office if they ever smoked marijuana. Some admit it, or at least partially. In 1992, Bill Clinton famously said he smoked but did not inhale as a university student. Having opened the issue of decriminalizing pot, Trudeau was asked about his own history with the drug. The Liberal Leader told the Huffington Post in August 2013 that he had smoked marijuana, and had in fact done so since becoming an MP. Interviewed by Huffington Post's Althia Raj, who authored a sycophantic biography of Justin Trudeau when he ran for the party leadership, he admitted to last smoking pot in his home in 2010 by the pool. "We had a few good friends over for a dinner party, our kids were at their grandmother's for the night, and one of our friends lit a joint and passed it around. I had a puff."

Raj also asked the other party leaders. Stephen Harper said he never smoked pot and Thomas Mulcair admitted to having done so but didn't offer details.

Trudeau, on the other hand, discussed his drug use with the Huffington Post for 20 minutes, saying it was in the interest of "full transparency" that he speak openly about the topic.

He said he smoked marijuana "five or six times" in Raj's words. Despite giving the reporter 20 minutes in his office, he followed up with an email: "It has never really done anything for me." He explained that, "When the joint went around the room, I usually passed it around to the next person," although sometimes, "I've had a pull on it." He said he sometimes had a buzz from doing so, but not always. "I'm not really crazy about it."

The Dauphin's first experiences with illicit drugs were on foreign soil. Backpacking in Europe when he was 18, he and a friend ordered hash, but had trouble heating it and "it was just a total disaster." While he had been around pot previously, it was not until he went to the Caribbean for a university class that he smoked his first joint. Trudeau said, "It's never really been a big deal," and he doesn't "keep a clear memory of it."

As a young man in his twenties living in Whistler, B.C., Raj reported, Trudeau "rarely smoked weed," "never bought drugs," and "never consumed enough to be asked to chip in." Trudeau explained, "I'm not someone who is particularly interested in altered states, but I certainly won't judge someone else for it."

Trudeau also said of his own disinterest in the drug, "I'm not one for dependencies, and I was always worried about that." While he won't judge others who use marijuana, he did implicitly suggest the downside of addiction when he suggests it could lead to dependency.

Trudeau said he has never tried hard drugs nor does he drink much alcohol; he claimed not to smoke cigarettes or drink coffee. He was mocked in social media for this admission and journalists speculated that a politician who is not fueled by caffeine might have a difficult time doing his job. Trudeau went to Twitter to joke: "Realizing I may have made a major mistake in my openness and transparency: vicious attacks coming because I don't drink coffee #oops."

Yet one wonders how honest Justin Trudeau was. During a summer stop in Prince Edward Island at the farm of Liberal MP Lawrence MacAulay the week after his admission of smoking pot, Trudeau told party supporters: "I admitted that a few times in my past I partook of marijuana. That sounds so formal. I took a puff on a joint a few times as a younger person." That doesn't jibe with his earlier admission that he smoked pot as an MP. Yet here he was trying to downplay his pot-smoking as a youthful indiscretion.

The Conservatives didn't find Trudeau's drug admission funny. Stephen Harper, asked about Trudeau's Huffington Post interview and pot use admission, said, "I think those actions speak for themselves." But other members of the government could not resist criticizing the Liberal Leader for breaking Canada's drug laws. Justice Minister Peter MacKay said Trudeau showed a "profound lack of judgement" and "is simply not the kind of leader our country needs." MacKay said in a press release, "By flouting the laws of Canada while holding elected office, he shows he is a poor example for all Canadians, particularly young ones."

Immediately after Trudeau's Kelowna comments, the Conservatives condemned him on their website: "These drugs are illegal because of the harmful effect they have on users and on society. We will continue protecting the interests of families across this country." The statement continued, "Our government has no interest in seeing marijuana legalized or made more easily available to youth." Trudeau's own words about the deleterious effects of pot suggest he does not, in fact, disagree that marijuana is harmful.

The *Surrey North Delta Leader* interviewed Blaine, Washington-based immigration lawyer Len Saunders, who said the admission of pot use could keep Trudeau out of the United States. "I couldn't believe it when I saw him admit to it," he told the Vancouver-area paper. "Justin Trudeau is inadmissible to the United States," Saunders said. "He's admitted to use of an illegal substance. If he's elected prime minister he can't come into the U.S. without a waiver." He said that despite some American states liberalizing their own marijuana laws, it was still "folly for any Canadian to publicly disclose their past pot use."

"Justin Trudeau could very well be barred from the US for admitting pot use," Fadi Minawi of Niren and Associates told *Yahoo! Canada News*. Niren explained that if U.S. customs asked him about his now public pot use and

Trudeau "admitted to the essential elements of this offence that would constitute of a violation of a law relating to a controlled substance and that would be problematic for him." Niren said that some Canadians have been barred for life from the U.S. for previous drug use, and that Trudeau may require an entry waiver that deems him rehabilitated to enter the United States. As Yahoo!'s Andy Radia stated, "This certainly could be problematic for a potential prime minister who might have to go to the United States to meet his American counterpart."

For his part, the Dauphin shrugged off the partisan criticism, saying that Canadians do not care about whether or not he smoked pot. His office did not return media inquiries about the potential of Trudeau being banned from the U.S. Trudeau would later tell reporters that it was not a mistake to admit his past drug use saying he made clear, "I am not a consumer of marijuana" because he only "tried it ... maybe five or six times in my life," nor had he "tried other types of hard drugs."

As a matter of policy, Trudeau reiterated, he thinks adults should be able to make the decision to toke up or not. "I think that the prohibition that is currently on marijuana is unjustified." Sounding like libertarian activist Marc Emery, Trudeau says, "I think that adults should be free to choose their behaviours in this particular case."

In four years, Trudeau went from an opposition MP who voted for mandatory minimum sentences for marijuana possession in 2009 to calling for legalization and admitting using pot. He also acknowledged that his own actions were incongruent with his voting record. He explained that his position evolved.

Trudeau also said in that lengthy Huffington Post interview that his deceased brother Michel was facing marijuana possession charges before his death in an avalanche in 1998, and that influenced his position that pot should be, at least, decriminalized. Trudeau claimed that Michel was caught with "just a tiny amount" and that having his younger brother die with a possession charge against him on the books, led him to think about the issue, although ultimately he would not support legalizing marijuana until late 2012. One of the benefits Trudeau claims for full-blown legalization, is that it can help authorities keep the drug out of the hands of children and combat organized crime that depends on the drug trade. His argument is that taking pot off the streets and the black market will help the government regulate the product like tobacco, which could prevent children from accessing the drug easily. He often vacillates between these pragmatic arguments and the libertarian case that adults can be trusted to make their own choices.

Trudeau said U.S. states such as Colorado and Washington have legalized marijuana without many problems – ignoring that the social experiments in those states began just two and three years earlier respectively – and that it could be done in Canada, too, quite easily. He also denied that legalizing pot would lead to a wide-open legal drug market in Canada. "I do not see this as a slippery slope. I see this as an issue of legislators slowly catching up to where public opinion and public behaviour actually is." Indeed polls have shown support for liberalization for some time.

Polling expert Eric Grenier noted in the *Globe and Mail* that according to numerous surveys, support for decriminalization exceeded 50 percent since 2003 and approached 70 percent, while there has been majority support for legalization since 2007. He also said that with the exception of seniors, there is support for liberalizing marijuana among all demographics, including Conservative voters. However, the polls do not indicate that liberalizing laws on marijuana are in any way a priority issue for most voters.

The Dauphin claims that most people support his position and that few have personally criticized him for his evolving position. The one exception, he acknowledges, are some ethnic voters who worry about whether making drugs easier to get on the street will make the streets less safe and their own children more prone to be exposed to the stuff. Trudeau reiterates his position that legalizing pot will keep it away from children.

Trudeau's evolving position and admitted drug use were applauded in many circles, especially by journalists. The Canadian Press called it frank. Yet the position, and even the admission of smoking a bit of weed himself, might also be calculating. Facing two older rivals for the job of prime minister, Justin might have been attempting to buttress his "cool" credentials and attract younger voters, especially when he was running for Liberal leader. He has admitted that, "I am certainly trying to make myself look different from the kind of politics that people have been suffering through for the past year." By distancing himself from the supposed stiff-shirt leadership of Stephen Harper and the angry father-figure of Tom Mulcair, Trudeau is appealing to a younger demographic that might not care much about policies and principles but are attracted to gestures that signal similarities, especially generational affinity.

For months after the Kelowna speech, Trudeau was repeatedly questioned by journalists about liberalizing marijuana. Trudeau would always answer, "We're number one out of 29 different countries in teen use," according some study, before reiterating his other talking points that legalization is the best way to keep marijuana out of the hands of teenagers because it would require people to show identification proving their age, which no one in the current black market for drugs is going to do. What Trudeau ignores, however, is that even if pot is legalized for adults, some unscrupulous people will still turn around and illegally sell their legal weed to minors, so the black market isn't going to disappear entirely. He says the current rules do not work, repeating the talking point that "prohibition has left us with a higher rate of use of marijuana in our teens than any developed country around the world … it can't get any easier now." He adds that for teenagers "it is easier to buy a joint than a bottle of beer." He repeated this line in Charlottetown, Winnipeg, and Vancouver in the summer of 2013 as he enthusiastically talked about his support for legalization. It is unimaginable to him that matters could become worse if Canada's drug laws were loosened. He talks about legalization as a panacea to prevent kids from toking up, but it won't be.

Trudeau also says that having a responsible regulatory framework will ensure quality control for the product. He said science should be the guide for the limit of tetrahydrocannabinol (THC) levels that could safely be sold; THC is the active intoxicant in marijuana which gives people their buzz when smoking pot.

But when talking about regulating marijuana, Trudeau has not spelled out whether he would permit marijuana to be sold in convenience stores like cigarettes, or in specialized marijuana stores, like most provinces sell alcohol. In fact, he offers no specifics about how legalization would work.

In September 2013, the Sun News Network reported that when pressed by members of the press on the specifics of his policy, "There are still a number of elements to put together on what the best process is, how to control it, what level to tax it at." He said he and his advisors needed to sit down with experts in the field, including law enforcement officials, to put the plan together. He reiterated his hope of keeping pot out of the hands of young people, but apparently was finding it difficult to develop a policy that simultaneously made it easier to acquire marijuana but made it more difficult for kids to do so. That same month, he told a crowd in Manitoba, "My vision of what the legalization of marijuana would look like, it's loosely based on how we control alcohol." One might sardonically note that teens never get their hands on beer.

Trudeau says that his position is vindicated by science and that his critics, those who favour continuing to prohibit illicit drugs, must provide evidence that their policy is sound, and not just a moralizing position. "They have to fall back on nanny state, 'We know what's good for you, we're telling you how to behave'," Trudeau characterizes the Conservative position. He claims it is not possible to muster facts to support maintaining the status quo – a status quo he supported before becoming Liberal leader, a status quo he voted for when he was a mere MP, a status quo he backed before becoming an MP. Now he says his policy is "grounded in evidence, one grounded in science, one grounded in liberty." He has also said, "I think that adults should be free to choose their behaviours in this particular case." On CTV's Question Period on September 8, 2013, Trudeau challenged Harper and his government "to explain why adults shouldn't be given the opportunity to make their own free choices and why they think the continued prohibition that's obviously failed in protecting our children is still justified." Both Harper and Justice Minister Peter MacKay said that liberalizing drug laws would make it easier for children to obtain marijuana.

Technically, liberalizing marijuana for recreational use and medical marijuana can be separate issues. And yet Trudeau suggests that once marijuana is legalized, it will be easier to do medical marijuana research. Many doctors and researchers say cannabis helps cancer patients undergoing chemotherapy, assists individuals with HIV/AIDS, and can help treat pain, but research on medical marijuana is limited because only recently has it been viable to study in the U.S. as more states permit pot for medicinal purposes. After his unprompted Kelowna comments in July 2013, Trudeau further defended his position on legalizing pot saying it would "allow for development of a medical marijuana industry." He would later explain in Winnipeg: "Our worries are that the current hyper-controlled approach around medical marijuana that actually removes from individuals the capacity to grow their own, is not going in the right direction."

Several U.S. states have experimented with medical marijuana without liberalizing it recreationally, most notably California, although there are studies suggesting many recreational users access medical marijuana under false pretences. Indeed, Canada permits medical marijuana, with 37,000 Canadians holding a Health Canada license to possess medical marijuana.

By linking liberalizing Canada marijuana laws to making it easier to access medical marijuana, Justin Trudeau is conflating the issues, perhaps deliberately to tamp down concerns about the ease with which pot might be accessed if Trudeau becomes prime minister.

It is either political naiveté or simple cloyingness to suggest, as Trudeau has, that liberalizing marijuana laws, "is maybe not the big issue of an election – I certainly hope it is not the big issue in an election – but it is not an insignificant issue." That's a little disingenuous. By endorsing a controversial position, Trudeau instigated a debate about the topic and he ensures questions about the legal status of marijuana will be asked leading up to and throughout the election campaign. And he made the issue fair game for his opponents in the election. Yet, Trudeau also says that he wants to continue speaking out against Canada's current marijuana laws as ineffective and unfair. Indeed, for a prime ministerial candidate who eschews talking about much policy, it is one of the few issues all Canadians know specifically where the Dauphin stands and would do if he became head of Canada's government.

Legalizing pot is not the only way Trudeau wants to make it easier to access or use drugs. He also supports expanding supervised drug injection clinics.

Insite is a supervised drug injection clinic in the crime and poverty-stricken Downtown Eastside neighbourhood in Vancouver that operates a needle exchange program for heroin, cocaine, and morphine users with the goal of reducing the harm the area's drug culture causes individuals. It is partially funded by Health Canada and operated from 2003 through 2008 under a special exemption to Section 56 of the *Controlled Drugs and Substances Act* granted by the Chrétien and Martin governments, and temporarily by Conservative Health Minister Tony Clement. When the Conservative government refused to exempt the facility from trafficking provisions of the law, the clinic sued, eventually winning a permanent exemption in the Supreme Court in 2011. The Conservatives introduced a bill, *The Respect for Communities Act*, which passed in the House of Commons in March 2015 and went to the Senate. If it becomes law, *The Respect for Communities Act* would regulate so-called safe injection sites, with provisions for certification and inspections, including reports on how facilities affect the local community, and require consultations with neighbours before new safe injection sites are opened. Trudeau and his entire caucus voted against the bill.

Trudeau has said he'll go with whatever the experts say. "I respect science, I respect scientists who have done studies and examined the consequences of different actions and recommendations." The studies, however, are often conducted by medical professionals who buy into the harm reduction philosophy. He praised the 2011 Supreme Court decision as a "victory for medical science, Charter rights, and common sense over narrow, right-wing ideology, and politicking."

Cities such as Calgary, Winnipeg, and Toronto are looking at setting up supervised injection sites, which Brian Lilley, then of Sun News (and now with TheRebel.media) called government-sanctioned heroin-shooting galleries.

When Trudeau was on the campus of the University of British Columbia on March 5, 2015, he was asked about his position on hard drugs, and he transitioned to supervised injection sites like Insite. He said: "I think there's much we can and should be doing around harm reduction, Insite's a great model of that and I certainly want to see more safe injection sites opened around the country."As The Rebel's Marissa Semkiw said, although Trudeau insists on labelling these facilities safe "there is nothing safe about injecting heroines into one's veins."

During that UBC event in March 2015, Trudeau said, "I disagree with loosening the prohibition on harder drugs" such as heroine, crack cocaine, and crystal methamphetamine. There is an inconsistency in saying he opposes loosening the prohibition when he supports government-funded, government-exempted facilities providing drug paraphernalia to drug users under the guise of harm reduction. But even if that didn't stretch credulity, recall that at the beginning of 2012 Justin Trudeau spoke out against liberalizing marijuana laws and within the year was for full legalization.

Chapter 20: Justin Trudeau on Abortion

For most of Justin Trudeau's first two years as leader, he evaded specific policy questions and offered platitudes that would offend as few people as possible while making his ideas and ideals sound lofty. But on a pair of divisive issues, Trudeau took positions in which he was crystal clear: legalizing drugs and protecting abortion.

When it came to abortion, Trudeau staked his ground early, as an MP. In February 2012 he told Radio Canada in Quebec that he could support Quebec separatism in order to defend abortion rights and same-sex marriage in Quebec. The Dauphin said: "I always say, if at a certain point, I believe that Canada was really the Canada of Stephen Harper – that we were going against abortion, and we were going against gay marriage and we were going backwards in 10,000 different ways – maybe I would think about wanting to make Quebec a country." In other words, breaking up Canada was something he was willing to do to defend abortion, at least in Quebec. The statement was odious, and unfitting for a man who would within a year seek leadership of a federal party with the hope of one day becoming the country's prime minister. It was also ridiculous; in 2012 Canada was not on the cusp of "going against" either abortion or same-sex marriage as polls showed support for legal abortion and gay marriage and the ruling Conservatives had avoided wading into such controversial issues.

Once the story broke in English Canada, there was a torrent of criticism. Trudeau initially refused to talk to the media, instead going to Twitter to explain: "Canada needs Qc to balance out Harper's vision that I (and many) just don't support." Again, Harper has avoided talking about abortion and same-sex marriage although he tolerates a sizable social conservative contingent within the Conservative Party caucus, so what vision is Trudeau talking about?

On February 14, some of those socially conservative Tories criticized Trudeau for his comments. Trudeau whisked himself away to the pool microphones after Question Period and dramatically but forcefully insisted: "The question is not, 'Why does Justin Trudeau suddenly not love his country?' Because the question is ridiculous. I live this country in my bones in every breath I take and I'm not going to stand here and somehow defend that I actually do love Canada because we know, I love Canada." He added: "Canadians shouldn't be asking, 'Who does Justin Trudeau actually want to separate?' Of course not. But will Justin Trudeau fight with his very last breath to make sure that this Canada stays the Canada that we collectively know it can be? Absolutely." To watch the video is to see a spectacle of the then goateed Dauphin referring to himself in the first person, dramatically insisting he did not say what he said just days earlier: he'd break up the country over abortion. Indignantly he tried to explain that what he really meant was that he would fight for abortion to his deathbed.

Just more than two year later, as the leader of the Liberal Party of Canada, he would illustrate what that meant. On May 7, 2014, the day before the National March for Life which attracts about 25,000 Canadian pro-lifers to Parliament Hill to call for an end to abortion, Justin Trudeau once again addressed a scrum in the halls of parliament. He said that all future candidates for the Liberal Party would have to support a "woman's right to choose" and same-sex marriage. Paradoxically, the Open Nominations process would ensure this by requiring the green-light committee to disqualify candidates who were pro-life or pro-traditional marriage. The handful of sitting pro-life MPs would be allowed to remain and run again, he explained, as the mandatory pro-choice policy would be grandfathered in, but he did not answer questions about whether or not they would be forced into line on future abortion votes or whether they could vote their conscience or represent their constituents on the issue. Trudeau said, "We [are making] sure that the people who are stepping forward are consistent with the Liberal Party as it is now, as it stands under my leadership and under the feedback we're getting from Canadians across the country." Trudeau added: "It is not for any government to legislate what a woman chooses to do with her body. And that is the bottom line." He said that the Liberal Party was the party of the Charter and therefore would protect abortion even though the procedure is not mentioned in the document his father foisted upon the country nor has the Supreme Court declared abortion a constitutional right.

Brian Lilley, a host at the Sun News Network, noted on his blog Lilley's Pad, said Justin Trudeau had his Charter history wrong. Lilley quoted a letter dated December 21, 2981, from Pierre Trudeau, Canada's Prime Minister at the time and architect of the Charter of Rights, to G. Emmett Cardinal Carter, Roman

Catholic Archbishop of Toronto, and later reprinted in the *Ottawa Citizen*. It said: "Since the November 2, 1981 Conference of First Ministers, parliament's authority has been strengthened by the addition of the notwithstanding clause to the Charter. Should a court decide at some future date that sections 7 or 15 do establish a right to abortion on demand, parliament will continue to legislate on the matter by overriding the court's decision and the specific Charter right as interpreted by the court." In other words, Pierre Trudeau did not consider abortion to be part of the Charter.

Campaign Life Coalition rated three sitting Liberal MPs as pro-life: John MacKay (Scarborough–Guildwood), Kevin Lamoureux (Winnipeg North), and Lawrence MacAulay (Cardigan), or about one in 11 members of the caucus at the time. CLC's National President Jim Hughes also noted that it was a dramatic and undemocratic turn for the Liberals, a party that had pro-lifers represent as much as a quarter of the caucus at times under Jean Chrétien and Pierre Trudeau. Hughes told The Interim at the time, "It is terribly troubling and totally undemocratic that members of parliament would not be allowed to vote their conscience on important moral issues." A few weeks later, Trudeau again clarified his position on the sitting MPs and how they would vote: they would have to back the party line, and MacAuley, MacKay, and Lamoureux all indicated they would fall into line: hardly profiles in courage.

It wasn't only pro-lifers who criticized the new tact. The CBC reported that former Liberal MP Rob Oliphant, an ordained United Church minister who supports abortion and was considering seeking the Liberal nomination in his old riding of Don Valley West, said he was troubled by Trudeau's hard-line policy. Oliphant said he had "a concern that people who hold another value or different religious view or whatever would be stopped from running, would not be green-lit." Oliphant said one of the strengths of the Liberals is that they are a "big tent party." But the Liberals were no longer a big tent. Former Liberal MP Tom Wappel (Scarborough West and later Scarborough Southwest) wrote in the *National Post* that he won his riding six times by upholding certain principles, including his pro-life stance, and that he was not alone among Liberals to uphold the sanctity of all human life. Wappel lamented, "People like us, are now, suddenly, *persona non grata* in the Liberal Party of Canada."

A few days later Trudeau tweaked his position, noting in a message on the Liberal Party website: pro-life Liberals could run for the nomination, but that they would have to commit to voting pro-abortion if they are elected; "Canadians of all views are welcome within the Liberal Party of Canada," but the Dauphin maintained that "under my leadership, incoming Liberal MPs will always vote in favour of a woman's fundamental rights." He insisted, "When it comes to actively supporting women's rights, our party must speak with one voice." CLC's Hughes said that Trudeau does not seem to understand the contradiction in trying to welcome pro-life voters while excluding pro-life candidates: "Why would a pro-life Canadian vote Liberal when its leader is so adamant that MPs could never represent their pro-life values?"

Numerous religious leaders condemned Trudeau's diktat. On May 14, Cardinal Thomas Collins of Toronto issued an open letter to Trudeau, who was raised Catholic, expressing his concern that pro-life individuals would be disqualified from running for the Liberals. Cardinal Collins noted that if Pope Francis, "as a young man, instead of seeking to serve in the priesthood in Argentina, had moved to Canada and sought to serve in the noble vocation of politics, he would have been ineligible to be a candidate for your party, if your policy were in effect." The Cardinal also noted that Catholics across the country would have difficulty countenancing Trudeau's policy: "It is not right that they be excluded by any party for being faithful to their conscience." He also criticized Trudeau for extending party discipline to areas of "conscience and religious faith," where traditionally MPs are free to vote on legislation as they see fit.

In his memoir *Common Ground*, Trudeau says that when he meets people who disagree with him on moral issues such as abortion and same-sex marriage, "especially newer immigrants," he refuses to pander to them, but instead says: "We disagree on this, and since we are both arguing from what we regard as our core principles, there is probably little room for compromise. I hope there is enough common ground on other issues, however, for you to consider voting for me." That sounds so reasonable, but is it? He is suggesting to people that they abandon core moral principles and support his political quest to become prime minister if on other less important issues, they might agree.

Trudeau's support of abortion knows no limits. When Marissa Semkiw of Sun News Network asked the Dauphin about sex-selective abortions which even the Canadian Medical Association has questioned, Trudeau said: "I will leave discussions like that between a woman and the health professionals that she encounters ... I don't think the government should be in the business of legislating away people's rights." Of course, government routinely legislates away people's rights from seat belt laws to limiting what private health care consumers can access. Is Justin Trudeau going to go full libertarian and vociferously oppose every intrusion into people's lives as he does any suggestion that abortion can be limited?

Trudeau could not even admit to Semkiw, however, any doubt about abortion even outside of a political context. She asked: "A woman comes to you. She says she's pregnant with a girl and she wants to terminate the life of the child because it's a girl. What would you say to her?" Trudeau replied: "My position has been very clear. The Liberal Party is the party standing up for people's rights. And the Liberal Party will always be the party of the Charter. So we will continue to stand up for people's rights and not legislate them away." She followed up: "So to be clear, you wouldn't discourage her from having an abortion because it's a girl?" He once again talked about his role as a parliamentarian.

Trudeau doubled down on abortion in his March 9, 2015 speech on the Canadian idea of liberty. Most of the coverage focused on his condemnation of Stephen Harper for fomenting division in the country over Muslim headscarves, but the Dauphin also made an outrageous statement about abortion: it was the greatest achievement in recent Canadian history. He said that women do not have full equality with men, but, "when you take the long view, it is impossible to be anything but awestruck by the progress we have made in creating a society where women are not just included, but vital to our economic and social progress." That's true, but his explanation for this progress might be disputed: "One set of policies in post-war Canada generated more liberty for more people than any other. It was the decades-long effort of the women's movement to gain control over reproductive health and rights. Indeed, let me be perfectly clear on this point. The Canada we know today is unimaginable without widely available birth control and the legalization of choice. Every conceivable measure of inclusion and progress has moved in the right direction since women gained legally protected reproductive freedom in Canada." It is hard to think of a bolder, more pro-abortion statement than claiming everything good about modern society stems from the legalization of abortion under his father.

He recommitted to defended abortion and defended his position on not allowing members of the Liberal caucus to be pro-life. He said his violation of their conscience rights was the correct thing to do because the rights of women to terminate their pregnancy exceeded any right of an MP to vote his conscience or to represent his constituents. "Let's be clear on this," said Trudeau. "For Liberals, the right of a woman to control her body is more important than the right of a legislator to restrict her freedom with their vote." He added that anyone who did not like this is welcome to run as a Conservative or independent. Of course, it is not just MPs and candidates who are offended by this policy, but citizens: voters. They have been given a clear signal that not only should pro-lifers reject the party but also anyone who cares about the independence of members of parliament to be free of the coercive hand of party leaders.

Chapter 21: Justin Trudeau on Moral Issues

In December 2013, the Supreme Court of Canada upheld an Ontario court's striking down Criminal Code restrictions on prostitution and ordered parliament to pass a new law within a year. During the Liberal Party policy convention held in Montreal in January 2014, a motion to commit the party to legalizing prostitution was brought to the floor for debate. Trudeau was noncommittal. He told reporters, "For now, I'm just very, very mindful that the Supreme Court came down very clearly that the current approach is not protecting extremely vulnerable women and sex workers and we need to make sure that we are finding a way to keep vulnerable Canadians protected from violence that surrounds prostitution but also is intrinsic to prostitution." The beginning of that phrase – "for now" – left him plenty of room to change his mind or adopt a new position. When speaking to reporters in French, however, he was less ambivalent. He said it was important to recognize that "prostitution itself is a form of violence against women." That didn't mean he would come out against prostitution, but hinted he might approach the issue with an eye to limiting it. He called for a "responsible, informed debate" on prostitution and said the party was "certainly going to look at" the so-called Nordic model, which focuses on penalizing johns who purchase sex rather than the women who sell it.

When the Tories introduced their legislative answer to the Supreme Court six months later, Trudeau dismissed Bill C-36 as incompatible with the requirements the justices set out for a permissible prostitution law. Trudeau claimed the new law was too similar to the old one the Supreme Court unanimously ruled was unconstitutional. Trudeau said the Liberals "have real concerns about this current government's approach, which we do not feel is consistent with what the Supreme Court had asked for."

But what precisely did Trudeau want the government to do? That wasn't clear. The *Ottawa Citizen* characterized the Liberal leader's position as having "danced around whether he favoured criminalizing or decriminalizing prostitution." He suggested the Liberals were looking for a bill that made "sure that the most vulnerable people – the workers in the sex trade – are protected from violence," which he made out to be the sole criteria of the Court in its ruling. But again, without being specific, he said, "We're looking forward to debating and trying to push this government into approving it according to what research and what citizen and advocacy groups across the spectrum have talked about."

When Sun News Network's Marissa Semkiw approached Justin Trudeau in Little Portugal during a by-election campaign shortly after the government introduced C-36 to the House of Commons and asked him specific questions about the bill, including whether he believed prostitution constituted violence against women, he had no answers. Asked three times specifically what policy he favoured, and what he would do to protect vulnerable women, Trudeau offered platitudes: "I think there's a lot of different ways of doing it. People have put forward different models and what we feel is that the government in its approach right now isn't living up to what the Supreme Court asked it to do which is to make sure that the most vulnerable people – the workers in the sex trade – are protected from violence."

"I think one of the things we need to do is see that we have a government that is actually taking on its responsibilities and we're looking forward to debating and trying to push this government into approving it according to what research and what citizen and advocacy groups across the spectrum have talked about."

"I think there's a lot of different ways of doing it. The most important thing to do is to make sure we are following the Supreme Court's guidance which this government certainly hasn't done with this bill."

This is typical Justin Trudeau. Asked about the specifics of policy, he has no ideas of his own. His default position is to defer to someone else, whether it be the Supreme Court or science or other so-called experts. But voters elect MPs and prime ministers to make decisions by sifting through the evidence and weighing various considerations. If Justin Trudeau is going to defer to the Supreme Court on what laws should exist, we don't need parliament to create laws and can dispense with elections. If he's going to let scientists and other experts dictate policy, we do not need parliamentarians debating these issues in Ottawa – just hand the power over to unelected experts in each field. (Never mind that they seldom agree the way Trudeau supposes they do.)

It is not so much Trudeau's position on prostitution, for it is clear that he isn't saying what he really believes should be the law governing the selling of sex. It is really about how he doesn't have many ideas about how Canada should be governed, only that it shouldn't be our elected officials who seem in Trudeau's mind beholden to follow whatever the experts – often vested interests – tell them to do.

When it came to euthanasia, Justin Trudeau again did not show where he stands. In 2010, as a first-term MP, he did not vote on C-384, a private member's bill that would have legalized euthanasia and assisted-suicide. In 2013, Trudeau told an audience at Ryerson University he did not want to discuss euthanasia until palliative care was improved in Canada.

At the Liberal biennial convention in Montreal in February 2014 Justin Trudeau merely acknowledged that delegates would vote on decriminalizing assisted-suicide but did not state his own position or even remain around for the vote. Yet during his keynote he used explicitly pro-euthanasia language, saying "death with dignity" challenged the party "to expand our idea of what it means to be a free citizen in a modern democracy." The resolution, which passed overwhelmingly, concluded, "Be it resolved that the Liberal Party of Canada commits to working with the professional medical community and relevant stakeholders in a collaborative effort to establish professional proto- cols in relation to de-criminalizing medically-assisted death in Canada." The party's website said at the time, "This convention will be a key milestone on the road to the next federal election in 2015," because "delegates will vote to adopt the policy resolutions that will inspire our next electoral platform." A month earlier, the Supreme Court of Canada agreed to hear a case challenging the Criminal Code prohibition on euthanasia and assisted-suicide. The *National Post* reported that Trudeau spokeswoman Kate Purchase said that because the issue is before the Supreme Court, "it would be inappropriate to prejudge the outcomes," and that the Liberal leader will "await their guidance." Having an opinion is not prejudging outcomes, but once again Trudeau would defer to the ermine-robed bosses at the Supreme Court.

About a year later, the Supreme Court handed down its decision, a unanimous ruling permitting doctor-assisted suicide with a direction given to the govern- ment to re-write a new law within the year. Justin Trudeau called on the fed- eral government to form a special committee to consider the issue in order to report back to parliament in July, so voters could pass judgement on the issue in the October 2015 election. Trudeau stated that he supported doctor-assisted suicide after watching his father's painful fight against pancreatic cancer when the former prime minister, also suffering from dementia at the time, refused treatment. It seemed odd that he was so reticent to share that story, instead maintaining the illusion of agnosticism on the issue. For a politician with such strong views on moral issues such as abortion, same-sex marriage, and legalizing drugs, it was more than a little unusual that he felt he could not initially voice his true opinion about euthanasia.

Chapter 22: Justin Trudeau on Coalitions

It is conventional wisdom that the attempted power-grab by the Liberals and NDP on November 27, 2008 hurt the Liberals and helped the Tories in the 2011 federal election. During the 2011 campaign, three years after the announcement of the formal coalition of the two left-wing parties, Conservative partisans referred to the agreement among the Liberals, NDP and Bloc Quebecois as a *coup d'etat*, an illegitimate and unholy alliance of opportunists, socialists, and separatists, willing to put their own interests ahead of the will of the people, as determined by the federal election just two months earlier when the Harper government increased its minority but still fell short of a majority. When the lame-duck leader of the Liberals, Stephane Dion, signed a formal agreement with Jack Layton and the NDP to form a coalition government, and sat for a photo-op alongside Bloc leader Gilles Duceppe, few Canadians could countenance the three losing parties dislodging the Conservative government. Indeed, every major polling company at the time found opposition to the coalition taking over government.

In the lead-up to the 2011 campaign, the Conservatives raised the spectre of a "losing" party making a deal with other losing parties to usurp the will of the plurality of Canadians and form a government. Harper's position was clear: only the party that won the most seats should be allowed to form government.

The shocking coalition of winter 2008 when the NDP and Liberals signed an agreement that divvied up cabinet posts and was propped up with the support of the separatist Bloc Quebecois made any discussion of formal cooperation on the Left a non-starter. Contenders favouring formal cooperation in both the NDP and Liberal leadership campaigns – the NDP in 2012 and Liberals in 2013 – finished poorly.

Nathan Cullen, the NDP MP for the British Columbia riding of Skeena-Bulkley Valley, finished third in the NDP race to replace the late Jack Layton, after running on a joint nomination process in ridings held by Conservatives where Greens, Liberals, and the NDP would choose a single candidate to represent the Left to avoid vote-splitting. Cullen garnered just under a quarter of the vote on the third ballot at the Toronto convention that ultimately chose Thomas Mulcair, a two-term NDP MP and former environment minister in Jean Charest's Liberal government in Quebec.

The following year during the Liberal leadership race, MP Joyce Murray (Vancouver Quadra), a former minister in Gordon Campbell's Liberal government in British Columbia, finished second to Justin Trudeau. She advocated voluntary run-off nominations among the Greens, Liberals, and NDP at the constituency level to pick a single candidate to face the Tories when the party riding associations agreed to cooperate. Murray said she would not impose the position on the party and would require the Liberal convention approve the scheme before urging local ridings to adopt it. She finished second to Trudeau with 11.8 percent of the vote, nearly double her nearest competitor (Martha Hall Findlay) but at the same time garnering just one-seventh of the support that Trudeau won.

These results surely contributed to the popular view among strategists and pundits that a formal coalition on the Left was a non-starter, despite arguments for cooperation by the so-called progressive parties to work together to defeat the Harper Conservatives. Paul Adams, wrote an entire book about it, *Power Trap: How Fear and Loathing Between New Democrats and Liberals Keep Stephen Harper in Power – and What Can Be Done About It.*

By December 2014, Ekos was finding that a sizable majority of Canadians preferred a Liberal-NDP coalition government led by Justin Trudeau to a Conservative government, as fully 60 percent favoured a left-wing coalition over another Harper term as prime minister, which was backed by 40 per cent of respondents. Frank Graves, the left-leaning pollster who runs Ekos, said in an iPolitics column, "The spectre of a coalition government that was used to effectively to strengthen Harper's fortunes in 2011 no longer seems to worry Canadians nearly as much." Despite such polling, Graves said that each party leader will insist that a coalition is not their goal as each party will seek to win enough seats to form government on their own.

That is until Thomas Mulcair raised the possibility on March 17, 2015, a mere seven months before the federal election. The NDP leader told reporters in Montreal that while he is running to win, he is open to a coalition with the Liberals because his goal is to get Stephen Harper out of 24 Sussex Drive. Mulcair said that the Liberals were not interested in the idea. "Whenever we have opened that door, Justin Trudeau slams it shut," Mulcair said. "My first priority is to get rid of Stephen Harper. The first priority of Justin Trudeau is Justin Trudeau."

Before Trudeau ascended to the Liberal throne and the NDP were polling ahead of the Grits, Mulcair repeatedly ruled out any form of coalition with the third-place party. While still insisting he can win power on his own – "We will win all the seats we already have in Quebec and we will add more, we are confident of that" – Mulcair began acknowledging the likelihood of the 2015 campaign being a three-way race, unlikely to produce a majority government by any party. It is unclear whether he hoped to create a mandate for formal cooperation between Liberals and NDP in case no party wins a majority, or whether he was buttressing his progressive bona fides and suggesting that Trudeau was first and foremost concerned about himself and not the country.

About a month after Mulcair mused about the possibility of entering a coalition with the Liberals, Justin Trudeau told the Canadian Press he would be open to forming a coalition government with the NDP but not if Mulcair was leading the party. "His style is anchored in the old ways of practicing politics. Politics needs to be rallying. And we have very different perspectives on how politics should be practiced." Asked if he would form a coalition if someone else was leading the NDP, Trudeau said, "I don't know … honestly, I don't want to get into hypotheses. Maybe. Maybe not." We should assume he meant hypotheticals, not hypotheses, but is it a hypothetical he had not pondered? He provided a response to the hypothetical notion of a coalition with a Mulcair-led NDP and thus evidence he has considered the possibilities. Why not share his thoughts about an NDP led by someone with a similar style of doing politics, which seemed to be his litmus test. Aaron Wherry of *Maclean's* said, "Next time I have an interview with Trudeau, I'm going to spend 20 minutes going through a list of possible NDP leaders to gauge his feelings on each one."

The next day, after an evening of nearly 24 hours of bad press, Trudeau clarified his position, contradicting to some extent his initial response which left the door open to a conditional coalition (with a new leader). During an April 15 press conference in Halifax, Trudeau closed the door to a coalition, and implied he had done so the day before in his CP interview: "What I said during that interview, what I've said for the past three years, is that I'm unequivocally opposed to any sort of coalition." And then he stressed, "The fact is, I'm opposed to coalitions."

The fact is, Justin Trudeau is not opposed to coalitions. If he was, he would not have signed his name, just as every other Liberal MP did, to the 2008 agreement between the Grits and NDP that divvied up cabinet posts to members of both caucuses.

Whatever. As Rex Murphy mused in the *National Post*, "It will be worth wondering, however, if that definitive and unqualified declaration will last a single day beyond the fall vote." Are there not electoral results which would induce

Trudeau to cooperate with the NDP, even with Mulcair as leader, to topple a Harper government? Trudeau said he was "opposed to coalitions," but at one time he was opposed to loosening Canada's marijuana laws and then he changed his mind enough to make it a topic he didn't stop talking about for two years. At one time he said he opposed C-51, the government's anti-terrorism bill, as he led the Liberal Party in voting for it. And after throttling the Harper Conservatives as a craven, crass, politically motivated, morally bankrupt government for years as both an opposition MP and Liberal leader, how could Trudeau not take the opportunity to prevent their return to power if given the chance?

Also, there is always an out. Coalition governments, with members of cabinet from more than one party, are rare in Canada, even at the provincial level. But parties do cooperate, both formally and informally. The Liberals and NDP could cooperate in any number of ways with just one party in power, but supported by the other on confidence votes. Even if Trudeau does not flip-flop, there is plenty of wiggle room in a seemingly unequivocal statement ruling out a coalition with the NDP.

Conclusion: Who is Justin Trudeau?

Justin Trudeau had an extra-long honeymoon as leader of the Liberals. For fully two years his Liberals led in nearly every public poll that was released. In some of those polls he opened up the sort of comfortable lead that had partisans and pundits talking majority, although the sober-minded Eric Grenier at FiveThirtyEight forecasting website never put the Grits in majority position. The Conservative onslaught of attack ads that defined and brought Stephane Dion and Michael Ignatieff down seemed to have no effect on Trudeau.

Perhaps the polls and the seeming ineffectiveness of the Tory's negative campaign against him led the Dauphin to consider himself invincible. He survived a few gaffes, including admitting admiration for the Chinese dictatorship and focusing on legalizing pot. It is possible that Trudeau thought he was not only hugely popular because of the fawning coverage of the Parliamentary Press Gallery, but untouchable politically. He confused the admiration of a bunch of like-minded journalists in the Ottawa bubble – the Stephen Mahers, Glen McGregors, Michael Den Tandts, and entire roster of reporters at the CBC and Canadian Press – with how millions of Canadians, whom he would depend on to be elected prime minister, see his performance. Trudeau was praised by political reporters and pundits for his charm, good looks, platitudes, and new style of politics, and the Liberal leader thought he had Canadians eating out of his hands. Heck, even former Prime Minister Brian Mulroney thinks Trudeau is magic, saying weeks before he became Liberal leader, "He's young, articulate, attractive – a flawlessly bilingual young man. What's not to like with this picture?"

The standard narrative is that Justin Trudeau's bubble burst following the fallout of the ISIS debate in October 2014 and his mishandling of C-51, the government's anti-terrorism bill. After years of doing no wrong, he suffered several serious missteps. That narrative in only partially true. Over the summer of 2014, Trudeau had an artificially high lead in the polls that was nearing double digits. It was a typical summer lull in the Tory polling numbers. Depending on the polling company, Trudeau's decline began in September before his crass CF-18 joke and looking weak on terrorism. But it did not help Trudeau's image when his immaturity was on display during a serious debate on an international crisis. All of a sudden Canadians took notice and certainly began to ask themselves: is Justin Trudeau up to the job of prime minister?

For the first eighteen months of Trudeau's leadership, he talked about legalizing pot and invoked the middle class a lot, but he did not offer substantial policies that addressed the concerns of Canadians. He specialized in the art of saying nothing. He would talk about health care and observe something would need to be done about it. Ditto youth unemployment. He talked about issues, but he never addressed them.

The nuance of environmental policy or defining who was actually part of the middle class took a back seat to maintaining the leader's celebrity status, the approachable guy who would stop anywhere for a selfie with an adoring fan – including at Jim Flaherty's funeral. Ezra Levant noted, "It was a funeral … and Trudeau thought it was an appropriate moment to get a little bit of love from a fan." Levant continued: "More than any other ritual … a funeral is about others. It's the ultimate anti-selfie," but not for Justin Trudeau. "Because he is a walking, talking selfie. That's all he is or knows." Later that summer, Trudeau would interrupt a wedding to kiss the bride and have his picture taken with her. This is classic egomaniacal behaviour: he makes other people's special times about himself.

Justin Trudeau has a certain style that many Canadians find charming. He is charismatic and optimistic. He appeals to the better nature of Canadian citizens. He is forward looking. He can appear non-ideological; *National Post* columnist Andrew Coyne says that Trudeau's mix of positions "artfully blend left and right in a way that makes it hard to categorize him as either." Trudeau often suggested he is merely an instrument to implement the aspirations of Canadians. When he became the leader of the Liberal Party on April 14, 2013, he said, "Leadership means service."

What it apparently does not mean is leading and making decisions.

He has too often deferred to experts and authority. Drug policy is based only on evidence and not on values. Science must dictate environmental regulations when in fact such decisions should be balanced by competing environmental and economic factors. Prostitution and assisted-suicide are issues that are decided by the Supreme Court without input from elected officials. Perhaps this is to hide his true intentions: the experts and courts to which he defers are often left-leaning, so he can claim that evidence guides what is really an ideological position.

Yet at times, this reliance on the experts reaches comic proportions. On December 4, 2013, Trudeau was asked in a scrum whether he thought the North Pole was part of Canada, an issue that the United Nations was considering at the time. The Dauphin's reply? "I'm going to defer to scientists. There has been an awful lot of work done over the past years and even decades on mapping out the undersea floor and the North Pole to align with the United Nations regulations on responsibility for it." That answer has everything that is wrong with Trudeau: deference to scientists on a question that is about a lot more than science, ceding authority on a question of Canadian sovereignty to a false authority like the UN. If anything is a political question, it is a country's borders. But Trudeau abrogated his responsibility on a question of Canadian sovereignty and did not have an opinion on something as simple (if disputed) as what the map of Canada should look like. As Brian Lilley has said, when Trudeau says, "I trust our scientists and oceanographers in terms of how we're mapping it," he is really saying, "Politicians should [not] have a say, and if a bureaucrat scientist tells him the North Pole isn't ours he will accept that."

Trudeau can deliver one heck of a speech and sound somewhat reasonable. But the impressive rhetoric, combined with the lack of policy and a focus on the superficial assets that make him a celebrity beyond politics, exposed the Dauphin as a lightweight the longer Trudeau served as leader.

Going into the 2015 federal election, both Conservative and NDP strategists mused privately about baiting Justin Trudeau into multiple debates, the assumption being that pressed by Stephen Harper and Tom Mulcair, and under the glaring spotlight of an intense national campaign, Trudeau would do what he has always done when he went off-script: make gaffes or expose himself as the leftist that he is.

Indeed, the Liberals must consider Justin Trudeau an intellectual lightweight; why else were they going through intensive debate practices "five or six hours a week" six months before the election, according to the *Hill Times*?

It is no sure thing Trudeau will fail in the debates. Polls and political commentators all agreed that President Barack Obama lost his first debate to Republican Mitt Romney in 2012. Former Obama advisor David Axelrod says in his autobiography *Believer: My Forty Years in Politics*, that he told the president before the second debate: "It's not a trial or even a real debate. This is a performance. Romney understood that. He was delivering his lines. You were answering questions. I know it's a galling process, but it is what it is."

The Conservative and NDP strategists must beware the fact that Trudeau, the former drama teacher, is a great performer. He is not great at improvising, as his forays into foreign policy jokes illustrate. But if he remembers his lines and stays on message, he can perform well enough to win over voters who might be attracted to his uplifting yet meaningless platitudes. The more debates strategy could backfire: if the Dauphin performs terribly in an early debate then expectations could be reset so low for the remaining debates that Trudeau can only look like he's improving.

But the election will probably not come down to the debates. Voters are making up their minds about whether Justin Trudeau is prepared for the job of prime minister and, if the polls are any indication, it seems many do not think he is.

Trudeau could be seen as immature and intellectually unready. That will be one problem. He is too much of a risk to hand the keys to 24 Sussex at a time of heightened economic anxiety and international uncertainty; the steady and adult presence of the incumbent, even if not beloved by the populace as Trudeau seems to be, could be preferred.

Justin Trudeau might have a bigger problem, however. He promised to change a party, not only in its sense of entitlement as seen in the Sponsorship Scandal, but in its default left-wing positions. Liberals like to brag that they are a centrist option to the extremes of the socialist NDP and *laissez-faire* Conservatives. In reality, they have been the party of Big Government since at least Lester Pearson and Pierre Trudeau, Jean Chrétien's budget surpluses notwithstanding.

National Post columnist Chris Selley has wondered whether Trudeau has really changed the party: "Underneath, is it a new party? Has it come to terms with its past failures? Is it willing to confront sacred myths?" Selley was looking specifically at the foreign policy file – "Will Liberals keep banging on about peacekeeping, honest-brokering, Kyoto and not going to Iraq, or are they ready to turn the page?" – but it is true of most policy. Justin Trudeau promises to be something new, but he is in many ways the same old, same old.

The Dauphin is committed to the clichés of liberalism on multiculturalism, the environment, daycare, foreign policy, infrastructure, and taxes, to name just a few. On pipelines, prostitution, and assisted-suicide he tries to appear moderate, taking nuanced positions or refusing to take one as he defers to experts and courts, but he ends up where one would expect a Liberal leader to be on every issue.

The Dauphin promised to be something new. But he isn't.

Looking at Trudeau's track record of speeches and interviews, it can sometimes be difficult to ascertain exactly where he stands. But time and again, he eventually proves himself to be a standard-issue left-winger. Maybe that is what Canadians want, but why hasn't Trudeau felt he could present his true beliefs?

The narrative by many on the Right has been that Justin Trudeau is an intellectual lightweight, but perhaps he is merely hiding his real agenda? It is said that no one is smart enough to be a good liar, and Trudeau's mistakes might simply be the errors one makes when the true self shines through the veneer of the public figure. The reason so many journalists in the Ottawa press corps gave Justin Trudeau positive coverage for so long was that they knew that underneath the celebrity was the second coming of Pierre Trudeau.

It is possible that Trudeau is both hiding his extreme left-wing agenda and is not terribly bright, a combination that would be especially dangerous to bring to power.

Justin Trudeau is inevitably compared to his father. It is commonly remarked that he does not have Pierre's intellectual acuity, but it is becoming increasingly clear that he shares his father's ideology and desire to remake Canada in his own liberal image. After two years as leader of the Liberal Party, enough of what the Dauphin would do as leader of the country is known to come to a conclusion about whether he should be entrusted with the responsibility of prime minister: one Trudeau was more than enough. There is no reason to risk another.

Bibliography

Books

Bliss, Michael. *Right Honourable Men: The Descent of Canadian Politics from Macdonald to Mulroney*. Toronto: HarperCollins, 1994.

Campbell, Colin. *Governments Under Stress: Political Executives and Key Bureaucrats in Washington, London, and Ottawa*. Toronto: University of Toronto Press, 1983.

Chretien, Jean. *My Years as Prime Minister*. Toronto: Knopf, 2007.

de Valk, Fr. Alphonse. *The Secular State*. Toronto: Life Ethics Centre, 1985.

English, John. *Citizen of the World: The Life of Pierre Elliott Trudeau, Volume One: 1919-1968*. Toronto: Knopf, 2006.

English, John. *Just Watch Me: The Life of Pierre Elliott Trudeau, Volume Two: 1968-2000*. Toronto: Knopf, 2010.

Granatstein, J.L. and Norman Bothwell. *Pirouette: Pierre Trudeau and Canadian Foreign Policy*. Toronto: University of Toronto Press, 1990.

Gwyn, Richard. *Northern Magus: Pierre Trudeau and Canadians*. Toronto, McClelland & Stewart, 1980.

Ignatieff, Michael. *Fire and Ashes: Success and Failure in Politics*. Toronto: Random House, 2013.

Jeffrey, Brooke. *Divided Loyalties: The Liberal Party of Canada, 1984-2008*. Toronto: University of Toronto Press, 2010.

Leduc, Lawrence, Jon H. Pammett, Judith L. McKenzie, and Andre Turcotte. *Dynasties and Interludes: Past and Present in Canadian Electoral Politics*. Toronto: Dundurn, 2010.

Litt, Paul. *Elusive Destiny: The Political Vocation of John Napier Turner*. Vancouver: UBC Press, 2011.

Martin, Paul. *Hell or High Water: My Life in and out of Politics*. Toronto: Emblem Books, 2009.

McCall-Newman, Christina. *Grits: An Intimate Portrait of the Liberal Party*. Toronto: MacMillan, 1982.

McDonald, Kenneth. *Red Maple: How Canada Became the People's Republic of Canada in 1981*. Richmond Hill, Ont.: BMG Publishing, 1975.

Nemni, Max and Monique. *Young Trudeau: Son of Quebec, Father of Canada, 1919-1944*. Toronto: McClelland & Stewart, 2006.

Nemni, Max and Monique. *Trudeau Transformed: The Shaping of a Statesman 1944–1965*. Toronto: McClelland & Stewart, *2011*.

Newman, Peter C. *A Nation Divided: Canada and the Coming of Pierre Trudeau*. New York: Knopf, 1969.

Newman, Peter C. *When the Gods Changed: The Death of Liberal Canada*. Toronto: Random House, 2011.

Panitch, Leo, and Donald Swartz. *The Assault on Trade Union Freedoms: From Wage Controls to Social Contract*. Toronto: Garamond, 1983.

Pammett, Jon H. and Christopher Dornan (editors). *The Canadian Federal Election of 2006*. Toronto: Dundurn, 2006.

Pammett, Jon H. and Christopher Dornan (editors). *The Canadian Federal Election of 2011*. Toronto: Dundurn, 2011.

Plamondon, Bob. *The Truth about Trudeau*. Ottawa: Great River Media, 2013.

Raj, Althia. *Contender: The Justin Trudeau Story*. Huffington Post Canada, 2013.

Somerville, David. *Trudeau Revealed: By His Actions and Words*. Richmond Hill, Ont.: BMG Publishing, 1978.

Trudeau, Justin. *Common Ground*. Toronto: HarperCollins, 2014.

Tuns, Paul. *Jean Chretien: A Legacy of Scandal*. Jordan, Ont.: Freedom Press, 2004.

Vastel, Michael. *The Outsider: The Life of Pierre Elliott Trudeau*. Toronto: MacMillan, 1990.

Weston, Greg. *Reign of Error: The Inside Story of John Turner's Troubled Leadership*. Toronto: McGraw-Hill Ryerson, 1988.

Zink, Lubor. *Trudeaucracy*. Toronto: Toronto Sun Publishing, 1972.

Zink, Lubor. *Viva Chairman Pierre*. Toronto: Griffin Press, 1977.

Zolf, Larry, *Just Watch Me: Remembering Pierre Trudeau*, Toronto, James Lorimer & Company, 1984

Articles:

(Scholarly articles and opinion columns are listed by author, but authors are not recorded for news stories. Dates may be online or print versions. Page numbers are therefore not included. This is a non-exhaustive list of source material.)

Adams, Paul. "Harper's Hail Mary: Fighting an election on terrorism." iPolitics, October 21, 2014.

Beare, Dan. "Liberals under Justin Trudeau: Will the new Liberal leader be good news for Canadian environmental regulation?" *Alternatives Journal: Canada's Environmental Voice*, May 3, 2013.

Brodbeck, Tom. "Trudeau forgets that dad brought in mandatory minimums." *Winnipeg Sun*, November 19, 2013.

Clément, Dominique. "The October Crisis of 1970: Human Rights Abuses Under the War Measures Act." *Journal of Canadian Studies*, Spring 2008.

Coyne, Andrew. "Justin Trudeau's appeal has NDP scrambling to the left ahead of election." *National Post*, September 15, 2014.

Goldstein, Lorrie. "Justin Trudeau naive to think he knows root causes of terrorism." *Toronto Sun*, April 25, 2013.

Gunter, Lorne. "Trudeau's carbon tax will hurt Canada's economy." *Toronto Sun*, July 8, 2014.

Hebert, Chantal. "Exile likely for suspended Liberal MPs." *Toronto Star*, November 18, 2014.

Hebert, Chantal. "Liberal-NDP alliance improbable but not impossible." *Toronto Star*, April 18,. 2015

Hebert, Chantal. "NDP has more to gain by refuting Bill C-51." *Toronto Star*, February 19, 2015.

Ibbitson, John. "Justin Trudeau's foreign policy is rooted in nostalgia." *Globe and Mail*, May 21, 2014.

Levant, Ezra. "Justin Trudeau's selfie life." *Toronto Sun*, April 19, 2014.

Lilley, Brian. "Pole position: Our PM-in-waiting defers, again, to experts on Arctic seabed issue." *Ottawa Sun*, December 4, 2013.

Lilley, Brian. "Trudeau Sr. and Trudeau Jr. on abortion and the Charter." *Lilley's Pad*, May 20, 2014.

Moffatt, Mike. "One thing Justin Trudeau and Stephen Harper agree on." CanadianBusiness.com, March 18, 2014.

Murphy, Rex. "Defeating Harper is his prime directive." *National Post*, April 18. 2015.

Murphy, Rex. "So much for due process." *National Post*, March 21, 2015.

Palacios, Milagros, and Charles Lammam, "Taxes versus the Necessities of Life: The Canadian Consumer Tax Index, 2014." Fraser Institute, 2014.

Raj, Althia. "Justin Trudeau smoke marijuana after becoming MP." Huffington Post, August 22, 2013.

Raj, Althia. "Liberals aresupporting Bill C-51 so Tories can't make 'political hay,' Trudeau Says." Huffington Post, March 9, 2015.

Robson, John. "MPs struggle to define terrorism." *London Free Press*, November 2, 2014.

Russell, Peter. "The Political Purposes of the Canadian Charter of Rights and Freedoms." *Canadian Bar Review*, 1983.

Selley, Chris. "Gen. Andrew Leslie's frank talk suggests the Liberals' foreign policy shibboleths are on their last legs." *National Post*, September 15, 2014.

Solberg, Monte. "Justin is beyond infinity." *Toronto Sun*, September 21, 2014.

Trudeau, Justin. "Canadian middle class left out of the growth equation," *Toronto Star*, October 31, 2012.

Trudeau, Justin. "Income splitting not a wise investment for Canadians." *Toronto Star*, November 4, 2014.

Tuns, Paul. "30 Years of Liberal Infighting." *Ottawa Citizen*, June 16, 2014.

Tuns, Paul. "Chretien's Survival Game." *Ottawa Citizen*, January 10, 2014.

Tuns, Paul. "How Pearson Created Modern Canada." *Ottawa Citizen*, April 6, 2011.

Tuns, Paul. "Trudeau's Third Walk in the Snow." *Ottawa Citizen*. February 27, 2014.

Tuns, Paul. "Why the abortion law was changed." *The Interim*, April 2009.

Walkom, Thomas. "Anti-terror law too much for Mulcair." *Toronto Star*, February 19, 2015.

Wherry, Aaron. "Justin Trudeau, heir to the politics of coalition." Macleans. ca, April 20, 2015.

Worthington, Peter. "Still seduced by Trudeau's magnetism." *Toronto Sun*, October 8, 2000.

"Airports, schools remain closed as thick smog blankets Chinese city of Harbin." CNN.com, October 22, 2013.

"American progressives surprised by Trudeau's support for Keystone XL." *Globe and Mail*, October 25, 2013.

"As an MP, Trudeau pocketed thousands in speaking fees." *Ottawa Sun*, February 14, 2013.

"B.C. Sikhs quit Liberals to protest Justin Trudeau's 'star' candidate." CBC.ca, December 9, 2014.

"Bertschi files suit against Trudeau over Orléans Liberal nomination." *Ottawa Citizen*, April 13, 2015.

"Bill Blair to seek federal Liberal nomination in Scarborough Southwest." CBC.ca, April 26, 2015.

"Brian Mulroney on Justin Trudeau: 'What's not to like'?" CTVNews.ca, April 8, 2013.

"Calling environment minister a 'piece of s**t' was ugly but it worked." Huffington Post, March 8, 2012

"Christine Innes Liberal candidacy rebuffed over deal, letter says." CBC.ca, March 14, 2014.

"Christine Innes fighting back against Trudeau." *Toronto Star*, April 3, 2014.

"David Bertschi supporters say Liberals' 'backroom politics' behind nomination." Huffington Post, November 17, 2014.

"Grit MP getting the boot?" *Toronto Sun*, March 19, 2015.

"Gun spat puts Trudeau's campaign to the test." CP24.com, December 3, 2012.

"How Canada has abandoned its role as peacekeeper." *Toronto Star*, October 30, 2014.

"Jean Chretien v. Paul Martin: now it's really war." *The Economist, June 2, 2002.*

"Jodie Emery's bid to run as federal Liberal candidate turned down." CBC.ca, January 16, 2015.

"Jody Wilson-Raybould, aboriginal candidate in B.C., caught in political crossfire." CBC.ca, August 18, 2014.

"Justin Trudeau admits that he 'won the lottery' with $1.2 million inheritance and successful speaking business." *Ottawa Citizen*, February 14, 2013.

"Justin Trudeau aims to strike balance between environment, economy with carbon policy." *National Post*, February 6, 2015.

"Justin Trudeau argues federal government needs to be more involved in city building." Edmonton *Metro*, January 26, 2014.

"Justin Trudeau defends performance as 2013 draws to close." CBC.ca, December 12, 2013.

"Justin Trudeau far from the only MP to make cash on the side." Huffington Post, June 17, 2013.

"Justin Trudeau favours Kinder Morgan expansion (if it's done right)" *Vancouver Observer*, February 26, 2014.

"Justin Trudeau: federal government must support auto industry." *Windsor Star*, January 22, 2015.

"Justin Trudeau fires back at Christine Innes in lawsuit." *Toronto Star*, May 28, 2014.

"Justin Trudeau may run deficit, but these candidates aren't seeing red." Huffington Post, February 22, 2014.

"Justin Trudeau might be better for business than Stephen Harper." *Canadian Business*, April 29, 2013.

"Justin Trudeau now says he is 'unequivocally opposed' to Liberal-NDP coalition." GlobalNews.ca, April 15, 2015.

"Justin Trudeau offers to pay back all public speaking Earnings." *Toronto Star*, June 16, 2013.

"Justin Trudeau plan taxes top 1% to cut taxes, boost benefits for middle class." CBC.ca, May 4, 2015.

"Justin Trudeau, Rob Ford stop for selfies at Jim Flaherty's funeral." *Toronto Sun*, April 17, 2014.

"Justin Trudeau talks politics, pipelines and pot with Metro Calgary." Calgary *Metro*, January 22, 2014.

"Justin Trudeau urges adoring students to question 'system'." *Windsor Star*, May 17, 2007.

"Justin wants to have a beer with you," *The Grid*, April 30, 2014.

"Justin Trudeau willing to breakup Canada over abortion." *The Interim*, February 14, 2012.

"Leslie acclaimed Liberal candidate in Orléans in chaotic meeting." *Ottawa Citizen*, December 7, 2014.

"Liberal hopeful feels Bill Casey bid pushed her aside." Halifax *Chronicle-Herald*, February 25, 2015.

"Liberal leader Justin Trudeau says Southwestern Ontario must move away from manufacturing," *London Free Press*, January 21, 2015.

"Liberal MPs Scott Andrews, Massimo Pacetti suspended from caucus amid harassment allegations." CBC.ca, November 5, 2014.

"Liberal nomination complaints lead to more resignations." CBC.ca, September 9, 2014.

"Liberal Party considers prostitution, euthanasia." *The Interim*, February 2014.

"Liberals accused of revictimizing MPs." *Globe and Mail*, November 7, 2014.

"Liberals reject Jodie Emery as Vancouver East candidate." *Vancouver Sun*, January 17, 2015.

"Liberals vote in favour of 'medically-assisted death' at party convention." *Toronto Sun*, May 21, 2014.

"Lots to do despite poll." Halifax *Chronicle Herald,* August 25, 2014.

"MacKay says Trudeau's answer to world threats is oversimplified." *Toronto Sun*, August 15, 2014.

"Mayors Want More Info On Liberals' Plans To Boost Infrastructure Funding." Huffington Post, August 20, 2014.

"Meir Medical Center honours Trudeau with award." *Canadian Jewish News*, April 7, 2014.

"Most Canadians want niqab banned in public, poll suggests." *Toronto Sun*, March 20, 2015.

"MPs in hot water." *Toronto Sun*, November 6, 2014.

"Municipalities need infrastructure dollars to succeed: Trudeau." *Welland Tribune*, May 30, 2014.

"Olivia Chow's mayoral candidacy has an unintended consequence: a lawsuit against Justin Trudeau." TorontoLife.com, April 15, 2014.

"Outgoing Police Chief Blair may seek federal Liberal nomination in Scarborough Southwest." *Scarborough Mirror*, February 17, 2015.

"Personal misconduct." *Toronto Star*, November 6, 2014.

"Pipeline projects need more than Ottawa's rubber stamp: Trudeau,." CTVNews.ca, June 18, 2014.

"Politics, Passion & Pipelines: An Interview." *Your McMurray Magazine*, May 29, 2014.

"Rival to Bill Blair's bid for federal Liberal nomination in Scarborough Southwest withdraws." *Scarborough Mirror*, May 13, 2015.

"Takacs acclaimed as federal Liberal candidate in Brantford-Brant." *Brantford Expositor*, August 21, 2014.

"Top B.C. aboriginal leader to run for Justin Trudeau Liberals in Vancouver Granville." *Vancouver Sun*, July 30, 2014.

"The Interview: Justin Trudeau's game plan." *Maclean's*, August 17, 2014.

"The lonely Liberal: Justin Trudeau and his quest for the (suspicious) West." *Alberta Oil Magazine*, October 6, 2014.

"The Rules Menu: Party Nomination Processes, Three Ways." Pundit's Guide, May 1, 2014.

"Thwarted Liberal candidate Christine Innes sues Justin Trudeau for defamation." CBC.ca, April 14, 2014.

"Trudeau admits he wrongly claimed expenses for speaking events; pays back money." *Ottawa Citizen*, January 16, 2014.

"Trudeau aims to make western inroads," *Edmonton Journal*, August 19, 2014.

"Trudeau backs Israel, slams Quebec charter." *Canadian Jewish News*, December 2, 2013.

"Trudeau calls for greenhouse gas limits on oil sands." *Globe and Mail*, April 10, 2014.

"Trudeau calls for new plan for new economic reality." *London Free Press*, January 21, 2015.

"Trudeau calls long-gun registry 'a failure'." CBC.ca, December 1, 2012.

"Trudeau has been doing dry runs of leaders' TV debates for months." *The Hill Times*, May 18, 2015.

"Trudeau joins peace initiative." *Montreal Gazette*, July 18, 2007.

"Trudeau might be open to coalition with NDP, but not with Mulcair as leader." *Toronto Star*, April 14, 2015.

"Trudeau picks lawyer to look at misconduct case." *Globe and Mail*, December 6, 2014.

"Trudeau says he was hired as a professional speaker, not an MP." *Toronto Sun*, June 20, 2013.

"Trudeau says he's doing it 'my way'." *The Hill Times*, October 26, 2009.

"Trudeau says incentives for carbon to help Keystone bid." Bloomberg News, June 26, 2014.

"Trudeau tells Iranian-Canadian newspaper that Harper's Israel position is all about votes." *National Post*, April 4, 2014.

"Trudeau would rethink Harper's mandatory minimum sentences." *Toronto Sun*, November 11, 2013.

"Trudeau's plan: Tax the rich to help the middle class." *Ottawa Citizen*, May 5, 2015.

"Trudeau uncritical of Suzuki's controversial comments." *Ottawa Sun*, July 13, 2013.

"Varinder Bhullar, Edmonton Liberal, accuses party of breaking open nominations pledge." Huffington Post, February 2, 2015.

"Who me? Conservative?" *Maclean's*, April 29, 2015.

Select interviews and speeches

Justin Trudeau interview, "Andrew Lawton Show," AM 980, January 20, 2015.

Justin Trudeau interview, "The National," CBC, April 16, 2013.

Justin Trudeau interview, "Question Period," CTV, January 5, 2014.

Justin Trudeau interview, "Winnipeg's Morning News," 680 CJOB, February 11, 2015.

Justin Trudeau, "Announcing bid for the Liberal Party of Canada leadership." October 2, 2012.

Justin Trudeau, "Reviving the Islamic Spirit Convention," December 22, 2012.

Justin Trudeau, "Leadership acceptance speech," April 14, 2013.

Justin Trudeau, "Fairness for the middle class," May 4, 2015

Justin Trudeau, "Canadian Liberty and the Politics of Fear," March 9, 2015.

Justin Trudeau, "Speech to the Calgary Petroleum Club," October 30, 2013.

Justin Trudeau, "Speech to the Calgary Petroleum Club," February 6, 2015.

CPSIA information can be obtained at www.ICGtesting.com
Printed in the USA
LVOW07s0707220615

443352LV00001B/5/P